Literature in Language Teaching and Learning

Edited by Amos Paran

Case Studies in TESOL Practice Series

Jill Burton, Series Editor

Teachers of English to Speakers of Other Languages, Inc.

Typeset in Berkeley and Belwe
by Capitol Communication Systems, Inc., Crofton, Maryland USA
Printed by United Graphics, Incorporated, Mattoon, Illinois USA
Indexed by Coughlin Indexing, Annapolis, Maryland USA

Teachers of English to Speakers of Other Languages, Inc.
700 South Washington Street, Suite 200
Alexandria, Virginia 22314 USA
Tel 703-836-0774 • Fax 703-836-6447 • E-mail tesol@tesol.org • http://www.tesol.org/

Publishing Manager: Marilyn Kupetz
Copy Editor: Marcella F. Weiner
Additional Reader: Ellen Garshick
Cover Design: Capitol Communication Systems, Inc.

Grateful acknowledgment is given to the following for use of copyrighted material:

Excerpts in chapter 2 selected from *Open Talk: Talking About Love and Sex,* by The Storyteller Group (storyteller@icon.co.za), 1994. Copyright © 1994 by The Storyteller Group. Reprinted with permission.

"Eveline" in chapter 3 from *Dubliners,* by J. Joyce, 1914/1967. Reprinted from Oxford World's Classics (2000) with the permission of the Trustees. Copyright © the Estate of James Joyce.

Excerpts in chapter 4 selected from *Talking It Over,* by J. Barnes, 1991, published by Jonathan Cape. Used by permission of The Random House Group Limited.

Sample cards in chapter 6 selected from the Tarot Pack. Created by and reprinted with permission from Pablo Otero Rodriguez.

"Carousel" in chapter 8 by L. Roy in *The Calling of the Kindred: Poems From the English-Speaking World,* edited by A. Barlow, 1993, Cambridge: Cambridge University Press. Reprinted here by permission of Lucinda Roy.

"Woodchucks" in chapter 9 by M. Kumin. Copyright © 1972 by Maxine Kumin, from *Selected Poems 1960–1990* by Maxine Kumin. Used by permission of W. W. Norton & Company, Inc.

ISBN 1931185247
Library of Congress Control No. 2005901720

Table of Contents

Acknowledgments

I would like to thank Jill Burton for her support, guidance, and feedback throughout the editing process of this book. I am particularly grateful to Marilyn Kupetz for her speedy and good-humoured response to queries, some of which must have seemed quite surreal (but at least we had some good laughs). Many thanks also to Marcella Weiner for helping the book over many niggling hurdles.

Series Editor's Preface

The Case Studies in TESOL Practice series offers innovative and effective examples of practice from the point of view of the practitioner. The series brings together from around the world communities of practitioners who have reflected and written on particular aspects of their teaching. Each volume in the series covers one specialized teaching focus.

◈ CASE STUDIES

Why a TESOL series focusing on case studies of teaching practice?

Much has been written about case studies and where they fit in a mainstream research tradition (e.g., Nunan, 1992; Stake, 1995; Yin, 1994). Perhaps more importantly, case studies also constitute a public recognition of the value of teachers' reflection on their practice and constitute a new form of teacher research—or teacher valuing. Case studies support teachers in valuing the uniqueness of their classes, learning from them, and showing how their experience and knowledge can be made accessible to other practitioners in simple, but disciplined ways. They are particularly suited to practitioners who want to understand and solve teaching problems in their own contexts.

These case studies are written by practitioners who are able to portray real experience by providing detailed descriptions of teaching practice. These qualities invest the cases with teacher credibility, and make them convincing and professionally interesting. The cases also represent multiple views and offer immediate solutions, thus providing perspective on the issues and examples of useful approaches. Informative by nature, they can provide an initial database for further, sustained research. Accessible to wider audiences than many traditional research reports, however, case studies have democratic appeal.

◈ HOW THIS SERIES CAN BE USED

The case studies lend themselves to pre- and in-service teacher education. Because the context of each case is described in detail, it is easy for readers to compare the cases with and evaluate them against their own circumstances. To respond to the wide range of language environments in which TESOL functions, cases have been selected from EFL, ESL, and bilingual education settings around the world.

 vii

The 12 or so case studies in each volume are easy to follow. Teacher writers describe their teaching context and analyze its distinctive features: the particular demands of their context, the issues they have encountered, how they have effectively addressed the issues, what they have learned. Each case study also offers readers practical suggestions—developed from teaching experience—to adapt and apply to their own teaching.

Already published or in preparation are volumes on

- academic writing programs
- action research
- assessment practices
- bilingual education
- community partnerships
- content-based language instruction
- distance learning
- English for specific purposes
- gender and TESOL
- grammar teaching in teacher education
- interaction and language learning
- international teaching assistants
- journal writing
- literature in language learning and learning
- mainstreaming
- teacher education
- teaching EFL in primary schools
- teaching English from a global perspective
- teaching literature
- technology in the classroom

◈ THIS VOLUME

The organic connection between language teaching and literature is brought to life in this volume, which also provides insights on how language teaching and literature are currently defined. Diverse teaching methods, Internet and canonical literary texts, sensitive approaches to cultural understanding—all have their place in the chapters in this book.

Jill Burton
University of South Australia, Adelaide

CHAPTER 1

The Stories of Literature and Language Teaching

Amos Paran

◈ INTRODUCTION

The story of literature and its relationship with second language learning is, like many others, not one story but many stories, changing according to its narrator and according to the perspective being taken. The received wisdom is that literature, once the mainstay of language teaching, being both its purpose and one of its main tools, was relegated to a marginal role with the advent of communicative language teaching in the 1970s. By the 1980s it had all but been "purged from the programme," as Widdowson (1985, p. 180) has put it. But then, in the late 1980s and early 1990s, glimmers of hope appeared. Carter and Long (1987) were able to talk of a "considerable resurgence of interest in the study of literature in relation to language" (p. 1). Publications since then include collections of academic papers (e.g., Brumfit & Carter, 1986), methodology handbooks and resource books (e.g., Bassnett & Grundy, 1993; Collie & Slater, 1987; Lazar, 1993; McRae, 1991; Whiteson, 1996), textbooks for learners (e.g., Carter & Long, 1987; Collie & Porter Ladousse, 1991; Lazar, 1999), and articles in collections and journals. There was some debate about the suitability of various approaches to the use and teaching of literature in EFL (e.g., Gower, 1986; Mackay, 1992; Weston, 1996), and the *ELT Journal* devoted a special issue to literature in 1990.

But there are other stories. One version is that literature had never really gone out of the classroom. As Gilroy and Parkinson (1996) and Maley (2001) point out, in many countries the EFL textbook is still a collection of literary texts; what had happened was that academic interest in the topic had died (Maley, 1989). This story continues with the thought that the return of literature was under a different guise from before, with a focus on the linguistic aspects of literature.

Another version of the story might view the resurgence of literature slightly differently and suggest that to some extent this renaissance may not have continued far beyond the mid-1990s. Whereas in the 1980s there were numerous articles on using literature in the language classroom in *TESOL Quarterly,* there were very few in the 1990s, and there have been none in the new millennium. Methodology textbooks present a mixed picture: Ur (1996) stands out among the crowd in actively encouraging teacher learners to teach and use literature and has specific units on the topic; Celce-Murcia (2001) includes a section on literature, as do Carter and Nunan (2000). But in Hedge (2000) and in Richards and Renandya (2002), there is no mention of literature (though extensive reading features quite prominently). Harmer

(2001), interestingly, includes quite a number of literary texts, but they appear in the chapter on reading. This relative absence from methodology textbooks is reflected in training courses: Belcher and Hirvela (2000) talk about the "conspicuous absence of a place for literature in the TESOL curriculum" (p. 33). Though there is little research on what actually goes on in classrooms, in some countries at least it is possible to have a university degree in English without having any exposure to literature (Qiping & Shubo, 2002).

My own teaching and teacher education experience, however, has shown me that learners and teachers, throughout the world, respond to literature in the second language (L2) of the learner or teacher with pleasure and enthusiasm, engaging with it on many levels. This volume of case studies is intended as evidence of that, as well as an attempt to contribute to the academic literature on this topic. In the first part of this chapter I discuss some of the current trends in teaching and using literature in the second language classroom, referring throughout to the various chapters in this volume. I then turn to issues in the use of literature in second language learning that I think are still unresolved, including a discussion of some of the criticism voiced in this area. I end with a short summary of the reasons literature is such a powerful tool in the hands of any language teacher.

◈ CURRENT TRENDS

Integrating Language and Literature

The major change that has occurred in the approach to literature is in its relationship with language. Language and literature are not seen as separate entities; rather, teachers now stress the way in which understanding one is part of understanding the other. The way in which the two can be integrated can vary. Some approaches may be based more on theoretical linguistic concerns than others, taking as their starting point a theory of grammar (as Lin does in chapter 8) or stylistics (e.g., Rosenkjar, chapter 9; Widdowson, 1975, 1992). In other cases there is a focus on general issues of language; however, the attention to language is not only based on practical language concerns or the learners' immediate needs (after all, we would expect some attention to language if only to acknowledge that learners may not know all the words in the text) but also embedded into the teaching, with a specific focus on the way in which language is used in the text. For Carter and Long (1991), language-based approaches entail a focus on the process of reading rather than a focus on the text as a set product. They use language-teaching tasks and activities with literary texts, thus bringing language into the focus of studying.

Various aspects of integration are a recurring theme in the chapters in this volume. Indeed, four of the chapters indicate this explicitly in their titles: Butler (chapter 2) and Lin (chapter 8) refer to integrating language and literature; Hess (chapter 3) discusses integrating skills; and Martin's (chapter 7) terms of integration refer to the integration of language and literature as well as to the integration of theory and practice, learning and fun—and other terms.

Extending the Range of Text Types

It is now widely accepted that there is no clear demarcation between literary and nonliterary texts but rather a cline of literariness. Thus it is possible to discuss the same phenomena in literary and nonliterary texts. This has resulted in a widening of the genres that are being used, with writers juxtaposing different genres in order to understand the way each functions. Apart from clearly nonliterary texts such as advertisements, which Butler (chapter 2) discusses, contributors to this volume include such genres as children's literature (McNicholls, chapter 6; Martin, chapter 7), fairy tales and their retellings (McNicholls, chapter 6), popular songs (Lin, chapter 8), various examples of popular literature such as Puzo's *The Godfather* (Schulte, chapter 12), and a variety of autobiographical narratives (Gordon, Zaleski, & Goodman, chapter 5).

Another development has seen films figure prominently in the language classroom, often together with literature. With more and more literary works being turned into films, there is a great deal of work that deals with filmed versions of literary works (see Jennings, 1996; Pulverness, 2000; Ross, 1991); this is reflected in this volume in the programme described by Schulte (chapter 12), where learners are encouraged to investigate the relationships between the literary and the cinematic text and are offered an extremely wide choice of films and texts.

Extending the Range of Writers Taught

In the past, the literature taught in the second language classroom included a very narrow range of canonical writers who were in turn represented by an even narrower range of works. For example, Beck (1995), investigating what English majors had read in English in secondary school, found Shakespeare and George Orwell well ahead of any other author; half of his 68 respondents had read the same Shakespeare play (*Macbeth*) and a third had read *Animal Farm*. Hermes (1995) reports similar findings, as does Nünning (1998), who found *Macbeth* mentioned by more than half of his group (see also Martin, chapter 7). *Animal Farm* also appeared as the second favourite in Engku Haliza's (1995) survey of EFL teachers in the United Kingdom to find which literary works they had had good experiences with (William Golding's *Lord of the Flies* came first). In most cases the writers chosen most often come from the inner circle (Kachru, 1985), they are mostly men, and the works taught have won critical acclaim and are overall within the canon. In yet another context, Banjo (1985) reports that the Nigerian schools in his survey tended to use the same texts; in his case these were mostly by African authors, but Shakespeare does make an appearance—as does the ubiquitous *Animal Farm*.

There may be various reasons for this phenomenon. Some works seem destined to be thought of as relevant to adolescents because the protagonists are adolescents— hence the popularity of J. D. Salinger's *The Catcher in the Rye* and Golding's *Lord of the Flies*. *Animal Farm* is a favourite because it is fairly short, not too difficult for upper intermediate learners to read in the original version, and perceived as relevant for its political content (see Elliott, 1990, for a discussion of the use of *Animal Farm* in EFL). Other books may fit neatly into a theme (e.g., F. Scott Fitzgerald's *The Great Gatsby* and the American dream). Beck (1995) suggests that many works are taught because they were relevant and topical when the teachers were themselves students, a situation that Schreyer (1978, as cited in Beck, 1995) suggests can create a vicious circle, perpetuating the same choices. I would also suggest that the availability of support materials, which may appear once a work shows promise of being popular, may also play a part in this phenomenon.

Against this background of reported conformity, there has been a recent widening of the range of works taught, from a number of aspects. There is the obvious chronological one, with an increasing number of works by living writers being included. There is the inclusion of works from the outer circle (Kachru, 1985), not only in outer-circle countries (e.g., Chan, 1999; Vethamani, 1996) but also in EFL situations. For example, in the syllabus for 2002–2003, the French Ministry of Education brought in work from South Africa (J. M. Coetzee's *Waiting for the Barbarians*) and from India (R. K. Narayan's *The Painter of Signs*). Some collections include translations as well (e.g., Segal, 1997; Shaffer-Koros & Reppy, 1994/1998). There is also an increasing engagement with young adult literature (e.g., Holzmann, 1997; Rönnquist & Sell, 1994).

The chapters in this volume reflect this trend very strongly. There is a wide variety of texts, from a variety of periods and countries, with a strong emphasis on contemporary texts—indeed, only three of the chapters do not include at least some works by a living writer. Although this was not planned, serendipity resulted in no duplication of texts in the programmes discussed in the various chapters, and even in those cases where the same writer was chosen, the contributors have selected different works to focus on.

Creating Space for the Learner

Many of the chapters in this volume discuss the previous experiences that learners have had with literature in the classroom, both in the first language (L1) of the learner and in L2, and the extent to which these experiences are often not very successful. Minkoff (chapter 4) points out that his students have previously experienced literature as dissection of texts, rather than as a living source of enjoyment and pleasure. Butler (chapter 2), Rosenkjar (chapter 9), and Tutaş (chapter 10) all include quotes from their students, who express their difficulties with literature and disappointment with literature teaching. This volume thus supports previous observations on the poor quality of literature teaching in many contexts, where "a dominating expert interrogates diminished learners about literature which they feel to be at a great distance from their lives" (Tomlinson, 1998, p. 177; see also Hall, 2003).

One way of understanding this situation and responding to it is through Rosenblatt's (1978) transactional theory of reading literature. Rosenblatt's choice of the term *transaction,* though it may seem odd to a TESOL/applied linguistics audience, was motivated by the wish to distinguish it from *interaction.* In her discussion of the relationship between the reader and the text, Rosenblatt explains that for her *interaction* indicates a dualistic view of separated factors, whereas *transaction* implies for her "an ongoing process in which the elements or factors are, one might say, aspects of a total situation, each conditioned by and conditioning the other" (p. 17). This ongoing process is also reflected in Rosenblatt's distinction between two types of reading: efferent reading, in which the reader focuses on the public meanings of the text, and aesthetic reading, in which the reader focuses on the lived experience and enjoyment of the reading. Reading a novel aesthetically, readers immerse themselves in the work and will live it, participate in its world. Reading it efferently, readers will be focusing on the plot to be remembered, the character analysis to be performed, and so forth. What is different between the two types of reading is thus the focus of the reader's attention and what the reader does during the reading. Some texts are clearly meant to be read efferently, whereas others need to be read aesthetically in order to achieve their impact.

In their previous schooling, second language learners have in many cases experienced a narrow view of literature, which sees it as having fixed meanings that the teacher needs to help learners to access or as teaching fixed ways of reading. These learners are being socialised into viewing the reading of literature as an efferent exercise and make no connection between what happens in the literature classroom (be it L1 or L2) and their own reading of fiction (and I would suggest that there are very few people who do not read fiction of any kind). The task for the teacher, then, is to find ways in which to help learners unlearn their previous attitudes, reengage them in texts, work with them to recapture the sense of enjoyment in literature, and help them see the relevance of what they are reading to their own lives.

What is apparent in this volume is the extent to which these ideas have filtered through to the TESOL world. Minkoff (chapter 4) and Gordon, Zaleski, and Goodman (chapter 5) refer to the distinction between efferent and aesthetic reading, and Tutaş (chapter 10) reports how teaching can change efferent responses to aesthetic responses.

Teaching Literature in Different Environments

Literature continues to be taught throughout the world—the 11 chapters in this volume come from 10 different countries, though this was not a factor in choosing them—in a large variety of settings. Some of these settings are more obvious than others: Both Rosenkjar (chapter 9) and Tutaş (chapter 10) describe programmes that are taught to literature majors at universities. Many of the settings are teacher education programmes (McNicholls, chapter 6; Martin, chapter 7; Vodičková, chapter 11), but there is a clear implication that a great deal of what is taught will be passed on to learners in primary classrooms. Lin (chapter 8) describes literature lessons in a secondary school environment, as does Schulte (chapter 12). Other settings are less immediately obvious. Thus Butler (chapter 2) talks about the way in which literature is integrated on a course that enrols English majors together with students who will not continue beyond the first year but are using the course as a way of improving their English. Hess (chapter 3) describes an approach that she has implemented in general English classrooms and also refers to the ways in which she has used literature in English for specific purposes (ESP) settings (see also Hirvela, 1990, and Kelly & Krishnan, 1995, for discussions of literature and ESP). Minkoff (chapter 4) discusses an elective course at a business school in France whose continued success is once again testimony that literature teaching and using can flourish in any environment.

Using Literature in the Classroom—Without Fear

In my own experience, many teachers, both literature majors and others, are still worried about the use of literature in the classroom. This fear is often a combination of two factors. One is a type of fear of the text, the feeling that if teachers do not provide a full explanation of the text (e.g., its meanings, symbolism, context), then they have failed. Thus, in many in-service training courses for teachers I have found that the teachers' main aim is to further their understanding of the texts that they will be teaching and amass background information and criticism that deals with them. These are also the teachers who are worried about using literature for language teaching (rather than teaching literature), possibly feeling that by doing so they are in some way degrading or desecrating the text. (This attitude is very similar to that which prevents many teachers from using extracts, for example.)

The other type of fear is a methodological one. If teachers see their role as teaching the text, they may realise that this does not sit comfortably with communicative methodologies that they may be accustomed to using. Other teachers feel that they do not know how to use literature or how to teach it. Finally, many teachers fear that the students will not enjoy literature. Ironically, the reverse may be true: Bouman (1983) recounts that in her experience when visiting schools in the Netherlands, "only too often the teachers, rather than the pupils, were afraid of poetry" (p. 14).

Some teachers may overcome their worries and find their own way into teaching and using literature—Minkoff's case study (chapter 4) is interesting as an account of how a teacher who is not a literature graduate has done this. But overall, given this situation, the role of the teacher educator is doubly important. In those chapters in this volume that deal with literature in teacher education, there is an implication that using literature with teacher learners works not only to improve their English (e.g., Vodičková, chapter 11) but also to introduce them to ways in which they could use literature in their classrooms (McNicholls, chapter 6; Martin, chapter 7).

Using a Variety of Approaches

I have argued elsewhere that there cannot be one correct methodology for incorporating literature into TESOL, but, rather, that the methodology used must be chosen after considering the text, the learners, the aim of the lesson, and the teacher (Paran, 1999). The various chapters illustrate this point, showing that it is possible to incorporate literature into TESOL successfully in a variety of ways.

The chapters in the latter part of the volume focus on different methodologies and approaches to the use of literature in EFL. Lin (chapter 8) discusses the way in which his approach is based on systemic functional grammar (Halliday, 1994) but goes on to say that the structure of his approach can be used with other theoretical frameworks as well. Rosenkjar (chapter 9) shows how it is possible to use a stylistic analysis with second language learners, thus refuting, to my mind, some of the arguments in Gower (1986) and strengthening the case made by Carter and Long (1987), Lazar (1993, 1995), and Widdowson (1975), among others. Vodičková (chapter 11) discusses the way in which it is possible to teach a Shakespeare play in class using a structured drama approach. Schulte (chapter 12) concludes this volume with an example of integration throughout the language curriculum. These chapters also illustrate the whole continuum of teacher control, from a highly structured experience (e.g., Lin, chapter 8; Rosenkjar, chapter 9) to a very open approach where the learners choose their own topics and texts (Martin, chapter 7).

Encouraging Creative Writing

Earlier in the chapter I discussed the way in which learners have gained space in the language and literature classroom. This has happened in part because the focus on reception of literature has moved on to include the creation of literature, giving voice to the learner. Bates (1999), in an anthology of poetry connected with EFL, includes a large number of poems by learners. Spiro (2004) is a resource book devoted to creative poetry writing activities. Drew (2001) reports on a similar course, and there have been anthologies of learner writing produced in many places around the world (see also Heath, 1996). In this volume, too, many of the programmes include creative writing. Butler (chapter 2) and Gordon, Zaleski, and Goodman (chapter 5) provide samples of their students' writing. McNicholls (chapter 6) specifically discusses the importance of creativity and of fostering it in young children.

Responding to Political and Social Changes

One clear message from the chapters in this volume is the extent to which political and social changes have influenced the teaching and the use of literature in EFL situations. In a number of cases, this has been in a negative way. Both Martin (chapter 7) and Vodičková (chapter 11) discuss the ways in which the need for greater numbers of language teachers has resulted in changes in courses. Butler's programme (chapter 2) was introduced in response to the changing population in the University of North West, in South Africa, following the fall of the apartheid regime.

But literature also provides a way to respond to the world. An example of the response to social issues in Butler's work (chapter 2) may be seen in the choice of a comic strip dealing with AIDS. Gordon, Zaleski, and Goodman (chapter 5) comment extensively on the demographic changes that are occurring in Long Island, in the United States, where their institution is located, and on what these demographic changes mean to the teacher education programme in which they are engaged. In their case the use of literature is directly motivated by these changes and is seen as particularly apt for the situation, as a way of dealing and reacting to political and social change.

Using Technology

With books entitled *Literature and the Internet* (Browner, Pulsford, & Sears, 2000), it is clear that technology is increasingly being harnessed to the teaching of literature—in this case in L1. One way in which technology is brought in is by providing different ways of carrying out activities that would have normally been done face-to-face. Thus, Towndrow and Vallance (2004) include activities such as using a chat room for role-play; using technology to prepare a piece of material illustrating a response to literature; and preparing materials for a Web site, which, in the past, would have been done through a poster. The large amount of both primary and secondary sources now at the disposal of teachers and learners is also a result of technology. There are Web sites and archives on many writers accessible through the Internet; these sites often include biographies, pictures, background information, and links to studies and monographs. In the case of writers whose works are no longer copyrighted, such sites may include full texts. Lesson plans are also available on the Internet, and often learners post their own materials on dedicated Web sites (see Martin, chapter 7, for examples of this). The accessibility of such a large amount of information has affected the classroom, through changing processes and method-ologies. In the past, it would have been the teacher's role to find materials for use in the classroom (e.g., background reading on the work being studied), and the choice would be limited for economic reasons. Using technology, the teacher can now provide the students with a list of options to choose from or may provide the learners with guidelines for finding their own materials. The webquest methodology, when used appropriately, results in a true shift of control of the learning process to the learners with the teacher taking on the role of an enabler and a manager of resources. Where resources allow, this can also be done through the use of CD-ROMs (see Schulte, chapter 12, for a discussion of webquests and CD-ROMs). Finally, technology has affected the teaching of literature by providing different ways of telling and reading—examples include hyperfiction (see Ferradas Moi, 2003) and web serials with interactive potential in which learners take part in the writing as well (see, e.g., British Council, 2000).

◈ CHALLENGES FOR THE FUTURE

Overcoming Divisions

In this chapter I have been referring to teaching literature versus using literature. To some extent, this distinction might be useful—for example, to distinguish between developing literary competence and the use of a literary text to encourage speaking. But just as teachers accept that there is a cline of literariness, they might want to think about literature in the classroom as part of a continuum—maybe a *cline of literary use* with developing literary competence at one end and use for language practice at the other end. Such a continuum might help teachers to realise that in a second language classroom neither of the two extremes exists on its own, and each always includes something of the other. Indeed, two other types of activity might be located on this continuum: extensive reading and storytelling. The separation of these two from literature is an artefact of a combination of the fear of literature that I have discussed and of teaching situations. Thus, some teachers may want their learners to read fiction but do not wish to teach it or to discuss its literary qualities, even though they may be doing this in a different guise (e.g., discussing characters). With young learners, for example, a teacher may want to come into the classroom and tell a story, rather than announce that the class will read or hear a piece of literature.

By viewing these activities as different manifestations of one preoccupation, I think language teachers will be better equipped to deal with critiques such as those by Horowitz (1990) and Edmondson (1997). One of the fallacies of Edmondson's position is that he sees language learning as focusing on language only. The language he uses to discuss this is revealing: He talks about "the business of language learning" (p. 42) and "the business of achieving proficiency or general competence in an L2" (p. 45) and talks of the learners as "educational consumers" and of specific learners as "the products of at least eight years school learning" (p. 43). He is thus an exponent of an isolationist position, whereby language learning is about acquiring competence in the L2 and nothing more. As the chapters in this volume clearly show, language learning is not only about language—it is about learning as well; it is not only about training but also about education. Indeed, integration is one of the hallmarks of many of the chapters. Understanding the role of literature in daily life, the way in which narratives function in learning, the role of literature and narratives in education, and the language-literature link is important in understanding why literature may have a place in second language teaching more than "history, geography, the economics or the architecture of other countries" (Edmondson, 1997, p. 46) or "philosophy, art, contemporary political issues or other subjects on the humanist agenda" (Horowitz, 1990, p. 162).

Broadening the Research Base

The extent to which literature has been allocated a marginal role within second language learning and teaching is most evident in light of the small amount of published research in this area, which is even more striking when contrasted with the burgeoning of research in other areas of language learning. In spite of the call in Quirk and Widdowson (1985) for more research "so as to discover the basis for learner preference, the factors which cause difficulty in interpretation, the effect on learners of different types of text, literary and otherwise, and in general the way in which the learning of language and literature could be seen as complementary" (p. 210), very little of this has been forthcoming. As both Edmondson (1997) and Maley (2001) observe, much of the discussion over the role of literature has been theoretical rather than empirical. Edmondson (1997) goes on to say that, because the method comparison paradigm has been discredited, attempting to decide what literature can offer second language learning cannot be established empirically. Of course, it is still possible to do this without attempting comparisons, and it is difficult to see how the issues that Edmondson raises can be discussed without looking at what happens with real learners in real classrooms.

Slowly, however, research is beginning to emerge. Hanauer (2001) examines the type of interaction and language that is produced by dyads discussing a poem, looking at the extent to which the discussion leads to extending linguistic knowledge. Though criticised by Mattix (2002) for not considering the affective side of reading literature, this is nevertheless an important marker in the research in this area. Kim (2004) provides interesting evidence of learner engagement with literature, whereas Isaac (2002) looks at the way in which learners engage with a literary cloze and their reactions to it.

The case studies in this volume provide valuable insights into what is happening in the classroom as well as information about the structure of programmes. I would argue, however, that some data gathering of the most basic type is still needed. The first type of research that is needed is, quite simply, descriptive. How much literature is in fact taught in the school systems around the world? How much literature are students reading? Research into materials is also necessary: To what extent do materials writers incorporate literary texts into course books? What types of materials are specifically being produced for literature in TESOL? Is there a difference between materials that are produced for a local market and materials that are produced for a global use?

What approaches are teachers taking to the use of literature in the classroom? How are learners reacting to this? Within this research, a better differentiation between learners is necessary. Rather than talk about EFL/ESL learners, teachers need to know what is happening with specific types of learners: adults, young adults, private language schools, primary and secondary education, and so on. Information is needed on what is happening in specific countries and in specific situations. (Indeed, in some theoretical discussions there is a blurring between L1 and L2, often through looking at activities suitable for first language learners and assuming that they will work with advanced second language learners.) In addition, researchers need to address the issue of what participants feel to be the advantage of the learning. Because one of the main reasons brought forward for the use of literature in the classroom is motivation, this question needs to be addressed directly, through investigating the learners' attitudes. Also urgently needed is research on testing literature in an L2, for which Spiro (1991) would be the logical starting point. Finally, a great deal of research on literature in second language learning is not in English, and it is vital that this information and research be shared more widely (see also Bredella & Delanoy, 1996).

◈ THE CRITICAL ROLE OF LITERATURE

In this chapter I have provided a broad description of the current state of literature in second language classrooms, with a focus on the case studies in this volume. I have looked at current trends and also what I perceive still needs to be done, especially in terms of research. I have dealt with some of the criticism levelled against practitioners and academics in this field. Ultimately, however, the most powerful reasoning for the use of literature lies in the simple observation that language teaching is an educational endeavour. Within educational systems teachers cannot view learners as consumers; they must take a more holistic view in their approach, a holistic view both of them and of the world. Literature demands that teachers make connections because, as Carter and Long (1991) say, "effective, and confident reading of literature is closely connected with a reader's ability to relate a text to his or her own experience" (p. 30). Many of the contributors to this volume stress the importance of relevance of the work to the students and have chosen literature that provides learners with opportunities to engage with important topics and themes. Indeed, Hess (chapter 3) calls her approach the *parallel life approach.*

Even in those cases where it might be argued that learners have purchased a product and are most like consumers (e.g., in many companies or when teaching business English), teachers would do well to remember the following quote from Dewey (1938, as cited in Littlejohn & Windeatt, 1989): "Perhaps the greatest of all pedagogical fallacies is the notion that a person learns only the particular thing he is studying at the time" (p. 155). It is the ultimate truth of this observation that is probably the strongest reason for using literature, in any classroom.

◈ ACKNOWLEDGMENTS

I would like to thank Pauline Robinson, Rosemary Wilson, and Jill Burton for their comments on a previous draft of this chapter.

◈ CONTRIBUTOR

Amos Paran taught EFL in secondary schools in Israel before completing an MA and a PhD in applied linguistics at the University of Reading, in the United Kingdom. He is the course leader of the MA TESOL by distance learning at the Institute of Education, University of London, and coordinator of the Literature, Media, and Cultural Studies Special Interest Group of the International Association of Teachers of English as a Foreign Language.

CHAPTER 2

A Brighter Future? Integrating Language and Literature for First-Year University Students

Ian Butler

I think Literature is a big difficult for me, because when I was at high school we used to do Macbeth and Julius Caesar the English in there is very complicated and it has no bright future. Maybe if I could read a very simple literature I can change my attitude towards literature. —Student's response to a questionnaire, University of North West

◈ INTRODUCTION

In this chapter I describe how I have attempted to integrate the teaching of language and literature in the first year of the English programme at the University of North West, in South Africa. My teaching is linked to an ongoing action research project, begun in 2000, which I have undertaken to develop and improve the English 100 course and my contribution to it. My work has included surveying current and recent theory on the integration of language and literature in ESL teaching, drawing up a curriculum, developing materials through which to translate the curriculum into classroom practice, being part of the team teaching the course, and attempting to gauge student and lecturer opinions of the success of this approach to English language teaching.

I argue that literature has a useful and important role to play in the teaching of English in an ESL/EFL context, even where the purpose for studying the language is purely instrumental and the students have little knowledge or experience of literature in English. Although the approach to language and literature described here was developed in a particular context, in response to specific needs, the principles underlying it could be applied in a variety of English language teaching situations and levels.

My discussion of the course will be accompanied by examples or descriptions of materials that I have used in teaching it. I hope that these will serve to give concrete expression to the methods and principles of the approach and also help to anchor it in the reality of the English language classroom.

Integrating language and literature in English studies is not, of course, unique to the programme at the University of North West. Any one familiar with developments in the use of literature in EFL over the last 20 years will have recognised the influences that have shaped the use of literature in the English 100 course. The attempt to demystify literature owes much to McRae's (1991) aptly named *Literature*

With a Small "l"; the technique of comparing literary and nonliterary texts draws on work by Carter and Long (1987); theoretical support for the multiple uses of a literary text comes from Stern (1991)—and these are only the first in a very long list of innovative and inspirational contributors to the field in recent years.

The context that provided the initial stimulus for the development of the course is not peculiar to South Africa either. Challenges similar to those facing us at the University of North West have been reported from as apparently diverse areas as Hong Kong and the Middle East (see, e.g., Chan, 1999; Haggan, 1999; John, 1986; Zughoul, 1987). Reading such accounts leaves the South African reader with a sense of déjà vu. The frequent mismatch between the expectations and interests of students and their lecturers, the conflicting demands of academic standards and practical necessity, ambivalent attitudes to the language and its literatures, and the pressure of external forces—all these are depressingly familiar.

Yet what has made the experiment in integrating language and literature at the University of North West interesting and exciting for me is the way in which it has forced me to examine my objectives in teaching English. When I was an undergraduate student, a university course in English was, in effect, a course in literature. And literature was, in effect, British literature, more specifically the canonical texts of the Great Tradition. This was the position at most South African universities 20 years ago, including those institutions at which most students spoke English as a second language. Clearly, a lot has changed since then.

◈ CONTEXT

The University of North West is a small university situated in a rural area of the North West Province, about 300 kilometres from the metropolitan centres of Johannesburg and Pretoria. It was established in 1980 as the University of Bophuthatswana in the then nominally independent Tswana homeland of Bophuthatswana. Its legacy as a creation of the policy of "grand apartheid" is still apparent today: The majority of students are Setswana speaking (in a response to a questionnaire in 2000, 70% of the English 100 class cited it as their first language) and come from the North West Province and neighbouring Botswana, although there are also a significant number from elsewhere in South Africa and from other African countries. Although English is the official language of the university and its medium of learning and instruction, nearly all the students and staff are second language speakers of English. Competence in English—among students, and increasingly among staff—is generally low. Many of the students come from economically and educationally disadvantaged backgrounds. Like most historically Black universities (HBUs) in South Africa, the university is chronically underresourced, and gross mismanagement and infighting in recent years have done little to improve the situation. There is little evidence of any culture of learning. Few students, even those who have the resources to do so, are prepared to spend money on books.

The challenges for the English teacher implicit in this context are added to by the nature of student enrolment in the Department of English. Most of the students at the University of North West who study English at the first-year level do so because it is a compulsory ancillary to another subject or a requirement in their programme of study. Few intend continuing to the second and third years of undergraduate study in the department, and even fewer continue to postgraduate study. The average enrolment at the first-year level is more than 1,000 students; in the third year it is 30. This situation can be ascribed to two contrary forces currently operating in South Africa. On the one hand, an increasing emphasis on science and technology in national planning has resulted in a corresponding neglect of social sciences and the humanities. This, together with a sharp drop in the number of students training to be teachers in recent years, explains the low number of senior students in the department and indeed of students at any level in other language departments within the faculty. On the other hand, the prestige that the English language enjoys in South African society and its position as a national lingua franca mean that it has an important instrumental role in education. This factor explains the relatively large number of first-year students.

The Department of English offers two different courses at the first-year level. English and Academic Studies (EAS) is a noncontinuing service course of one or two semesters, compulsory for most students at the university. It focuses on their needs as students studying through the medium of a second language. English 100, the focus of my attention here, is a more general course, the foundation year for the 3-year major in English. Approximately 300 students register for this course, usually in addition to EAS. Some in this group (a minority) hope to major in the subject; the rest do not intend remaining beyond the first year. English 100 must therefore serve a double purpose: to give a grounding in the discipline and to provide a self-contained course that is both interesting and useful. The course also requires the teacher to reach a (sometimes uneasy) compromise between meeting students' practical linguistic needs and meeting the demands of academic respectability.

The English 100 students deal with the fact that they are "conscripts," taking the course in compliance with the academic requirements of their programmes of study, in a variety of ways. For some it is a source of resentment, often linked to ambivalent feelings about the language itself. The following extract from a student's journal, although not typical, suggests a view of English that is shared to varying degrees by many people in South Africa:

> Though English is an international language it doesn't favour people [who] do not know it for example some overdoze [on] drugs (medicine) and end up losing their lives due [to] English. Maybe English was meant to exploit Africans. English originate in England, from history white use to cheat our grand parents. That is why developing countries still depend on them, though [they are] independent.

Other students adopt a more pragmatic approach; a few, however, actually welcome the opportunity to use and study English. The following poems, like the previous extract, were written by first-year students in their journals. Read together, these three texts capture nicely the range of attitudes to English among the students. The first poem suggests a stoic acceptance of English:

> I am forced to use English
> I use it everywhere, even at my own village
> People are surprised: "Why you use English?"
> I am forced to use English

> I am forced to use English
> I said, "Hello," to my friend
> "Do you think you are smart?" he said to me.
> "Practice makes better, my friend, you better start now."
>
> I am forced to use English
> Most jobs need English
> You panic, you fail their interview
> With English you are already an employee.
>
> I am forced to use English
> Because of the situation I'm in
> I want to prosper in life
> English is an answer.

Another student was much more enthusiastic:

> I dwell upon English as often as possible,
> When I meet you for the first time,
> It's English you will hear me speak.
> Although it is not my first language,
> It's visibly beginning to seem like it.
> . . .
>
> I have a great passion for English,
> And where it may take me,
> I will forever follow!

Poems like these aside, the English 100 course might not seem to offer very fertile ground for the teaching of literature. But the comment of another student— used as the epigraph to this chapter—points to the way in which literature has, in fact, been used in the course. Literature is still an object of study, as it is in more traditional university courses in English, but the aim is to make it more accessible to the students. This has involved a careful selection of the works to be studied, with a focus on their relevance to the students' needs and interests, rather than on the degree to which they represent any literary canon. More significantly, literature is made accessible through its integration with the study of language. This combination of two elements traditionally separated in the teaching of English aims at benefiting both of them. Knowledge of the way in which language works makes literature seem less intimidating; in addition, literature itself provides an ideal resource for the teaching of language. The inclusion of literature in the English 100 syllabus, in other words, depended not just on justifying it as an area of study in its own right but also on its usefulness in teaching language.

The inclusion of both language and literature in the current syllabus is not in itself a radical departure from earlier practice. Both had always been components in the English programme at the University of North West from its foundation, a time when at most South African universities studying English was more or less synonymous with studying literature. (Then it had been the inclusion of language studies that had marked the university's English courses as innovative; today the pendulum has swung so far in the opposite direction that, throughout South Africa, it is the continued study of literature at tertiary level that is most at risk.) Over the years the two components had, however, drifted apart. Lecturers specialised in either language or literature and were generally indifferent to or ignorant of others' work. The two disciplines were taught and examined separately. Students often complained of the conflicting demands made on them by language and literature lecturers. Assessment criteria and grades were often perceived as being unfairly inconsistent. By the late 1990s members of the Department of English felt that they needed to overhaul the syllabus to remedy the situation and, at the same time, address the needs of the first-year students. This conveniently coincided with calls from the national Ministry of Education for universities to restructure their programmes in light of the major educational changes that were being implemented throughout the country. The whole English programme consequently underwent a process of revision. An important element in the changes was the integration of language and literature.

In the sections that follow, I describe the integration of language and literature in the English 100 course, which has been the focus of my research since 2000.

◈ DESCRIPTION

English 100 is made up of four consecutive 8-week modules:

- ENG 101: Introduction to English Studies
- ENG 102: Introduction to Textual Analysis
- ENG 103: Introduction to Literary Genres
- ENG 104: Grammar Awareness

Throughout the course the emphasis is on the development of practical analytical and observational skills rather than rote learning of facts and information. Students are continually encouraged to draw on their existing knowledge and experience, becoming active creators of knowledge rather than passive consumers of it. Learning of this kind should ideally take place in small groups, where a learner-centred approach is possible, but the limited number of staff available to teach the course means that this is not always possible. To compensate for this, self-study tasks and activities have been built into the teaching materials (see Figure 1). The outcomes-based education approach (which is used in compliance with national education norms) also emphasises the need for students to take control of their own learning. Every unit of work has its own set of outcomes, against which the students are able to assess their own progress.

Each module includes four 40-minute contact periods per week. Assessment is continuous, by means of tasks, assignments, and examinations.

◈ DISTINGUISHING FEATURES

The form that language/literature integration takes in each module varies, depending on the focus of that module. In the first two, the integration is made within each module through the use of literary texts, used on their own or in conjunction with nonliterary texts. ENG 103 and ENG 104, although specialising in literature and language respectively, are integrated through a cross-fertilisation of texts and activities.

- Think about the names of streets and places with which you are familiar, especially names that have changed recently. What do these names reveal of the history and politics of our country? (from a unit entitled "Language Around You")

- In the short story, "The Mute Companions" (Narayan, 1985), Sami and the monkey portray various characters and situations. How do you think they were able to do this without the use of language? In the same story the servant "explained by signs that the master of the house wanted the monkey to be brought to his presence" (p. 151). What signs do you think he used? And later, how did Sami try "to explain that he had no designs on the boy but only wanted to get the monkey" (p. 151)? (from a unit entitled "Communication")

- In the literary extracts that you have been given, analyse the ways in which different varieties of English are used to characterise people in the texts as regards to social status and education. Do you think that it is right to do this? Are some varieties better than others? Think about similar judgments made about varieties of any other language you know (e.g., the dialects of Setswana). (from a unit entitled "Standards and Standard English")

FIGURE 1. Sample Tasks and Activities in ENG 101: Introduction to English Studies

ENG 101

The main aim of the first module is to raise and develop the students' language awareness as well as develop the skills of reflection, observation, and analysis that they will need later in their studies. Here literature is used primarily as a means to introduce ideas and concepts. Short stories, poems, and extracts from longer works are chosen for their ability to illustrate and exemplify topics touched on in the module. There is a minimum of literary analysis; the focus at this stage is rather on content (see Figure 2 for examples). The role of literature here, in other words, is premised on one of the most basic arguments for its inclusion in language learning: It provides a pleasant and entertaining way of learning about something that might otherwise appear dull and boring. Literature appeals to the emotions and imagination as well as the intellect. It can, in Sydney's (1595/1973) phrase, "both teach and delight" (p. 101). It can also provide a useful way of concretising and particularising abstract concepts.

A requirement of the first module is that students keep a journal to give students an opportunity to write in English as well as a means to encourage self-reflexivity and language awareness. Here they are also encouraged (but not forced) to express themselves through literary forms. The poems quoted in the previous section show that some do take up the challenge.

ENG 102

The ability to recognise and use different styles of language in the appropriate context is a vital skill for language learners. This is what the second module aims at developing. Through the analysis and creation of different kinds of text, the awareness of language that was introduced in ENG 101 is consolidated. Here, as in the first module, literature has a role to play by providing a rich resource for a wide range of language styles and registers.

However, in ENG 102 integration of language and literature is aimed at

- An extract from Shaw's (1941) *Pygmalion* is used to illustrate the idea of social styles and registers. Once students get past the immediate strangeness of the text, they are able to find parallel examples from their own experience. The famous line from the film, *Pretty Woman* (Marshall, 1990), where the heroine says that she enjoyed the opera so much that she almost "wet her pants" also helps to bring Eliza Doolittle up to date.
- Narayan's (1985) short story, "The Mute Companions," provides a stimulating introduction to a section on verbal and nonverbal communication.
- A folktale from Cameroon written in pidgin English gives concrete expression to the theme of English as a world language. At first glance the text appears incomprehensible and completely unrelated to standard English. By making the effort to understand it, however, students are taught the importance of close, careful reading.
- Extracts from works by Achebe (1958, 1960) and Fugard (1980) provide examples of regional and social variation within the English language.
- A poem entitled "On Learning Sotho" by South African poet van Wyk (1995) encapsulates the affective dimension of language learning.

FIGURE 2. Examples of the Use of Literary Texts in ENG 101

developing both linguistic and literary skills. The module can therefore also be seen as preparing students for the study of literature in ENG 103. Second language students are often intimidated by the mystique surrounding literature, especially poetry. By combining the analysis of literary texts with others traditionally regarded as nonliterary, literature is taken down from its pedestal.

Comparing literary with nonliterary texts enables the teacher to demonstrate that although literary texts are, in many ways, different, they also share many features with other, more familiar, discourses. Carter and Long (1991) propose the idea of a "cline of literariness" (p. 101). In other words, literature should not be seen as a phenomenon isolated from other language uses (as it might often appear to those without literary experience); instead, literariness exists on a scale, with many kinds of discourse possessing some of the features traditionally associated with literature. Identifying such texts may provide students with a way into literature. Advertisements, billboards, and slogans (such as those in Figure 3, copied from billboards in the streets of Mafikeng) are part of everyday life, yet they employ many of the

ARRIVE ALIVE
(from a poster in a national campaign for road safety)

WORK HARD — PLAY HARD — COCA COLA
(billboard advertisement)

There's more reward in an award-winning beer
BLACK LABEL
(billboard advertisement)

FIGURE 3. Advertising and Billboard Texts

techniques traditionally associated with poetry, such as alliteration, assonance, and parallelism.

In addition, some of the distinctive characteristics of literature are also revealed through the technique of textual comparison and contrast. For instance, students are presented with two texts describing the effects of European colonialism on Africans: One is an extract from a history textbook in which the effects are presented in impersonal, abstract, and generalised terms; the other is a passage taken from Achebe's (1958) novel *Things Fall Apart*. Here two characters discuss the devastating effect that the arrival of the White man has had on the social fabric of their village; the details are specific and personal, the language emotive and richly textured. Not only is the language different; as a literary text it also provides the reader with information and insight not found in the factual account.

Other texts that I have contrasted in this way include

- Eliot's (1927/1963) "The Journey of the Magi" and the biblical accounts of the same journey

- a recipe for cooking a chicken and a fictional account in which a child describes her horror at having to eat a chicken she had regarded as a pet

- a historical account of the Zulu hero, Shaka, and a translation of a traditional praise poem recited in his honour

- a poem expressing the speaker's love for South Africa and an extract from a reference book listing various statistics about the country

Figure 4 contains a task in which the students are invited to consider the power of the literary text in comparison with other kinds of writing. Gordimer's (1970) comment implies the ability of literature ("the story of one individual who lived through that") to move and persuade the reader, in a way that many other kinds of information, such as statistics ("the figures, how many people moved, how many jobs were lost") cannot. Here, unlike in the earlier tasks, the students are not actually given two texts to compare. The comparison is implicit, with the focus of the analysis on the literary text and the way in which it transforms and transcends the bare facts of the situation.

ENG 103 and ENG 104

Although ENG 103 and ENG 104 are separate modules, each with a clear literature or language bias, integration is effected through the multiple use of texts. Literary texts, prescribed for the ENG 103 module, are also used in ENG 104 as a stimulus for writing skills development and to provide a meaningful context for the teaching of grammar. Conversely, raising awareness of how knowledge of grammar enables one to understand and create meaning is incorporated into the teaching of literary genre from the start.

The use of popular literary forms also makes integration of the two modules possible. Fables, comic strips, traditional stories, and other popular forms of narrative discourse are, as many language teachers know, ideal vehicles for teaching language. In this context, I also use them to bring the rarefied world of literary terminology into contact with the language of everyday life. Such popular forms are not only part of a continuum that includes serious literature, traditionally the focus of literature teaching, but, as narrative, also represent a form of discourse found in

---

The Power of Literature

The facts are always less than what really happens . . . . If you get a law, like Group Areas, under which various population groups are . . . uprooted from their homes and so on, well somebody may give you the figures, how many people moved, how many jobs were lost. But to me it doesn't tell you nearly as much as the story of one individual who lived through that.

Nadine Gordimer, *The Listener*, 21 October 1970
(epigraph in *Dance With a Poor Man's Daughter*)

Pamela Jooste's (1998) novel, *Dance With a Poor Man's Daughter*, is the kind of story that Nadine Gordimer might have had in mind. It depicts the destruction of Cape Town's District Six and the forced removal of its "coloured" inhabitants to the Cape Flats, as seen through the eyes of an 11-year-old child.

Now attempt the following task:

Read chapter 14 of the novel, where the narrator describes her feelings as she and her family wait to receive their notice of eviction.

With this chapter in mind, decide whether you agree with Nadine Gordimer. Explain your answer.

FIGURE 4. Task for Considering the Power of Literature

the daily use of language, giving rise to such mundane and apparently trivial uses of language as gossip, anecdotes, and jokes. Narrative is, in fact, one of the most fundamental uses of language known to humans. To demonstrate this, I make narrative—or, put more simply, the telling of a story—the first of the writing skills to be covered in the module.

Two examples illustrate how this kind of integration is possible. In an assignment, students have to rewrite a comic strip story (The Storyteller Group, 1994) as continuous prose narrative. The story is taken from an educational comic strip promoting AIDS awareness (see Figure 5) and was chosen because its theme (a mother and daughter learning to talk to each other about sex) is reminiscent of one of the short stories studied in ENG 103, Rifaat's (1987) "An Incident in the Ghobashi Household." In a subsequent assignment, the same themes and preoccupations provide the rough data for an argumentative essay, the second stage in developing the students' writing skills. The activities are intertwined in a way that allows them to complement each other and provide mutual stimulation. Writing a prose narrative based on a comic strip involves the transfer of information from an easily accessible, popular narrative form to one that requires more linguistic skills to produce. The argumentative essay represents a further step in the process of developing writing skills: The concrete world of the narrative has to be translated into more abstract, objective discourse. And, linking language to literature, the form and content of the comic strip story and the students' own prose versions of it pave the way for a greater appreciation and understanding of the short story as a literary genre.

All these activities also provide meaningful and motivating contexts for the study of the grammatical forms and functions typically found in narrative and argumentative writing. On the basis of students' written work, I am also able to perform a needs analysis to identify areas that need attention. The texts—those prescribed for study

Continued on p. 21

and those generated by the students themselves—thus provide a focus and context for the grammar component of the language module.

In another class exercise I used a traditional story as a vehicle for developing both literary and linguistic skills. By applying the techniques of cloze and multiple choice, I was able to teach and test content comprehension, vocabulary knowledge, verb tenses, and the use of direct and indirect speech using the story as an authentic

Figure 5. Two Excerpts From *Open Talk: Talking About Love and Sex* (The Storyteller Group, 1994)

and meaningful context. The story was also examined from a literary point of view: For example, students were asked to identify in it some of the stylistic conventions of oral storytelling and to infer the moral typically found in traditional stories. They were then given an assignment to find and retell a traditional African short story.

Teacher Perceptions of Effectiveness

At the end of 2001 I drew up a questionnaire in which I attempted to gauge my colleagues' opinions on the success of our experiment in integrating language and literature in the first-year course. Nine of the 11 questionnaires that I distributed were returned. These responses indicated almost unanimous overall support for the integrated approach. Seven respondents believed that the experiment had been a success, and eight expressed a desire to continue their involvement in the project. Eight respondents were confident of their ability to teach both language and literature, and seven expressed their satisfaction with the approach adopted in the sample materials that I had provided.

In the second part of the questionnaire (see Figure 6), I asked my colleagues to express their views on the benefits to be gained from an approach that integrated language and literature teaching. I provided a list of 14 statements based on my reading in the field and my own teaching experience. Following the lead of many writers in the field, I arranged them into two categories, according to the focus in each statement: language through literature or literature through language (see, e.g.,

Language Through Literature

1. Literature provides a resource/authentic context for the teaching of grammar and vocabulary.

2. Because of its appeal to the learner's imagination and emotions, literature provides motivation for language learning.

3. The themes and plots of literary works provide stimuli for meaningful debates, discussions, and other language tasks that develop the learner's linguistic and communicative competence.

4. Literature provides learners with authentic models for the norms of language use.

5. Literature assists learners in developing their overall language awareness and knowledge about language.

6. The study of literature helps develop the learner's interpretive and analytical skills (e.g., skills of inference), which can be applied to other language-related activities.

7. Literature represents language at its best and thus provides an ideal model for language learning.

8. Literature provides learners with insights into the norms and cultural values embodied in the language.

9. The study of literature educates the whole person in a way that more functional approaches to language teaching do not.

Literature Through Language

10. Comparing literary and nonliterary texts allows the learner to move from the known to the unknown; in this way, literature is made more accessible to him or her.

11. Linking the study of literary texts to creative language activities (e.g., as rewriting the endings to stories, role playing, or rewriting a narrative from a different point of view or in a different genre) makes the text more accessible to the learner and removes some of the intimidating mystique that often surrounds literature.

12. Applying basic ESL/EFL techniques (such as cloze, multiple choice, and jigsaw reading) to the study of literature develops language skills and promotes engagement with the text.

13. Learners cannot develop literary competence without an adequate competence in language. Integration of language and literature helps compensate for any inadequacies in the learner's linguistic competence.

14. Developing the learner's sensitivity to how language is used in a literary text (e.g., through elementary stylistic analysis) provides him or her with a way in to the text, a starting point for the process of comprehension and appreciation.

FIGURE 6. Statements Used to Explore Teachers' Attitudes to Using Literature

Carter & Tomlinson, 1985, p. 9). The respondents were asked to indicate whether they agreed, disagreed, or felt that they were not able to comment. Here again, they indicated their general support for the integration of language and literature. The number of responses in agreement with each of the statements never fell below seven. In a number of instances, agreement was unanimous (Statements 4, 6, 11, and

14); in others, those respondents who did not agree with the statement indicated that they were not able to comment rather than expressing outright disagreement (Statements 5, 8, 9, 10, 12, and 13). Only in four instances did any respondent explicitly disagree with a statement (Statements 1, 2, 3, and 7). Even here, the limited extent of the disagreement may be deduced from the fact that it was limited to one negative response in each case, expressed by only two of the nine respondents (one disagreed with Statements 1, 2, and 3; the other, with Statement 7).

Student Responses

The response to both parts of the questionnaire clearly indicated broad support by the teaching staff for the principles underlying the English 100 course. But to what extent did the students themselves share our views on literature and the way in which it had been integrated with language?

In the course of the 2000 and 2001 academic years, I attempted to find the answer to this question through the use of questionnaires and self-reflective tasks given to the English 100 students. I investigated three related key issues:

- What did students expect and want from a course in English?
- Did this include literature?
- What did they think of our approach in integrating language and literature?

The initial findings, based on the responses of 114 new students at the beginning of 2000, seemed to confirm our original perceptions: The motivation for studying English was instrumental rather than integrative, in spite of a number of expressions of personal enjoyment and appreciation. A strong sense of English as a (or possibly the main or only) language of empowerment emerged, coupled, significantly, with a concomitant sense of personal inadequacy that they hoped the course would address.

For one student studying for a bachelor's degree in communications, this practical bias made literature redundant. In her response to the questionnaire she commented:

> As a student of English I do not see the reason why we should study English literature because I see it as not important and relevant to the course. I think that only grammar can help as a student of communication because it helps and teaches us how to communicate.

A comment like this, expressed with such confidence and certainty, could not be ignored. To test the extent to which her views were shared by others in the class, I devised a task that conveniently combined pedagogy with action research. I asked the students to write a short essay in which they explored their attitudes to the study of literature. The comment just quoted, and others expressing different views, were used as points of departure.

My subsequent analysis of the essays suggested that the student who saw no point in studying literature represented only a tiny minority within the class. Of the whole 114-strong group, only 6 students rejected the inclusion of literature in the syllabus outright, and one did not have any strong feelings either way. The rest believed that literature should form an integral part of any course in English and offered various reasons to support this view. Some mentioned general benefits such as the broadening of knowledge and experience, stimulation of the mind and emotions, and promotion of creativity. Many of the responses, however, tended to emphasise the idea of literature as *language in action*. For this reason, they suggested that reading and studying literature could contribute to the development of grammar, vocabulary, and general language skills. Reasoning of this kind in fact reinforced the instrumental motivation: Literature was valued precisely because it complemented and contributed to the acquisition of practical language skills. It was not seen as undermining this goal, as had been implied by the student quoted previously. It therefore came as no surprise that when, at a later stage, we asked a sample of students to comment on our integrated approach, 86% were in favour of it.

◈ PRACTICAL IDEAS

Choose Texts That Are Appropriate to Your Learners

The texts you choose need to be relevant to the learners' knowledge and experience and to appeal to their imagination and emotions. In my choice of texts I tended to emphasise African and Commonwealth literature; however, the idea of relevance can be applied to age, gender, social background, political interests, and so on.

Extend the Definition of Literature

The genres you choose can include popular literature, traditional stories, narratives, and comic strips. These forms need not replace "serious" literary texts but can serve as a means of introduction to them, enabling the learners to move from the known to the unknown.

Compare and Contrast Literary Texts With Other Nonliterary Texts

This is an extremely effective technique that helps develop the learners' sense of the choices available within the language. It also helps demystify literature. The contrast could be between markedly different uses of language (e.g., a novel and a reference book) or texts that differ only in certain crucial ways (e.g., an advertisement and a poem).

Use Literature as a Resource

Use literature to teach language awareness, the rules of grammar, and vocabulary. Such apparently mundane activities should not be seen as a desecration of the text. On the contrary, they enable the learners to look at literary technique from the writer's point of view and develop an appreciation of his or her literary technique. You can also use the themes and plots of literary texts as a stimulus for communicative activities, such as essays, letters, discussion, and debates. In addition, you can use literature to develop cognitive and academic skills needed by all students: problem solving, close reading, and inference. The advantage of using a literary text to develop these skills is that, if well chosen, it can engage the learner in a way that is less likely in other kinds of text.

❧ CONCLUSION

As I indicated at the beginning of this chapter, my work on the English 100 course is an ongoing project. Feedback from students and colleagues, my own observations, and the constantly changing demands of tertiary education in South Africa have all influenced the course's development since its initial implementation in 2000. Further changes still need to be made. Whereas integration has been successful in some areas, it has left other needs unanswered. For instance, the extent to which the course provides an adequate foundation for students wishing to continue their studies in English language or literature is still a matter for concern.

On the whole, however, results are promising. Clearly, literature still has a meaningful role to play in the teaching of ESL or EFL. My colleagues and I are now considering the possibility of including literary texts in the EAS course as well. A well-chosen novel could go a long way in concretising the abstractions of law or sociology. Our main concern, however, remains that of the student whose comments introduced this account: taking the complication out of literature and giving it a brighter future.

❧ CONTRIBUTOR

Since writing this chapter, Ian Butler has left the University of North West, in South Africa, and now teaches English at the North American International School in Pretoria. He is completing his doctoral research on the integration of language and literature in TESOL at the University of South Africa.

CHAPTER 3

The Short Story: Integrating Language Skills Through the Parallel Life Approach

Natalie Hess

The study of literature cannot bring about moral excellence nor prevent moral degeneracy, yet without literature I think that we would find it more difficult to live well and act virtuously. —Wayne C. Booth, *The Company We Keep*

On late afternoons in the sixth or seventh period, when I am just about ready to collapse, the only thing that can keep me going is a story. There is just nothing quite like a good story. —EFL teacher in an urban high school

❖ INTRODUCTION

The return of literature as a rich and worthwhile source for language study has been observed and appreciated over the last 20 years by the ESL/EFL community (Brumfit & Carter, 1986; Duff & Maley, 1990; Kramsch, 1993; Lazar, 1993; Olson, Torrance, & Hildyards, 1985) as well as by the *ELT Journal*, which in July 1990 devoted an entire issue to the teaching of literature. In the introduction to that particular issue, Whitney (1990) writes:

> It has never occurred to me that learning and teaching literature or even learning and teaching about literature (in any language) should not be a source of enjoyment, or that they should not in some vaguely educational sense, be anything other than beneficial. (p. 171)

I am one of those teachers who, in spite of structuralist admonitions, managed throughout the years to insert literary islands into all my courses, including English for specific purposes (ESP) courses for doctors from Hungary, flight attendants from Japan, and nuclear engineers from China. My students have invariably found both profit and pleasure on such forages and, to my knowledge, have never filed a complaint about lack of language input as a result of literary excursions.

I enjoy teaching every kind of literary genre but find particular pleasure in working with short stories. Storytelling, as Krashen (1981) notes, has long been a compelling human activity. The genre offers endless exploration in a cultural and linguistic miniworld that offers entry into a broad universe of shared discourse.

I call my approach to teaching literature the *parallel life approach*. It is a process through which the understanding of a story brings illumination and self-awareness. It works through a constant dialogue between reader and text, pulling the voice of the individual from a social context. As readers move from intensive to extensive readings on the premise that every creative writer needs a creative reader, their discussions easily float from text to life and either strengthen or challenge their belief systems.

◈ CONTEXT

In this chapter, I describe how I have used the short story in an advanced ESL reading class at the Center for English as a Second Language (CESL) at the University of Arizona in the United States. The class was the typical CESL mix of 18 students heralding from countries as diverse as Mexico, Japan, Saudi Arabia, and Germany. Although the class was labeled *advanced,* it was, as these groups generally are, very multileveled. Some students were excellent speakers but could not write a coherent sentence, whereas others, with a high degree of grammatical and spelling proficiency, were completely tongue-tied. In between these extremes, there were many other variations.

Besides being multileveled, the class was, of course, multilingual and multicultural. It was an interesting and fortuitous mix, and it is because of such heterogeneity that all of my activities have become open ended. There can be no slots to fill, no display questions to be answered, and no worksheets to be completed. Everything in such classes has to be structured so that each student can learn and grow at his or her own level and pace.

Although I locate description of the lesson in this chapter within a particular context, I have taught all levels of EFL/ESL in multiple settings, from large, urban high schools in a country where English was a foreign language to ESL preacademic centers and adult education environments. I have also worked as a teacher educator in six countries. I have used literary islands in all of these settings. There is always a poem, a novel, a play, or a story that sheds light on the world and opens windows to genuine communication. For the group of Hungarian doctors, it was William Carlos Williams's poignant story "The Use of Force" that loosened tongues and stimulated pens. A group of lawyers found much to say after reading the speech of Atticus in Harper Lee's novel *To Kill a Mockingbird.* A group of travel agents were extremely intrigued by Macon's advice to travelers in Anne Tyler's novel *The Accidental Tourist,* whereas a class of business students, looking at the problem of time management, thoroughly enjoyed the discussion and writing surrounding the poem "Leisure" by W. H. Davies. The largely Mexican American group of elementary teachers in my culture class today find much to identify with in Victor Villaseñor's novel *Macho!* as they struggle to find their place in the tension between assimilation and isolation.

◈ DESCRIPTION

The particular story that I have chosen for demonstration here is Joyce's (1914/1967) "Eveline" (see the Appendix for the full text of the story). It is a short story that is frequently used by ESL practitioners. It serves the purpose of language learning well because it is intense; universal in message and meaning; and, best of all, truly a very short story, taking up about four pages. Typically, teaching such a story would take three to five 2-hour lessons. For the sake of convenience and because of space restrictions, I have here projected all the material into three lessons, but many of the exercises can well take considerably more time, and flexibility is the essence of the procedure.

The central theme of this story is decision making. The plot involves a young Irish woman who, at the opening of the story, has ostensibly made the decision to leave her family and the responsibilities tied to family life to accompany her sailor boyfriend to a new life in Buenos Aires. The dilemma comes with her misgivings about the decision and her subsequent prevarications.

Teaching the story has allowed me to integrate the four skills (listening, speaking, reading, and writing), produce a lot of interesting language activity, stimulate reflection, bring out different opinions, and energize absorbing thought processes.

The following section describes three 2-hour lessons.

Lesson 1, Part 1

Starting With a Content Schema

The first few paragraphs of the story are the port of entry and should be explored slowly and intensively, moving from the life of the students to the life of the text and back to the life of the students. I take my time in investigating those opening paragraphs. Doing such discovery carefully makes the rest of the story much more interesting and accessible for my students. Thus, I dedicate the first two lessons to rigorous exploration of the first four paragraphs.

My immediate task is to enable the students to comfortably enter the literary miniworld that we are about to discover. I do this by creating an appropriate schema, one of the "building blocks of cognition" (Rumelhart, 1980, p. 34) that help us to interpret and arrange new knowledge.

Using Visualization

I begin the story with a visualization to help students enter the first image presented in the story. Students are asked to relax and close their eyes, but I admonish them to stay alert and not fall asleep. Here is what I say:

> Imagine a window. Decide how large it is and how it is decorated. Are there curtains? What kind? I want you to see this window very clearly in your mind. Are there flowers in the window? What kind of a house is this window a part of? Is the window open or closed? Is the glass of the window clean or dirty? Do you see anything else? (*Pause.*) Now I want you to imagine a person who comes and sits at the window. (*Pause.*) Please see this person very clearly. Is it a man or a woman? How old is your person? How is your person dressed? What is he or she doing at the window? (*Pause.*) Please nod when this picture is like a movie in your mind and you see it very clearly.

Once I have received nods from everyone, students open their eyes and, in pairs, describe to their partners what they have imagined. When I see that the pair conversation is completed, pairs combine with pairs, and each classmate tells the foursome about his or her partner's vision. The partner corrects when necessary. We follow this with a whole-class, teacher-fronted discussion on how and why windows are often used as symbols. We bring out expressions such as *a window of time, a window of opportunity, a window of hope,* and *the eyes are windows of the soul.*

Building a Language Schema

We are now ready to move on to the next stage. In this stage, I want to build a language schema for the first paragraph of the story. The first paragraph of most short stories is a significant one because it is here that mood, setting, character, and theme can be established. Joyce (1914/1967) does so masterfully in what has to be one of the shortest of first paragraphs, and I do not want my students to miss the design. Here is the first paragraph of Joyce's "Eveline":

> She sat at the window watching the evening invade the avenue. Her head was leaned against the window curtains and in her nostrils was the odour of dusty cretonne. She was tired. (p. 25)

Before we look at the paragraph, I dictate its last sentence: "She was tired." I then ask the students to write a paragraph that ends with this sentence. After the students write their paragraphs, they sit in pairs and read them to each other. We post the paragraphs around the walls of the classroom. Students walk about reading the paragraphs and writing comments. The only instruction I give is that anything written, including suggestions for improvement, should be phrased positively. Here the first part of this lesson generally ends, and students go out for a break.

Lesson 1, Part 2

Continuing Content and Language Schemata

When students return, we generally choose one or two of the paragraphs that they have produced to be read out loud. The following is a typical example:

> My mother had cleaned house all day. She to wash the windows, bake cake, made me favrite soup, and mend shirt. Now she resting and listen to me read homework in English. It hard to listen because she so tired.

We follow the readings with a discussion of what makes people tired. The suggestions always begin with "hard work," and it takes a bit of time to get to things such as exercise, boredom, illness, sadness, starvation, and depression. Once these have come up, students are usually willing to provide plenty of examples.

I now present the students with the word *evening* and ask them to produce a verb that might belong together with this noun. They generally produce some of the following combinations:

- The evening came.
- The evening came softly.
- The evening ended.
- The evening went slowly.
- The evening was fun.
- The evening was boring.
- The evening never ended.
- The evening crept.

We then talk about the word *invade* and its military implications. Students produce sentences such as

- The soldiers invaded my country.
- McDonald's has invaded the world.

Only then do we read Joyce's first paragraph. I read it three times. The first time students just listen. During the second reading, they follow along in the text, their task being to note how the word *evening* is used. During the third reading, they are to notice how strangely the word *leaned* has been posited.

We follow this with a discussion of the exhaustion and passivity that Joyce has created. Eveline does not simply lean her head. It is as if even this action of pure fatigue must be done for her; thus, "her head" is "leaned." She is at a window, which may imply hope, but what comes to her is a dusty smell that adds to the sense of exhaustion. She is so passive here that even the evening, which my students have seen as coming softly, "invade[s] the avenue." Does Eveline feel the evening as an invasion because she must do something this evening that she would rather not do?

Working With Content

The next paragraph is full of information. I again read it three times. The first time students again only listen. The second time, I ask them to look for all the information that we are given. The third time, they are asked to look for a verb formation that is seen many times over.

In the discussion that follows, we learn that Eveline's neighborhood has changed because so many people have gone away to other countries. We also learn that Eveline's mother has died and that her father was the bully of the neighborhood. It was he who, during his daughter's childhood, was the angry ogre that chased the neighborhood kids with his blackthorn stick. We also learn that Eveline is about to leave her home.

The discussion that follows deals with all the problems presented here: how it must have felt to have a father that all your playmates feared; how difficult it must be to see everyone you know move away and the scene that you have known change; how terrible it must be for a daughter to lose her mother.

The language point in the paragraph also supplies interest. The verb formation that I looked for was *used to*, which Joyce employs five times in this paragraph:

- "there used to be a field there in which they used to play"
- "The children of the avenue used to play together in that field"
- "Her father used often to hunt them in out of the field with his black-thorn stick"
- "little Keogh used to keep *nix*"

It does not take my students long to see that this form demonstrates actions that happened repeatedly in the past, and they are able to produce sentences about their own lives using this form.

In the third paragraph, we are introduced to three objects that are among those Eveline has dusted weekly always wondering, "where on earth all the dust came from." The objects—the picture of a priest, the print of a self-sacrificing saint, and a broken harmonica—are all thematically related to religion.

Before we read the paragraph, I ask the students, who are all away from their permanent homes, to recall a significant object from their own homes, visualize the object, and write a paragraph describing it. Later, in pairs, they talk about their remembered objects. As we read, we compare their object with the three objects Eveline is dusting. The religious nature of Eveline's objects brings us to a discussion of the setting of the story. Here, with elicitation and occasional help from students, we weave the cultural and religious background of Ireland. I tell them a bit about the life of Joyce and the love/hate relationship he had with his homeland. We talk about the pull Eveline's religion must have had on her decision.

Moving From Intensive to Extensive Reading

Our first lesson ends. We have been doing some very intensive reading, and it is time that they read extensively on their own. Their assignment is to read the following five paragraphs before our next lesson. I divide the class into three groups, and each group is assigned a different question to be answered in writing. I tell them that the answers are not given directly in the story but that they will have to infer their answers from what is written there. There are usually many questions about the idea of reading between the lines of the story. One of the students pointed out that people tend to do this even when they meet real people. We learn a few facts about a new person, and we make a great many inferences.

The questions for homework are as follows:

- Who is Frank? What kind of a person is he? Why do you think that Eveline has fallen in love with him? Why do you think that she has not talked to him about how confused she is when she thinks about leaving home? Does anything in the relationship between Frank and Eveline remind you of anything in your own life or of anything else you have read about? (to be answered by the first group)

- What kind of a man is Eveline's father? Is he justified in his feelings about Frank? What kinds of memories does Eveline have of him? Why are these memories important to her? Does anything in Eveline's relationship with her father remind you of anything in your own life or anything else that you have read or heard about? (to be answered by the second group)

- What do we learn about Eveline's mother? What kind of relationship do you think that she had with her daughter? How is Eveline both pushed toward her mother and pulled away from her mother? Does anything in Eveline's experience remind you of anything in your own life? (to be answered by the third group)

Lesson 2, Part 1

Beginning With a Jigsaw Activity

We begin this lesson with a jigsaw activity. Students gather in groups with those who have answered the same questions. I tell them that in the next configuration, each student will become a teacher. It is, therefore, their responsibility to make sure that everyone in the group knows and understands the material that each has read. Students then summarize the content of their reading, talk about their answers, and compare reactions. These answers and reactions are often extremely varied. The groups serve the added purpose of helping those students who have not done their assignment.

Students then form groups of three. In each group there is a representative of each question. Each representative brings his or her own ideas, as well as the ideas that he or she has heard in the previous group, to this new configuration. All students then reread the homework paragraphs to find one sentence that impressed them, that they thought was interesting or important, or that reminded them of something. Volunteers read their sentences out loud and explain their choices.

Incorporating a Walkabout

We continue the lesson with a walkabout. In this exercise, I have posted a number of statements around the walls of the room. In pairs, students walk about the room, reading and talking about the statements. When they have finished the entire circle of statements with one partner, they switch partners and do the circle again. Possible walkabout statements include the following:

- Eveline's father knows what is good for his daughter.
- Eveline promised her mother to take care of the family. She has no right to leave.
- Eveline can trust Frank.
- Eveline's father is a very prejudiced man.

When the students finish the walkabout, they take down any statement from the wall that they found particularly interesting. These statements serve as a trigger for the ensuing class discussion.

Sharing Opinions

This is the moment that lends itself to the introduction of Maslow's (1987) concept of the ladder of human needs—survival, safety, society, status, and self-fulfillment. The concept draws out many interesting questions and reactions. I ask the students to think about how many of these needs are met in Eveline's life. We note that Eveline's fears make her appreciative of bare survival needs: "In her home anyway she had shelter and food; she had those whom she had known all her life about her." The discussion ends this lesson and spills over to the next period.

Lesson 2, Part 2

Making Decisions

Once the discussion of the previous lesson has reached a natural conclusion, we move on to the story's central theme: making decisions. This is an example of one way in which my approach calls for an intermingling of life with literature. The students are given ample opportunities to hear the opinions of others, and many do develop the ability to understand different perspectives.

In pairs, students develop a list of important decisions most people have to make during their lives. With class contributions, we compile the following on the board:

- which friends to choose
- what school to attend

- what career to choose
- how to choose a partner
- where to live
- what to buy
- whether or not to have children
- how many children to have
- how to handle money

Students share a good decision that they have made in their own lives and, if they can, a bad decision. I illustrate by choosing from my own life, pointing out that the decisions they choose to tell about should be nontrivial but not so personal that sharing would be too difficult.

A discussion on why decisions are so difficult to make ensues, and students typically express some of the following ideas:

- You never really know what the end result of a decision is going to be.
- You might hurt other people through your decision.
- The decision might change your life for the worse.
- You have to live with your decisions. (Here a student noted that she had spent many years of her life blaming her parents for having made bad decisions concerning her life, until at a certain age, she was forced to make her own decisions and noted that she, too, was quite capable of making the wrong choices.)
- Whenever you choose one thing, you give up other things. (We learn the idiom *to have your cake and eat it, too.*)

Eveline, in the story, has made a decision to go away with Frank, but she is not at all sure about the wisdom of her decision. I ask students to advise her. Why should she go? What benefits and advantages are there to going/staying, and what are the disadvantages of each?

Students work in groups on the decision-making process, and as we listen to each group, we find that Eveline has very little to keep her at home. Her job offers no satisfaction, and her working life is full of endless petty humiliation. Her family life is full of thankless drudgery, and she seems to have no friends. She works very hard at pulling out the few happy memories that she has of her father and holds on to these as if they were precious gems not to be lost.

Frank, on the other hand, has been kind and generous. He has taken her to the theater, where, for the first time, she sat in an expensive seat and enjoyed the show. He fascinates her with his stories and offers her hope of a better life in Buenos Aires. And yet, she hesitates before the unknown. She knows what she has at home in Ireland. She understands the cultural code. She speaks the language and knows the customs; perhaps her father is right about "these sailor chaps." Who knows what awaits her in that strange country? Perhaps her prince will desert her. Then how will she manage in completely strange surroundings? Then, of course, there is the deathbed promise that she made to her mother, and she has always been a dutiful daughter. We spend some time talking about how and why deathbed promises are so much more serious than other promises.

Reading Closely

We take a closer look at the fourth paragraph, which gives us a glimpse of Eveline's situation at work. Before rereading the paragraph, we talk about things people want from their daily work and, again, create a class list that looks something like the following:

- money
- vacations
- nice people to work with
- a chance for advancement
- a chance to be creative
- a sense of security
- good retirement plans
- benefits
- a sense of belonging

We read the paragraph and reach the conclusion that Eveline has very few, if any, of those desires.

Extending Through Writing

We finish the lesson with a writing assignment for the next day. Students are to imagine that Eveline has left for Buenos Aires with Frank and that, 5 years later, she writes a letter to her father. Students are to compose that letter.

Lesson 3, Part 1

Using the Letter

We begin by having students read their letters to their partners. Later, students nominate letters that should be read out loud to the whole class. All the letters are then posted on the walls, and students circulate writing comments and suggestions about the content of the letters. Again, the instructions are that all comments and suggestions should be put in positive terms. I demonstrate suggestions about what might be written, for example, "I really liked what you wrote about Buenos Aires, but are you sure that you want things to have turned out so happily? Is this realistic?"

Role-Playing

We move from the letter to a role-play exercise. Half of my class is assigned the role of the father, while the other half is assigned the role of Frank. All who have been assigned the role of the father sit together in a group, as do all those who have been assigned the role of Frank. I explain that we will soon have conversations between Eveline's father and her boyfriend. Each father will face a boyfriend. Frank will want to convince the father that his daughter should leave with him, while the father will adamantly refuse and think of all the reasons why she should not go.

In the *Father* and *Frank* groups, the students are asked to think of all possible arguments their character might use. I move between the two groups, giving assistance as needed. When I feel that each group has accumulated enough ideas, Father/Frank pairs are created, and they role-play the two characters in what usually turns into a lively conversation.

I circulate, listening in here and there, and take note of any pairs who would not mind showing off a bit. When the activity seems to run itself dry, I stop it and invite one pair to perform before the entire group. As that group performs, any student who wants to come up front to replace an actor simply has to move up to either Father or Frank, touch the actor on the shoulder, take his or her place, and continue the conversation.

Considering Cultural Concerns

At this point in the lesson, we consider some of the cultural constraints that influence Eveline's decision making as well as our own. On the board I draw a line, which becomes our continuum. At one end of the line, I write the word *individual*. At the other end I write the words *family and society*. I ask students to consider any important decision they have made and to think about what influenced them most— thoughts about themselves as individuals or as members of a family and a society. We spend some time talking about the meaning of the word *society* (e.g., school, religious institutions, national affiliations, political and social groupings). Students then move to the board and write their name anywhere on the continuum where they feel it belongs.

Once all the names are placed, students explain their placements. They can do this in pairs, in small groups, or with the whole class depending on the mood of the class and time constraints. We contemplate Eveline's placement on the continuum. Students choose different spots and defend their reasoning.

Lesson 3, Part 2

We return to a group writing project. We now assume that Eveline has run away with Frank and that the police have posted a missing person announcement in the local press.

Creating a Missing Person Announcement

We spend some time talking about how such announcements are phrased. This brings us to a review of physical features, clothing, and "last seen" place possibilities. I share one or two missing person announcements from the local newspaper. (Teachers who do not have access to an English newspaper could easily create such an announcement.) In their groups, students talk about their ideas, agree on the phrasing of the announcement, and have a group recorder write it up.

The interesting aspect of this exercise is that Eveline is never described in the story. Thus, it is up to the students to decide just exactly how she should look. This usually brings about a great deal of discussion and compromise.

Here is a typical missing person announcement, produced by a group of students:

Missing

Eveline Hill, 21 years old. She slender and small (5'2"). Has blue eyes and light brown hair and none distinguishing marks. She last see in O'Hara department store. She work as salesclerk. Last see she on blue skirt, and white blouse.

Anyone who knows young woman to contact Mr. James Hill, father.

Reading and Analyzing the Last Paragraphs

The last section of the story is filled with signs of distress. Joyce creates the tone of anguish through metaphor, symbol, and literal meaning. Currents of guilt and doubt are unleashed. The black boat becomes a threatening monstrosity. Eveline's desire for happiness becomes a need to do her duty. She cannot possibly leave the "dust" of her present life to enjoy the metaphorical good air of "Buenos Ayres." The bell of duty clangs "upon her heart." The man who, in the previous paragraph, was going to "save her" is now going to "drown her . . . all the seas of the world tumbled about her heart." She is bewildered and trapped behind an iron railing.

I read the last section three times. The first time, students simply listen. The second and third time, I ask them to underline all the signs of confusion and unhappiness. We follow this with a group discussion that evolves into a full class discussion about why she did not go. Many students see her as paralyzed by cultural restrictions as well as psychic wear and tear. Others think that she did make a decision and the right one at that.

Looking at the Story as a Whole

At this point, I provide a few activities in which we look at the story as a whole. The first activity relates to the language of the story. In a chart, I present students with examples of the varieties of language used by Joyce (see Figure 1). Can they see the difference in language use as displayed in the two columns? They usually note that the left side has much simpler language because we are inside Eveline's head and listen in on her thoughts. The rich metaphorical language on the right belongs to the implied author and narrator.

In another exercise, I give students a card on which they can write anything they feel about the story. It can be an interpretation describing how they feel about plot or character. It can also be a question. Once students have completed their cards, they stand and mingle. Each student approaches a partner to read and explain his or her card. Then cards are exchanged, and students find a new partner to whom they talk about their own card as well as the new card that they received in the exchange. The card switching continues as long as there is high interest.

• There used to be a field there.	• A bell clanged upon her heart.
• Tizzie Dunn was dead.	• All the seas of the world tumbled about her heart.
• They used to play.	• passive, like a helpless animal . . .

FIGURE 1. Language Analysis: Can You See Any Difference?

At this point, students in some classes were eager to reread the entire story. They partner-read, taking one paragraph each and giving each paragraph a name (e.g., "Dreaming About a Better Life," "Woman at the Window," "Dust in Her Nostrils").

As an additional exercise, I give students another chart to rate Eveline, her father, and Frank on a 1–5 scale (5 being the best rating) for the qualities listed (see Figure 2). Once they have completed their rating, they stand up and mingle. They talk with several partners about how and why they rated their characters as they did. I have found this to be an excellent review of the entire story.

Other exercises that work well for general review of the story are Who Would Buy What? and What Would They Say?

In Who Would Buy What? I list a set of objects, for example, a bottle of rum, a Bible, a book of stories, a white dress, and a suitcase. Students are to decide which character in the story might want to buy each object and explain why they think that such an object would be needed by or suited to the character.

In What Would They Say? I list several professionals, for example, a doctor, a teacher, a psychiatrist, and a policeman. Students are to decide what these people might, in today's context, say about each character in the story.

◈ DISTINGUISHING FEATURES

Four Skills Incorporated

One important distinguishing feature of the approach is that it incorporates work on all four skills, usually moving from listening and speaking to reading and eventually writing. It is clear that language learning always involves a tremendous amount of repetition. I have tried to avoid the monotony that comes with such repetition by varying some small element in the procedure. For example, a new task is created during the listening to or reading of the same passage so that students listen for something completely different each time the passage is read (as was done with the second paragraph in the story). Another variation is identifying a different audience (group, pair, or individual) for each speaking task.

Structure Used in Meaning-Related Tasks

I have also attempted to use language structure in meaning-related tasks, as when tying the structure of *used to* with the theme of leave-taking and change in the story. I have found that students are willing to share their thoughts and expand their

	Eveline	Father	Frank
generosity			
sensitivity			
intelligence			
kindness			
responsibility			

FIGURE 2. Chart for Rating

language when they are asked to speak of a personal idea first in general terms. This is perhaps best seen where the class first talks about decisions generally made by people throughout a lifetime, before moving into a decision in their own lives.

The parallel life approach is greatly enhanced by the technique of visualization, which was used here at the opening of the story but which can enhance student perception at any point in a literary work. Collie and Slater (1987) have noted that the printed page is often a cold and distancing medium. Visualization can help students to convert print into living color.

The notion of open-endedness, which allows students to use the full potential of their present language skill, is crucial to the parallel life approach. There are no right answers; instead there is always a multiplicity of possibilities, which is part of my teaching tactics. Such an assortment of possibilities is, of course, also found in the conundrum of life, and it is here that literature, in its wealth of emotional content and linguistic intricacy, offers expressive potential to the language learner as well as heightened interest for the teacher.

◈ PRACTICAL IDEAS

The techniques and activities used in this chapter can be readily applied to any text (including nonliterary texts). The following four ideas are those that I have found to be extremely flexible and useful.

Use Jigsaw Activities to Practice All Four Skills

Jigsaw activities allow for both extensive and intensive reading and give students the chance to function as both teachers and learners. As used in Lesson 2, Part 1, a jigsaw activity includes the following steps:

1. Students individually read and work on specific sections of a shared text.

2. In peer groups, students interact with those who have read the same material.

3. In expert groups, students share material with those who have worked on different sections.

4. With the whole class, students discuss the entire shared text.

Use Walkabout Activities to Maximize Discussion Opportunities

In the walkabout, students discuss issues from the text with one or several partners as they move about reading short texts posted on the walls of the classroom. The technique was demonstrated in the concluding section of Lesson 2, Part 1, for a review of the story. The activity can also be used very effectively as a prereading strategy.

Use Card Exchange as Another Technique for Exchanging Ideas

As illustrated in Lesson 3, Part 2, the ideas can also be created by the students, as well as reacted to, thus adding greater flexibility and possibility for expression.

Use the Continuum With Cultural Focus Activities

This type of activity, illustrated in Lesson, 3 Part 1 (under the section Cultural Concerns), is a strategy that works well for any text that calls for cultural examination. By placing themselves on a continuum that moves from individual to family to society, students are encouraged to see themselves within a cultural framework and to analyze literary characters and situations within such a framework. It is a technique that I have applied to historical, sociological, and psychology-based readings as well as to literature.

❖ CONCLUSION

The short story is a rich source for language development that goes far beyond the written page. Students talk and write a great deal about themselves as they vicariously inhabit literary lives. A good story offers elasticity for evocative stretching that moves students toward interesting language use.

But teaching the short story is an exciting and fruitful process for other reasons, too. In my work with other teachers, I have noted that most of us entered the profession because we were inspired by a role model—a significant teacher in our own lives. When teachers recall these significant educators, they will often not recall the lessons or the classroom organization of their mentors but refer to how these teachers made them feel. Emotion is a powerful motivator, and literature helps teachers spur such motivation. Thus good literature, while promoting language learning, also inspires emotion, provides models and materials for cultural understanding, and opens student voices to issues of relevance and to expanding horizons.

❖ CONTRIBUTOR

Natalie Hess is a professor of bilingual/multicultural education at Northern Arizona University, in the United States. She has taught ESL/EFL and served as a teacher educator in six countries. She is the author and coauthor of several ESL/EFL textbooks and teacher resource books.

❖ APPENDIX: "EVELINE" (Joyce, 1914/1967, pp. 25–29)

SHE sat at the window watching the evening invade the avenue. Her head was leaned against the window curtains and in her nostrils was the odour of dusty cretonne. She was tired.

Few people passed. The man out of the last house passed on his way home; she heard his footsteps clacking along the concrete pavement and afterwards crunching on the cinder path before the new red houses. One time there used to be a field there in which they used to play every evening with other people's children. Then a man from Belfast bought the field and built houses in it—not like their little brown houses but bright brick houses with shining roofs. The children of the avenue used to play together in that field—the Devines, the Waters, the Dunns, little Keogh the cripple, she and her brothers and sisters. Ernest, however, never played: he was too grown up. Her father used often to hunt them in out of the field with his blackthorn stick;

but usually little Keogh used to keep *nix* and call out when he saw her father coming. Still they seemed to have been rather happy then. Her father was not so bad then; and besides, her mother was alive. That was a long time ago; she and her brothers and sisters were all grown up; her mother was dead. Tizzie Dunn was dead, too, and the Waters had gone back to England. Everything changes. Now she was going to go away like the others, to leave her home.

Home! She looked round the room, reviewing all its familiar objects which she had dusted once a week for so many years, wondering where on earth all the dust came from. Perhaps she would never see again those familiar objects from which she had never dreamed of being divided. And yet during all those years she had never found out the name of the priest whose yellowing photograph hung on the wall above the broken harmonium beside the coloured print of the promises made to Blessed Margaret Mary Alacoque. He had been a school friend of her father. Whenever he showed the photograph to a visitor her father used to pass it with a casual word:

—He is in Melbourne now.

She had consented to go away, to leave her home. Was that wise? She tried to weigh each side of the question. In her home anyway she had shelter and food; she had those whom she had known all her life about her. Of course she had to work hard, both in the house and at business. What would they say of her in the Stores when they found out that she had run away with a fellow? Say she was a fool, perhaps; and her place would be filled up by advertisement. Miss Gavan would be glad. She had always had an edge on her, especially whenever there were people listening.

—Miss Hill, don't you see these ladies are waiting?

—Look lively, Miss Hill, please.

She would not cry many tears at leaving the Stores.

But in her new home, in a distant unknown country, it would not be like that. Then she would be married—she, Eveline. People would treat her with respect then. She would not be treated as her mother had been. Even now, though she was over nineteen, she sometimes felt herself in danger of her father's violence. She knew it was that that had given her the palpitations. When they were growing up he had never gone for her, like he used to go for Harry and Ernest, because she was a girl; but latterly he had begun to threaten her and say what he would do to her only for her dead mother's sake. And now she had nobody to protect her. Ernest was dead and Harry, who was in the church decorating business, was nearly always down somewhere in the country. Besides, the invariable squabble for money on Saturday nights had begun to weary her unspeakably. She always gave her entire wages— seven shillings—and Harry always sent up what he could but the trouble was to get any money from her father. He said she used to squander the money, that she had no head, that he wasn't going to give her his hard-earned money to throw about the streets, and much more, for he was usually fairly bad of a Saturday night. In the end he would give her the money and ask her had she any intention of buying Sunday's dinner. Then she had to rush out as quickly as she could and do her marketing, holding her black leather purse tightly in her hand as she elbowed her way through the crowds and returning home late under her load of provisions. She had hard work to keep the house together and to see that the two young children who had been left to her charge went to school regularly and got their meals regularly. It was hard work—a hard life—but now that she was about to leave it she did not find it a wholly undesirable life.

She was about to explore another life with Frank. Frank was very kind, manly, open-hearted. She was to go away with him by the night-boat to be his wife and to live with him in Buenos Ayres where he had a home waiting for her. How well she remembered the first time she had seen him; he was lodging in a house on the main road where she used to visit. It seemed a few weeks ago. He was standing at the gate, his peaked cap pushed back on his head and his hair tumbled forward over a face of bronze. Then they had come to know each other. He used to meet her outside the Stores every evening and see her home. He took her to see *The Bohemian Girl* and she felt elated as she sat in an unaccustomed part of the theatre with him. He was awfully fond of music and sang a little. People knew that they were courting and, when he sang about the lass that loves a sailor, she always felt pleasantly confused. He used to call her Poppens out of fun. First of all it had been an excitement for her to have a fellow and then she had begun to like him. He had tales of distant countries. He had started as a deck boy at a pound a month on a ship of the Allan Line going out to Canada. He told her the names of the ships he had been on and the names of the different services. He had sailed through the Straits of Magellan and he told her stories of the terrible Patagonians. He had fallen on his feet in Buenos Ayres, he said, and had come over to the old country just for a holiday. Of course, her father had found out the affair and had forbidden her to have anything to say to him.

—I know these sailor chaps, he said.

One day he had quarrelled with Frank and after that she had to meet her lover secretly.

The evening deepened in the avenue. The white of two letters in her lap grew indistinct. One was to Harry; the other was to her father. Ernest had been her favourite but she liked Harry too. Her father was becoming old lately, she noticed; he would miss her. Sometimes he could be very nice. Not long before, when she had been laid up for a day, he had read her out a ghost story and made toast for her at the fire. Another day, when their mother was alive, they had all gone for a picnic to the Hill of Howth. She remembered her father putting on her mother's bonnet to make the children laugh.

Her time was running out but she continued to sit by the window, leaning her head against the window curtain, inhaling the odour of dusty cretonne. Down far in the avenue she could hear a street organ playing. She knew the air. Strange that it should come that very night to remind her of the promise to her mother, her promise to keep the home together as long as she could. She remembered the last night of her mother's illness; she was again in the close dark room at the other side of the hall and outside she heard a melancholy air of Italy. The organ-player had been ordered to go away and given sixpence. She remembered her father strutting back into the sickroom saying:

—Damned Italians! coming over here!

As she mused the pitiful vision of her mother's life laid its spell on the very quick of her being—that life of commonplace sacrifices closing in final craziness. She trembled as she heard again her mother's voice saying constantly with foolish insistence:

—Derevaun Seraun! Derevaun Seraun!

She stood up in a sudden impulse of terror. Escape! She must escape! Frank would save her. He would give her life, perhaps love, too. But she wanted to live. Why should she be unhappy? She had a right to happiness. Frank would take her in his arms, fold her in his arms. He would save her.

. . . .

She stood among the swaying crowd in the station at the North Wall. He held her hand and she knew that he was speaking to her, saying something about the passage over and over again. The station was full of soldiers with brown baggages. Through the wide doors of the sheds she caught a glimpse of the black mass of the boat, lying in beside the quay wall, with illumined portholes. She answered nothing. She felt her cheek pale and cold and, out of a maze of distress, she prayed to God to direct her, to show her what was her duty. The boat blew a long mournful whistle into the mist. If she went, to-morrow she would be on the sea with Frank, steaming towards Buenos Ayres. Their passage had been booked. Could she still draw back after all he had done for her? Her distress awoke a nausea in her body and she kept moving her lips in silent fervent prayer.

A bell clanged upon her heart. She felt him seize her hand:

—Come!

All the seas of the world tumbled about her heart. He was drawing her into them: he would drown her. She gripped with both hands at the iron railing.

—Come!

No! No! No! It was impossible. Her hands clutched the iron in frenzy. Amid the seas she sent a cry of anguish!

—Eveline! Evvy!

He rushed beyond the barrier and called to her to follow. He was shouted at to go on but he still called to her. She set her white face to him, passive, like a helpless animal. Her eyes gave him no sign of love or farewell or recognition.

CHAPTER 4

Talking It Over in Class
Philip Minkoff

◈ INTRODUCTION

This case study describes an 18-hour literature course in a French graduate business school, Audencia, Nantes School of Management. It examines the reasons for setting up the course, the difficulties encountered, the course content, and an evaluation of the course. As an illustration of the pedagogical approach taken, I look in some depth at a number of extracts from Barnes's (1991) *Talking It Over*.

◈ CONTEXT

Before students enter Audencia at the age of 20, they go through a tough selection process that includes a 2-year intensive postbaccalaureate preparation (the *classe préparatoire*) from 18 to 20 years of age for a highly competitive entrance exam. In spite of the heavy emphasis placed on math in *classe préparatoire*, students are expected to be good all-rounders. This includes being proficient in two foreign languages—one of which must be English—as well as having a sound cultural background, with an emphasis on history, geography, philosophy, social sciences, and current affairs.

French is given high priority, but the study of literature at both baccalaureate level and *classe préparatoire* level is often stilted. A methodological dissection of texts is taught at the expense of getting students to see literature as a source of pleasure and personal growth. This *lecture méthodique* (methodical reading approach), while developing a sense of rigour that can be applied to other subjects such as philosophy and history, hinges on the supposition that students have already acquired a literary culture, which in many cases they have not. Some, of course, have read widely in French and are very sensitive to literature. Others read occasionally and have acquired the basic critical skills. Few, on the other hand, have had more than a fleeting contact with literary texts in English.

The obstacle race for entry to a top management school means that students are usually conscientious, open-minded, innovative, pragmatic, and demanding. These qualities do not, of course, automatically lead to an overwhelming desire to read, let alone study, literature, and experience has shown me that imposing literature on business students is likely to meet with a certain amount of resistance, albeit passive. Perhaps there is a problem of face validity (how will studying literature help me negotiate a sales contract?); perhaps it brings back unhappy memories of having to plough through, then minutely dissect, pages and pages of obscure poetry to get a good grade at the baccalaureate. Whatever the reasons, the resistance is there. This is why the course that finally emerged, entitled Literature and Language, is not offered in the core curriculum but as an elective, with a strict warning that students who opt for it should be prepared to put in about 2 hours of out-of-class reading each week.

◈ DESCRIPTION

Like my students, I am a nonspecialist. I am an ex-business major with no formal training in, and no previous experience of, teaching literature. Given this, the absence of external constraints (e.g., a national curriculum or exams set by an outside body) and the fact that studying literature is not every business student's cup of tea, what, then, led me to want to set up a literature course? The answer is that after 10 years of teaching business English and communication skills, I needed to take on something more intellectually stimulating.

Deciding Why, What, and How to Teach

I was fortunate insofar as my desire to get out of a rut coincided with the school's new policy of encouraging diversity in its intake of students and in the courses offered (e.g., nonbusiness electives such as the history of art, ethics, and morals). Encouraged by this trend, I began putting together a course. I was also fortunate in being enrolled in a postgraduate programme at Nantes University entitled Educational Science and Didactics. This gave me access to the university library, and I was able to get advice on background reading from one of the English literature professors. However, being a very busy person, her guidance was not ongoing and I was left to fend for myself. I began to plough my way through what I was told was essential background reading in what turned out to be a naïve quest to establish clear objectives and develop a sound pedagogical framework. I read Roland Barthes, Wolfgang Iser, Umberto Eco, Christopher Brumfit, Henry Widdowson, and others, and the more I read, the more I felt out of my depth. The experience was frustrating for three reasons. First, there is so much to read on the subjects of literary criticism and methodology. Second, so much of it is dry, and even more of it is undecipherable—to a neophyte at any rate. Third, the parts that are decipherable, interesting though they may be, seemed mainly irrelevant to my immediate needs. What I was really looking for was for somebody to tell me, "This is *why* you should teach literature, this is *what* you should teach, and this is *how* you should teach it." Cooking recipes, I suppose.

The experience was, as I say, frustrating, but by no means a waste of time. The first part of my quest, "Why teach literature to nonnative learners?" has, at least, been partially answered. The study of literature, if dealt with from a linguistic perspective, will, it is hoped, help students become a little more aware of the ways language is used to create meanings other than the direct transfer of information. A sensitivity to style and register is a necessary component of language acquisition, especially at an advanced level.

As for the second part of the quest, "What to teach?" many of my guiding principles came from Kramsch (1993), who introduced me to the distinction between efferent and aesthetic approaches to reading. The efferent approach (decoding forms and information in texts) is what the students I teach are rather good at, having spent 10 or so years doing just that. The aesthetic approach, on the other hand, deals with the particularities of style, the use of genres and registers, and the fractured symmetries and ambiguities of a literary text. Students who use only the efferent approach to reading will be deceived into believing that all they have to do is retrieve a meaning that is already in the text. It does not account for the fact that a text creates its reader through its very structure or form and that readers, in turn, create the text as they themselves give it meaning.

However, Kramsch (1993) does go on to warn that it is not easy to predict what kind of reading a text will encourage:

> A linear, predictable narrative structure on a familiar theme with easy-to-fill silences elicits more readily a response from a foreign reader, but it can be deceptive and tempt students into reading it only on an efferent level. A linguistically easy text might present a narrative sophistication that is unfamiliar to the students, thus raising their aesthetic curiosity. (p. 138)

Regarding the third part of the quest, "How to teach?" there was really very little I came across that actually helped me, or at least not directly. Perhaps there simply cannot be any systematic, step-by-step approach to dealing with literature in the classroom, all texts and all readers being different. However, I found the following simple model by Kramsch (1996) quite useful:

> A literary narrative yields meaning in three ways:
>
> • Story: What does the story tell? (setting, characters, events/plot)
>
> • Text: How does the text tell the story? (vocabulary and grammar, discourse structure, textual time and space, parallelisms, etc.)
>
> • Narration: How do the narrator and reader give meaning to the story? (narrative voice, point of view, reader response, etc.)
>
> All three ways should be explored because the overall meaning depends on all three. (n.p.)

What I came up with in the end was an eclectic mix of texts that I chose because I really like them. In this, too, I followed Kramsch's (1993) advice:

> The teacher's initial reaction to the text will be his most valuable asset in teaching it. Ideally, a teacher should never have to teach anything to which he or she is totally indifferent; even hating a text can be the best incentive to find out something about that text and oneself as a reader. (p. 138)

Why, though, choose a text you hate? I felt that having carte blanche entitled me to choose only texts I liked. My second consideration, and an equally important one, was to choose texts that were accessible and at the same time rich enough to arouse great interest and sustain a class discussion for 90 minutes. It is important to bear in mind that the difficulty of a given text is not necessarily in the vocabulary and grammar but in the meaning students are required to find in it. In two cases (extracts from Joyce's [1922/2002] *Ulysses* and Pinter's [1979] *Betrayal*), I chose texts that clearly illustrate a particular style. As for Shakespeare, I felt that no programme could be complete without at least a fleeting glimpse of this great writer. The programme, after several modifications, is currently as shown in Figure 1. The order is of no particular importance, except that our study of Tom Stoppard's (1967/1991) *Rosencrantz and Guildenstern Are Dead* has to follow on from the lecture and discussion of Shakespeare's (1603/1992) *Hamlet*. Another consideration was beginning the programme with very accessible texts so as not to discourage weaker students.

The programme, given its short duration, is fairly varied in that it touches on three of the four main genres. I had originally included some poems by T. S. Eliot but dropped them because I could not get enough response from the class. There is now no poetry included. Other works, such as an extract from Lewis Carroll's *Through the Looking-Glass*, were dropped for similar reasons. The programme is mainly contemporary with a brief glimpse at Shakespeare and James Joyce. White males dominate, for which I apologise; I have no excuse except to say that sex and ethnic origin were not uppermost in my mind when I chose the texts.

Launched in 1996, the programme is an 18-hour elective and is offered twice a year to students in their final or penultimate year of study. About 20 students enrol

Lesson 1	• What is literature? How important is it to you? Why bother studying English literature? • Identifying and discussing short extracts from a range of genres and periods	
Lesson 2	• "Crickets" (Butler, 1992a) • "Lamb to the Slaughter" (Dahl, 1953/2002)	Short stories
Lesson 3	• *Talking It Over* (Barnes, 1991), chapter 1	Extract from novel
Lesson 4	• "The Chinese Lobster" (Byatt, 1995)	Short story
Lesson 5	• *Ulysses* (Joyce, 1922/2002), extracts	Extracts from novel
Lesson 6	• "The Trip Back" (Butler, 1992b) • "My Son the Fanatic" (Kureishi, 1997)	Short stories
Lesson 7	• *Betrayal*, part 1 (Pinter, 1979)	Drama
Lesson 8	• *Betrayal*, part 2 (Pinter, 1979)	Drama
Lesson 9	• Shakespeare lecture • *Hamlet* (Shakespeare, 1603/1992), extracts	Drama
Lesson 10	• *Rosencrantz and Guildenstern Are Dead* (Stoppard, 1967/1991), part 1	Drama
Lesson 11	• *Rosencrantz and Guildenstern Are Dead* (Stoppard, 1967/1991), part 2	Drama
Lesson 12	• *The Remains of the Day* (Ishiguro, 1989), extracts	Extracts from novel

FIGURE 1. Programme for Literature and Language Course, Audencia, Nantes School of Management

for each session, which means that 15 or so students turn up for any given class. The class is small enough to have frontal lessons and still involve all students, and I never ask students to work in pairs or small groups, except for part of the first lesson, which involves having to identify genres.

Reflecting on the Nature of Literature

The first lesson begins with a reflection on the nature of literature. What is literature? What can be included as literature? I find that this is a good way to open as it allows students to express themselves in front of classmates they may not know, while I can play the devil's advocate, arguing, for example, that literature means great books by great authors, preferably men, preferably White, and preferably dead, or that literature includes love letters, biographies, essays, and sermons. It is also an opportunity for me to introduce the concepts of aesthetic and efferent reading by using Widdowson's (1975) comparison of scientific and literary texts. Presented in the form of a table, the class can see that literature, unlike scientific texts, foregrounds language and exploits ambiguity to create something dynamic and destabilising.

The rest of the first lesson involves identifying genres. In pairs, students have 15 minutes to read eight short extracts and classify them under the following headings: biography, contemporary classic, 18th-century novel, 19th-century novel, science fiction, spy novel, textbook, and thriller. They are also expected to justify their choice. This activity allows us to look at a number of interesting points, such as

- the choice of vocabulary (The opening paragraph of James's [1986] *A Taste for Death*, with its obsession for detail, also contains vocabulary associated with death such as *wax, brass,* and *dust.*)

- the evolution of the novel and the changing role of the narrator (as discussed later in the section Exploring Narration)

- literary devices in works of nonfiction

My preferred teaching approach is to ask questions to elicit a number of responses. I try to comment on each response or ask others to react to a classmate's comment. In this way, short discussions can emerge. It is sometimes necessary for me to give prompts or clues to help students see a particular point I consider important. By asking questions and offering prompts, I am able to guide the discussion in a way that will encourage interaction and help students reach a deeper level of understanding.

Beginning a Text

I have chosen to focus on Barnes's (1991) *Talking It Over* to illustrate how literature can be used in the classroom. The students in this course have 1 week to read the first chapter, entitled "His, His or Her, Their." The only instructions I give are to read the text carefully and be prepared to talk about it in class. I avoid guiding them at this stage as I want each reader to develop a personal appreciation of the text. (In the following paragraphs, I have italicised the questions I ask the students.)

The lesson begins with my usual questions: *Did you like it? Why? Why not?* Apart from warming up the class, this 10-minute introduction helps me to gauge the mood of the group, to see who has understood the nuances (and on whom I can rely later on) and to reassure those who had a hard time understanding what it was all about.

Exploring Narration

In a previous class, 2 weeks before this one, the class will have discussed the changing role of the narrator in the English novel. The class will have seen that the intrusive, omniscient, 19th-century narrator provided an authoritative view of reality, wider than any of the characters' individual consciousness. The class will also have seen that this intrusive, omniscient narrator is eclipsed early in the 20th century and replaced by passages of introspection and self-analysis. When I ask the class to talk about the unusual structure of Barnes's chapter (and, indeed, the entire novel), the response is not difficult to elicit. There are three narrators who take turns to speak. The structure is interesting because the reader learns about each of the three characters by what they say about themselves (what they choose to say and what they choose not to say), what the others say about them, and, most important, how they say it—the language they use.

It is clear to most readers that the three narrators do not speak the same way, and this is a point that is worth exploring. The following extract is the first narrator's (Stuart's) introduction:

> Stuart   My name is Stuart, and I remember everything.
>   Stuart's my Christian name. My full name is Stuart Hughes. My *full* name: that's all there is to it. No middle name. Hughes was the name of my parents, who were married for twenty-five
> 5   years. They called me Stuart. I didn't particularly like the name at first—I got called things like Stew and Stew-Pot at school —but I've got used to it. I can handle it. I can handle my handle.
>   Sorry, I'm not very good at jokes. People have told me that before. Anyway, Stuart Hughes—I think, that'll do for me. I
> 10   don't want to be called St John St John de Vere Knatchbull. My parents were called Hughes. (p. 1)

What do we learn about Stuart from the way he speaks in these few opening lines? Perhaps there are slightly fewer contractions than we would expect in spoken language (Lines 1 and 2); perhaps less use of possessives and more use of prepositional phrases with "of" (Line 4). It is not much, but the impression we have is of a slightly stilted style, a rather conventional, slightly apologetic Englishman.

If we compare Stuart's introduction to Oliver's introduction later in the chapter, the difference is striking:

> 210   Oliver   Hi, I'm Oliver, Oliver Russell. Cigarette? No, I didn't think you would. You don't mind if I do? Yes, I *do* know it's bad for my health as a matter of fact, that's why I like it. God, we've only just met and you're coming on like some rampant nut-eater. What's it got to do with you anyway?
> 215   In fifty years I'll be dead and you'll be a sprightly lizard slurping yoghurt through a straw, sipping peat-bog water and wearing health sandals. (p. 8)

How does Oliver come across? Do we immediately warm to him? No reader is blind to Oliver's informal, chatty style (note, e.g., that there are more contractions here than in Stuart's introduction, though the latter is longer). But what for some is an aggressive streak (Line 214), others recognise as good-humoured provocation. Oliver's wit is something that many students simply do not see at first glance.

Stuart and Oliver, then, speak very differently, and this chapter provides the reader with many opportunities to compare and contrast. In the following passage, Oliver is talking about Stuart, his "oldest friend":

> In my view the jugular podge wouldn't show up so much if he had longer hair, but he never gives that coarse mousy matting of his any *Lebensraum*. And with his round face
> 320 and friendly little circular eyes peering at you from behind those less-than-state-of-the-art spectacles. I mean, he looks *amicable* enough, but he somehow needs *work*, wouldn't you say? . . .
> . . . Maybe he seeks a more thrustful mien so that when he goes to his nasty little hutch in the City and glares at his neurotically blinking little screen and barks
> 330 into his cellular telephone for another *tranche* of lead futures or whatever, he comes over as just a trifle more macho than we all know him to be. (p. 12)

Why does Oliver use so many foreign words (coup de grâce, fundador, Lebensraum, mien, tranche)? Is it a mark of sophistication, is it an example of his tongue-in-cheek wit, or is he being ostentatious or pretentious? The students' reactions to this vary, of course. *How might Stuart react to Oliver's style of speaking, in light of what Stuart has already told us about simplicity and pretentiousness?* Incidentally, the only foreign words that Stuart uses are from Latin (e.g., *sine die*, Line 94), a dead language.

Exploring Conflict and Freedom

One of the main themes of this chapter is the impending conflict between the three characters, Oliver and Stuart, who are old friends, and Gillian, who is Stuart's wife. The seeds of conflict are best seen in the ongoing and good-natured discussion they have regarding the rights and wrongs of *his, his or her,* and *their.* I start this discussion by asking the students to fill in the correct pronoun in the following sentence:

One of the delegates has parked _____ car in front of the entrance.

Students are often surprised to learn that all three are commonly used. Our three characters, however, each have a different opinion. Oliver opts for *his*, Stuart prefers *their*, whereas Gillian goes for *his or her*. *What do these differences reveal?* The possessive, singular nature of Oliver's choice may reflect his own singularity and masculinity. Or it may be that he enjoys being provocative and politically incorrect. The plurality of Stuart's choice may reflect a passive, slightly clumsy neutrality. Gillian's choice, while reflecting her desire for equality, may also be interpreted as sitting on the fence; perhaps she will be forced to make a choice later on in the story.

As Stuart later goes on to say:

> 96 Here we were, three reasonably intelligent people discussing the merits of his and his or her and their. Tiny little words, yet we couldn't agree. And we were friends. Yet we couldn't agree. Something about this worried me. (p. 4)

What does Stuart's comment imply? The implication is that behind the words lies something else, something possibly sinister, which is, as yet, only vaguely hinted at.

If one of the main themes of this chapter is conflict, another is freedom—the freedom, for example, to choose your name and how your choice of name defines who you are. Whereas Gillian and Oliver changed their names (for reasons that students rather enjoy discussing), Stuart, as we saw earlier, sees no reason for upsetting the status quo. Others may have tried to change his name for him, but he learned to get "used to it" (Line 7) in a way that Gillian and Oliver never could.

What other freedoms are discussed in the chapter? The freedom to choose what to remember is also discussed. Stuart claims that he remembers everything (Line 129), whereas Oliver insists that he remembers only the important things and that most people's minds are like "a monstrous skip crammed with trivia" (Line 238). Whatever the pros and cons of a finely honed selective memory versus a monstrous tip, there are certainly huge discrepancies in what is actually retained. *What does a comparison of Stuart's and Oliver's recollections of the wedding ceremony reveal?* The differences, shown in Figure 2, are striking, and their significance is worth discussing.

Whose memory is the more accurate? There is no way of telling, especially as Gillian complicates matters by telling us that the ring was "sitting on a fat burgundy cushion" (Line 206). The class then looks in more depth at Oliver's recollections of that wedding ceremony. Before reading the following passage aloud, I draw the students' attention to its importance. They will have a minute or so after the reading to identify what is important.

> So I believe in coddling my memory, just slipping it the finer morsels of experience. That lunch after the wedding, for
> 265 instance. We had a perfectly frisky non-vintage champagne chosen by Stuart (brand? search me? *mis en bouteille par Les Vins de l'Oubli*), and ate *saumon sauvage grillé avec son coulis de tomates maison*. I wouldn't have chosen it myself, but then I wasn't consulted anyway. No, it was perfectly all
> 270 right, just a little unimaginative . . . Mme Wyatt, with whom I was *à côté*, seemed to enjoy it, or at least to relish the salmon. But she pushed rather at the pinkish translucent cubelets which surrounded the fish, then turned to me and asked,
> "What exactly would you say this might be?"
> 275 "Tomato," I was able to inform her. "Skinned, cored, de-pipped, cubed."
> "How curious, Oliver, to identify what gives a fruit its character, and then to remove it." (p. 10)

	Stuart	Oliver
the weather	a beautiful day, soft, gentle	swirling clouds, too much wind
the registrar	dignified, correct degree of formality	oleaginous, crepuscular, little, full of dandruff
the ring	the ring I'd bought, a plum-coloured cushion	like an IUD, a damson pouffe
Gillian	whispered her vows	could scarcely vocalise her responses, was crying

FIGURE 2. Stuart's and Oliver's Recollections of the Wedding Ceremony

What is the importance of this passage? We have a coming together of many of the ideas previously raised: foreign words, memory, conflict, names, identity. *Is Oliver simply describing a meal, or is there something else behind the words?* The tomato, like Stuart, has kept its name but every other identifying feature has been removed and all that is left is something pinkish, translucent, and unimaginative.

Freedom, then, is the freedom to live as you please, to choose who you want to be and avoid ending up "skinned, cored, depipped, cubed" (Lines 275 and 276). There is, however, one part of life over which people have no control and that, of course, is death. *How does Oliver view death?* At first he gives the impression that it is inevitable, that everybody has got to die, so let's make the most of living while we're alive, let's smoke to our heart's content. This bravado, however, cracks in the closing paragraphs of the chapter:

> Have I told you my Theory of Life, by the way? Life is like invading Russia. A blitz start, massed shakos,
> 415 plumes dancing like a flustered henhouse; a period of svelte progress recorded in ebullient despatches as the enemy falls back; then the beginning of a long, morale-sapping trudge with rations getting shorter and the first snowflakes upon your face. The enemy burns Moscow and you yield to Gen-
> 420 eral January, whose fingernails are very icicles. Bitter retreat. Harrying Cossacks. Eventually you fall beneath a boy-gunner's grapeshot while crossing some Polish river not even marked on your general's map (p. 15)

Behind Oliver's facade of bravado, then, how does he really view death? Death is anything but honourable. People are not shot neatly through the heart by a professional soldier in uniform but by a mere boy-gunner who uses not bullets but grapeshot. Death is unheroic, sordid, degrading, and meaningless. Death is not spectacular. People die alone, anonymously, while trying to cross some obscure, unmarked Polish river.

And what about life? What does each of Oliver's metaphors refer to? The "plumes dancing like a flustered henhouse" (the excited and colourful frivolity of adolescence? a crowded nightclub?); "rations getting shorter and the first snowflakes upon your face" (the slow physical decline through middle age? missed opportunities? going grey, realising that things are only going to get worse?); "the enemy burns Moscow" (your dream in life—a cottage by the sea, a long and happy marriage, health and strength, fame and fortune—is simply not going to happen?); and "bitter retreat" (let's go back and try and recapture something of our youth, we'll go out more, travel more, spend more time with friends—but the world has changed and we cannot return?).

Exploring Friendship

So as not to end the class on too depressing a note, we can take another look at the relationship between Stuart and Oliver. Oliver's speech is full of not only direct swipes at his oldest friend ("I'm afraid I couldn't tell you whether Stuart was wearing his medium-dark-grey suit or his dark-dark-grey suit for the ceremony" [Lines 281–283]) but also indirect assaults ("Like that deep trog of a bank manager" [Line 372]).

Consider the following passage:

> Like that deep trog of a bank manager I went to
> see at the end of my first term at university. The sort of fellow
> who gets an erection when he hears the bank rate's gone up a
> 375   tenth of a percent. Anyway, this trog, this . . . Walter had me into
> his panelled wankpit of an office, classified my request to
> change the name on my cheques from N. O. Russell to Oliver
> Russell as not central to the Bank's policy for the 1980s, and
> reminded me that unless funds were forthcoming to camouflage
> 380   my black hole of an overdraft I wouldn't be getting a new
> cheque-book even if I called myself Santa Claus. (p. 14)

What does this tell us about Oliver's feelings toward Stuart? Well, perhaps nothing. After all, the object of Oliver's condescension here is not Stuart or, at least, not directly. However, we do know that Stuart has a top job in a bank, so there may well be some transfer of Oliver's feelings from him to the bank manager. If the reader is prepared to go along with this, the sexual references ("erection" and "wankpit") take on a deeper significance in the context of the love triangle that we can see emerging.

When two males are vying for one female, it helps if one can undermine the other rival's virility. Oliver's speech is full of references to Stuart's sexual inadequacy, without him ever saying it in so many words. *Can you identify any of these references* (e.g., the mousy hair, the wedding ring like an IUD on a damson pouffe, the name *Stuart Hughes* destined for a career in soft furnishings, the black hole of an overdraft that needs to be camouflaged)? *How does this compare with Oliver's idea of himself?* Consider the following passage:

> then matadored the old charm around in front of
> him for a few minutes, and before you could say *fundador*
> 385   Walt was on his knees begging for the *coup de grâce*. So
> I allowed him the honour of endorsing my change of name. (p. 14)

The image of the matador conjures up grace, power, and, above all, virility.

Wrapping Up

The lesson ends with a recapitulation of the idea raised at the beginning, namely, that the way each of the characters speaks reveals as much as—if not more than—what each of them actually says. Furthermore, the oral style of the text, with its vocabulary and syntax characteristic of spontaneous, colloquial speech, seems authentic at first glance. However, on closer examination, this seeming authenticity reveals itself for what it is—an illusion behind which Barnes, the invisible ventriloquist, cleverly steers readers into a reflection on who they are and how they choose to live and die.

◈ DISTINGUISHING FEATURES

A Literature Course for Business Students

The main distinguishing feature in this course is in its context, namely, that it is offered to business students for whom literature is not necessarily a major preoccupation. The design of the course may not be special, innovative, or different, but from the students' point of view, it may be a refreshing change from the rather academic approach taken by their high school teachers earlier on in their studies. Sitting around in a circle, airing their point of view, and reacting to their classmates is something that not all French business students have had the pleasure of experiencing.

It is probably also unusual for a literature course to be taught at university level by a nonspecialist. Not only do I not have the formal training that other literature teachers enjoy, but I teach literature only twice a year (for a total of 36 hours), which, at the beginning at least, made me feel slightly unsettled.

Other features of the course worth mentioning are that, contrary to many other courses, there is no poetry on this course and that I include extracts. From a methodological point of view, I have stressed previously that most sessions are conducted in a frontal manner. In addition, students are expected to prepare many of the readings on their own before they are tackled in class.

Two-Way Evaluation

Evaluating a course of this nature is no easy matter. Most students enrolled in the course come to class most of the time, so I suppose I must be doing something right. They also come to class having read the assignments carefully, although there have been times when this has not been the case (see my comments in the Practical Ideas section). There is an out-of-class written assignment of two or three pages in which the students are expected not simply to regurgitate ideas that were discussed in class but to add some original ones. The results are generally very good and in some cases absolutely striking. The informal feedback I receive is, on the whole, positive.

I have also begun asking students to hand in a written appraisal at the end of the course and this, I am pleased to say, has been extremely positive. Here are some of the comments from December 2001:

- Although not directly relevant to my professional projects, the course has been very enriching for my personal development.

- It allowed me to learn about a subject which I wouldn't have done alone.

- An opportunity to study English in a more relaxed, less academic context than usual.

- The course has made me want to extend my reading of English literature.

- I feel more confident about taking on novels in English.

- Even though some of the texts were too difficult for me, I enjoyed being stretched.

- The course offers a cultural dimension which is appreciated.

- An opportunity for me to think about important themes in some depth (living in a foreign culture, betrayal, depression, death, artistic creation, etc.).

- The course is analytical rather than descriptive, and this develops our awareness.

- The course lacks a historical perspective which outlines the main literary movements in English literature.

- It would be interesting to do more work around the texts (more about the author, the period, the literary context).

- It would have been better to study fewer works, but study each in more depth.

The term that comes up most often in these evaluations (written in French) is *ouverture d'esprit.* The English equivalent, *awareness,* hardly does justice to the image of the mind and spirit opening up.

◈ PRACTICAL IDEAS

Select Texts That You Really Enjoy

Selecting texts you enjoy is preferable to trying to cater to students' perceived tastes. Many of the students in my class read Stephen King's novels, but I would feel uncomfortable including these in my course because I do not really like them. It does not bother me to hear a student at the beginning of a lesson say, "I didn't like the assignment very much." In fact, I see this as a challenge and hope that by the end of the lesson my enthusiasm will have rubbed off on them. The material, though, has to be fairly accessible to the students and lend itself readily to classroom discussion.

Create an Atmosphere in Which Students Are Encouraged to Express Their Ideas

Although not all interpretations are valid, an exchange of ideas is essential, and you should not shy away from eccentric responses. Nevertheless, ask students to justify their position, call on the others to comment on a classmate's point of view, and share with the class your own understanding of the text, but never tell a student that he or she has missed the point.

Make Sure You Focus on How the Text Achieves Certain Effects

Bring to your students' attention the ways in which language is used (e.g., the sound of words, ambiguities, metaphors, registers, parallels, pauses, silences, withholding of information). Sometimes a single phrase or a single word can be the focus of a 10-minute discussion. For example, in "Lamb to the Slaughter" (Dahl, 1953/2002), the policemen's voices are described as being "thick and sloppy" (Line 314), with all the associations that these two adjectives spark off.

Be Prepared to Think on Your Feet

Putting together a course such as this requires an enormous amount of thought, but no amount of preparation can guarantee its success. The main danger is that students do not always prepare the reading that has been assigned or do not read it carefully enough to be able to sustain a meaningful discussion. When this happens, you have to adopt other techniques to keep the lesson moving. For example, you may have to play the devil's advocate to prod students into responding, using a role-play situation. Thus, you may present students with the following:

OK, you're Stuart . . . happily married, pretty secure, lucrative job, down to earth. I shouldn't really be telling you this but, well, the other day I bumped into your old friend, Oliver, and apparently he's been telling everyone that he finds you boring and unimaginative. I mean does he always talk about you like that?

A similar tactic, again addressing the students as Stuart but dealing with another part of the novel could be to say to them, "You were telling us once that at your wedding he got up and toasted the bride. How did you feel? I mean isn't it the groom who's meant to toast the bride? How do you reckon Gillian finds him?" Similarly, dealing with students' unexpected responses can be difficult, more so, I find, than in a class discussion on current affairs or social issues.

◈ CONCLUSION

The questions of why teach literature, what to teach, how to teach, and how to evaluate the course have not been—cannot be—answered precisely, although raising these issues is, I believe, an essential part of the process of setting up a course. What I have learned, and what teachers preparing a similar course may want to bear in mind, is the importance of establishing a guiding principle. For me, this included the need to move away from the teaching approach that uses texts as pretexts for comprehension and grammar exercises or for teaching culture. It meant my having to learn how to understand and appreciate the peculiarities of a literary text and how to share them with the students in a way that is not too directive yet structured enough for students to feel that the programme has brought added value.

◈ CONTRIBUTOR

Philip Minkoff has been teaching English at Audencia, Nantes School of Management, in France, since 1985. He is the author of *Executive Skills* (Prentice Hall, 1994) and has written a number of articles on language teaching and culture.

CHAPTER 5

Stories Lean on Stories: Literature Experiences in ESL Teacher Education

Tatiana Gordon, Joan Zaleski, and Debra Goodman

❧ INTRODUCTION

Oral histories, memoirs, biographies, historical fiction, narrative fiction, prose, and poetry have found their way into the constructivist teacher education classrooms. The use of autobiography (e.g., Abbs, 1974), imagery (e.g., Clandinin, 1986), metaphors (e.g., Tobin, 1990), and imaginative literature and media (e.g., Brunner, 1994) has been explored and documented. Continuing the work of those who experiment with the use of narrative ways of knowing in teacher education, this chapter provides an overview of the ways in which Hofstra University's TESOL program incorporates the use of literature in the preparation of second language teachers. Relying on various types of literature response (e.g., construction of and reflection upon their own language learning stories) and various modes of engagement with the text (e.g., book clubs), the program empowers teacher learners to bridge cultural and social disjunctures (Ball, 1998) and become more effective second language educators.

For this chapter, we define literature as embracing fiction, poetry, and creative nonfiction. Definitions of literature are multiple. Formalists and structuralists base their definition of literature on the use of specific literary devices in the text. New critics speak of a literary canon, privileging some works over others (Eagleton, 1983). We work with a constructivist definition that interprets literature as "a particular kind of utterance that a writer has 'constructed' not for [practical] use but for his own satisfaction" (Britton, 1982, p. 36). According to Britton, this satisfaction comes when readers assume the roles of "spectators" and reflect on their lives.

❧ CONTEXT

Hofstra University is located in the town of Hempstead, on Long Island, east of New York City, in the United States. Leading to the New York State certification to teach ESL, Hofstra's TESOL program is designed to prepare second language educators who will be working with young and adolescent language learners. The majority of the program's graduates become employed as elementary- and secondary-level ESL teachers in various school districts in Long Island's Nassau and Suffolk Counties. A sizable group of graduates teaches in New York City schools.

Long Island, the home of Hofstra University, is experiencing a striking shift in its demographics. This suburban area, which formerly had only a few immigrant enclaves, is becoming increasingly diverse. According to the Immigration and Naturalization Service (1996), the number of immigrants moving to Long Island is steadily increasing. Whereas in 1995, 8,039 immigrants relocated to Long Island, in 1996 the number grew to 10,594—a 32% increase. Two of the largest and fastest growing groups are Latino and Asian. The U.S. Census Bureau (2000) indicates that Latino immigrants account for 10.0% and 10.5% of the total population in Long Island's Nassau and Suffolk Counties respectively; Asian immigrants are reported to constitute 4%. Long Island residents are acutely aware of the changes in the area's population profile; *Newsday,* a local newspaper, has been running articles with headlines such as "Island's Little El Salvador" (Jones, 2001) and "Surge in LI's Asians" (Endo, 2001).

Cultural Disjunctures

The abrupt shift in the demographics of the area is accompanied by cultural rifts— or in Ball's (1998) words, *disjunctures*—between language minorities and the communities where immigrant families live and immigrant children are being schooled. These disjunctures can be profound and manifest themselves in nativist outbursts, such as the clash of local residents with Mexican American immigrants in Nassau County's town of Farmingville (Smith, 2001). They may be more covert and reveal themselves in the segregation in Long Island's residential patterns (Peracchio, 1990).

The makeup of Hofstra's TESOL program student body is congruous with the ethnocultural configuration of Long Island's population. Although the majority of teacher learners are suburbanites who have been raised locally and educated in Long Island's schools, a sizable number (almost 30%) are immigrants from a variety of cultural and ethnic backgrounds, such as Brazil, Chile, China, Colombia, Greece, Haiti, Israel, Korea, Peru, Puerto Rico, Russia, and the Ukraine.

To some extent, the cultural disjunctures found in the Long Island area affect Hofstra students, with a few tendencies particularly prominent. Teacher learners who have been educated in suburban Long Island schools speak and write with some concern about their insufficient familiarity with immigrant cultures and their lack of understanding of the immigrant community perspective. They also are wary about their ability to function successfully in the New York City schools. As for teacher learners who were educated outside the United States, they tend to speak and write about having missed out on the education and experience necessary to appreciate some of the educational issues explored in the classroom.

As is clear from this account, Hofstra's TESOL program operates in a context characterized by multiple disjunctures. These disjunctures between the local communities and the communities of language and cultural minorities or between the experiential and cultural backgrounds of teacher learners and those of their future students need to be considered when decisions for the TESOL program are being made, as it is to the teacher learners enrolled in the program to whom the job of bridging these disjunctures is eventually going to fall.

Theoretical Framework

The decision to integrate literature and creative writing into the program has a lot to do with the context in which the program is being implemented. Given that home cultures of the teacher learners and their would-be students are strikingly dissimilar, faculty made the decision to pair up modes of inquiry traditional in academia with heuristic tools that are more capable of evoking an emotional response, more open ended, and more universally meaningful. Narrative ways of knowing have been integrated into the program to enable teacher learners to bridge cultural, educational, and emotional disjunctures while achieving multiple program goals.

First, literature and personal narratives serve as a means for exploring cultures and building complex cultural meanings. By reading literary texts and narratives, teacher learners begin to develop a less ethnocentric stance toward cultures other than their own and also develop understanding of the "enabling and constraining dimensions of culture" (Giroux, Shumway, Smith, & Sosnoski, 1988, p. 144). Most important, TESOL students build a more complex and profound understanding of U.S. culture as it relates to the education of language and cultural minorities.

The capacity of literary discourse and narrative to encode cultural meanings and to make them legible to the outsider is widely recognized in anthropological research (e.g., Rosaldo, 1989). Personal narratives in particular have been pointed to in numerous ethnographic studies (e.g., Bruner, 1986) as artifacts through which cultures become intelligible to others. Significantly for the program goals, personal stories have been demonstrated (Ball, 1998) to serve as rich repositories of entextualized knowledge that can be used to inform the process of reforming the schools' curricula to meet the needs of cultural minorities.

Further, literature is relied on in the program because of its capacity to stimulate reflection. Through encounters with literature, teacher learners embark on a process of reconstructing and reorganizing their personal theories of language and literacy learning. Teacher learners also begin to question common educational practices and reflect critically on institutionalized ways of teaching.

Much has been said about the power of literature to stimulate thinking. As researchers of literary discourse (e.g., Lotman, 1972) point out, literature does not provide answers; rather, it poses questions and provokes the thought process. Notably, literary discourse has been demonstrated (e.g., Buchman, 1988; Brunner, 1994) to be an effective instrument for stimulating teacher learner reflection. Buchman (1988) speaks of the capacity of literature to evoke contemplative response in the teacher education classroom. Similarly, Brunner (1994) suggests that "openness, incompleteness, and contradiction," the features of books that call for "constructive, interpretive activity" (p. 98), make literature an effective means for stirring reflection that reveals to the teacher learner the arbitrariness of the culture of schooling.

The use of literature also has a lot to do with the affective goals that we strive to achieve, namely, with the program's effort to foster the teacher learners' sense of connectedness with their would-be students and to promote the pedagogy of caring. We are concerned with engaging teachers learners in the kind of knowing that Dewey (1933) describes as the "fusion of intellectual and emotional" (p. 118) and Maxine Greene (1978) refers to as "committed rationality" (pp. 21–23).

This goal is made possible because of the nature of the transaction that takes place during the reader's encounter with literary discourse. In contrast to the predominantly efferent, public meaning-oriented reader stance that occurs during the reader's encounter with scholarly discourse, the stance adopted by the reader who is experiencing a literary text has been described as predominantly aesthetic, evoking personally associative, emotional sensations and value-laden meanings of the words (e.g., Karolides, 1999; Rosenblatt, 1938). Personal narratives in particular have been pointed to as discursive events endowed with powerful means of establishing the emotional bond between the writer and the reader. Narratologists (e.g., Bal, 1997) argue that the explication of the narrator in the narrative presumes the presence of the interlocutor or the narratee to whom the narration is addressed. By virtue of its idiosyncratic structure (i.e., author → narrator → imaginary reader → reader), the narrative is capable of establishing a connection with the reader. Notably, narratives have been demonstrated to promote "connectedness, trust, teamwork" in the teacher education classroom (Brody, Witherell, Donald, & Lunblad, 1991, p. 261).

Finally, the literature component is used in the program as a source that inspires teacher learners to action. Literature is significant in this regard, because it can speak in the language that Giroux (1988) describes as "a language of possibility" (p. 113). In her study of the use of stories in teacher education, Brunner (1994) demonstrated the usefulness of stories for educating the empowered teacher; that is, the teacher who "sees possibilities for affecting his or her environment and for making a contribution to society" (p. 50).

◈ DESCRIPTION

The program's literature component is meant to impart the historic and cultural flesh to the academia-generated conceptual backbone, provoke reflection, evoke feeling, and stimulate action. We use the narrative mode of inquiry to break out of the artificial discipline constraints, to avoid the false dichotomy between academia and nonacademia, or, in Freire's (1997) words, to combine "reading of the word" with "reading of the world," "reading of text" with "reading of context" (p. 46).

To accomplish these goals, the program uses twofold ways of knowing, in which meaning construction moves between the academic and the literary idioms and in which scholarly texts are supplemented by narratives. The types of literary oeuvres used in the program are varied; they include poetry and children's literature, biographies and autobiographies, and historical fiction and fictionalized biographies.

The double-pronged (literary cum nonliterary) inquiry is undertaken in most courses in the program. For instance, the sociolinguistics course uses poetry to initiate discussion on language variation. The narrative poem "Rayford's Song" (Inada, 1992) illustrates the potential of literature to raise and examine complex issues without losing sight of the deeply human, cultural, and personal nature of language and language learning. In initial class reflections, teacher learners report that they typically correct children's language variants (whether stemming from home dialect or second language influences) without giving much thought to their own actions. But suddenly the teacher learners hear Rayford, the protagonist of Inada's poem, ask,

Miss Gordon, ma'am—
we always singing your songs.
Could I sing one of my own? (p. 43)

Inada writes that Rayford sings about "suh-whing a-looow su-wheeeet ah charr-ee-
oohh" (p. 44) in a way that had "the whole world focusing on that one song . . .
making even Miss Gordon's white hair shine in the glory of it" (p. 44). After insisting
that Rayford repeat *chariot* correctly, Miss Gordon asks if anyone else would "care to
sing a song of their own?" (p. 45):

Our songs, our songs were there—

. . .

but they just wouldn't come out.
Where did our voices go? (p. 45)

Inada's poem illustrates the connection between language, culture, and family
background, allowing teacher education students to explore the critical role of
teachers in considering the potential of all students to sing their own song.

In the multicultural curriculum class, while exploring legislation and litigation
that has shaped the education of language and cultural minorities, teacher learners
read excerpts from *La Causa: The Migrant Farmworkers' Story* (De Ruiz & Larios,
1993). By participating vicariously in the life and work of the migrant farmworkers,
teacher learners begin to understand some of the grievances of minority communities, which brought forth the Bilingual Education Act of 1968. Following up with
reading *Voices From the Fields: Children of Migrant Farmworkers Tell Their Stories*
(Atkin, 1993), a collection of interviews with the children of today's migrant
farmworkers, teacher learners get to hear the voices of today's immigrant students.
When one of the interviewees, Mari Carmen Lopez, says, "My parents feel bad about
my working in the fields, but they don't have the education to be able to work in
anything else. But education is very important to them. They always tell us we need
to go on studying so we don't have to work in the fields" (p. 88), she speaks to the
teachers of tomorrow.

Literature is also integrated into the program's assessment course. Teacher
learners read excerpts from Lemann's *The Big Test* (1999), which combines social
analysis with personal history, and become familiar with the "time—roughly
speaking 1890–1920—when eugenicist views were common among enlightened
Americans" (p. 23). It was the time when the idea that intelligence is quantifiable first
captivated the imagination of the U.S. public. TESOL students learn about the wave
of nativism that was spurred by the East European immigrants' poor performance on
the first IQ tests and the subsequent Immigration Act of 1924, which, in effect,
stopped immigration to the country. TESOL students also get to know James Conant
and Henry Chauncey, the architects of the SAT, who embarked on the "idealistic and
hubristic" (Lemann, 1999, p. vii) campaign to proliferate standardized testing in the
name of meritocracy. By reading selections from Lemann's work, teacher learners
begin to find the answer to the intriguing question why standardized assessment
tools that have been proven to possess strikingly low validity have come to dominate
the educational scene in the United States.

Although TESOL students experience literature throughout their master's degree
program, one course in the program is particularly designed to use engagements with

literature as a means of fostering understanding of language teaching and learning. The course, entitled Introduction to Literacy Studies, encourages teacher learners to consider what role race, culture, gender, class, and the institution of schooling play in language development and learning. The distinguishing features of the Hofstra TESOL program's literature component, such as the emphasis on self-examination through narratives or interpretive engagement with literature, are particularly prominent in this course. These important characteristics are discussed in the Distinguishing Features section.

◈ DISTINGUISHING FEATURES

Constructing and Reading the Texts of Students' Own Lives

TESOL students begin our program trying to find the answer to a commonsense question: How do I teach various language skills to students whose first language (L1) is not English? We contend, however, that such a question cannot be answered without first shifting to a more uncommonsense way of thinking, which requires that students examine their own literacy and language histories. Thus, the question becomes recast as a number of queries with different foci: What was it like for me to learn to read and write? What early experiences with language do I remember? What role did my family play in these experiences? What school experiences shaped my language learning?

Thinking in uncommonsense ways, that is, as learners as well as teachers, is facilitated through telling and making sense of language learning and literacy stories. When students create their stories, they address the complexity of learning in ways that help them see themselves and their worlds differently. Such stories open up possibilities, spark imagination, and stir storytellers to *wide-awakeness* (Greene, 1994). But stories are also interpretive, rooted in students' own personal experiences. In constructing their own narratives and own autobiographies, storytellers have no innocent eye (Bruner, 1994); rather they develop hypotheses, versions, and expected scenarios. Through being exposed to stories told by others, students begin to consider alternative interpretive frames or different ways in which their own stories might be told (Bruner, 1994).

TESOL students start out in the literacy class by thinking about the L1 and literacy experience in their lives. They tell how they got their names and explain their significance. The sharing of name stories is initiated by reading the children's picture book *Chrysanthemum* (Henkes, 1991), a humorous yet thoughtful story of a young child's tension between the unconditional love of her parents, who see her name as truly beautiful, and the problems she faces in school as she tries to write her long name in the tight spaces, as well as withstand the teasing of her peers. After reading the story aloud, the teacher learners stop to write short essays that recount the stories of their own names. As they share these stories, they learn that naming is often a cultural practice, that the spelling of names reflects cultural traditions, and that names carry a very strong significance in terms of pride and self-identity.

Responding to published stories and poems gives TESOL students another opportunity for introducing themselves. This is how one TESOL student, Ana Burgio, introduces herself in her original piece written in response to George Ella Lyon's (1999) poem "Where I'm From":

Where I'm From

I am from the land of sun
24 hour sun, toasting, sweating, muggy.
I am from dirt streets
Where we could smell the scent of earth
After a torrential 5 minute rain.
I am from a dry land
Where the sun set before we knew if we
Would have enough water for tomorrow.
Is the water truck coming?
I am from the beach with palm trees
That danced to make me cool and refreshed.
I am from my mother's arms
Where I heard songs that nobody knew
I am from the cashew land
Where I had cashew ice cream, juice,
And loved the smell of the tree.
I am from Ceara, Sao Paulo, Rio. . . .

Introductions are followed by activities in which teacher learners are asked to create *literacy timelines,* visual representations of their language and literacy learning experiences. The timelines include all the language learning events teacher learners can remember leading up to their experiences as graduate students. They exhibit these illustrated stories in class and talk about them with others. One experience is highlighted as a *critical incident;* that is, one about which the storytellers had particularly strong feelings and which influenced their language growth and development in a powerful way. That incident, written up as a narrative piece, is submitted to the instructor, in addition to being shared in class.

Literacy timelines and critical incidents become talking points for considering aspects of language and literacy learning at home and in school. As students visit the timelines and share their critical incidents with each other in small groups, they begin to discover other possible ways of telling language learning stories and to question their preconceived notions of language competence and literacy learning.

In a reflection discussion that follows viewing the literacy timelines, European American TESOL students tend to talk about the similarities that they see in home and school literacy experiences: They were read to as young children; they were typically successful in school. In a number of occasions, teacher learners from other backgrounds have spoken up, disrupting the dominant vision of what it means to be literate. One TESOL student from a Mexican immigrant family spoke up, almost in shame, saying that her mother never read to her. As the teacher learners examined her timeline with her, however, they could see that her mother had told her stories every night before she went to bed. Analyses like this one help teacher learners realize that there are many "roads to literacy" (Goodman, 1997, p. 56) and make them aware of the tendency of schools to privilege some literacy experiences over others.

The stories also serve as a reminder of the importance of teacher understanding of the resources that language minority students bring to school (Moll & Gonzalez, 1994; Ruiz, 1988). Catalina Otero shared a story of her first-grade experience entering school speaking primarily Spanish:

> The first Parent Teacher Conference was held in November. My teacher pretty much told my mother that I was not learning and could not be helped in the classroom. . . . she suggested to my mother, whose own English skills were poor, that she read to me every night and sign a sheet to make sure that she was indeed reading to me. Night after night my mother would sit down with my "I Can Read" primer and tirelessly recite the pages with me. . . . By the second Parent Teacher Conference in March my teacher was absolutely astonished at how much I had progressed. To this day my mother still tells me how proud she felt that day; she felt that she had proven that her lack of English fluency did not necessarily mean that she was incapable of teaching me how to read.

Stories like the one told by Catalina make it possible for teacher learners to view language minority children and their parents in a new light. As teacher learners listen to these stories, they begin to wonder about their own preconceived ideas and stereotypes regarding immigrant children and their parents.

The critical incident recounted by one student helped the class to experience other facets of immigrant experience: the longing to participate and the cultural confusion:

> I can remember vividly when I was in first grade, all the students used to bring in books for story time from the local library and I didn't understand how they got them. I thought their parents used to go to the library to purchase them. Well it made sense to me because we went to the supermarket and that is where we purchased all different types of food. So I asked my mother to take me. At that time my parents didn't have a lot of money, and they were new immigrants in a new world. My mother took my younger brother and I both to the local library in Lynbrook. My mom brought with her a pencil and some pieces of paper. When I got there I was amazed to see all the tall shelves stacked with all different kinds of books. My mother said to look around and try to find one that she would copy for me. So I found one. It was *A Bargain for Frances* by Russell Hoban. My mother sat down at a long wooden table and began to copy the book for me. She couldn't read it to me because she spoke only Italian, and when I looked at the book I couldn't even recognize a word that I might know. When my mother was finished copying the book we walked back home. She gave me the book she made, and I began to draw the pictures that I remembered were in the story. The next day I brought the book I made into my class for story time. I thought this would be the best book that the teacher would ever read aloud to the class. The teacher called all of the students onto the back carpet. When all the students were sitting quietly on the carpet, she asked for the book. I handed it to her and then the students began to laugh at me and the teacher said that this was not a book from the library. She wouldn't read it to the class. I was so upset and embarrassed. I took back the book, put it in my school bag, and brought it home for my brother to enjoy.

As students engage in a transaction with stories (Rosenblatt, 1938) like the previous two students' stories, they begin to see which situations are supportive for language learners and which are negative and painful. Teacher learners begin to realize that language learning is socially situated. By sharing stories, teacher learners begin to develop their theories of language and literacy development that are endowed with humanity, authenticity, and complexity and are not simplified into abstract models. Telling their own stories also prepares teacher learners to enter into published texts with new understandings and new questions.

Side-by-Side Reading

As teacher learners share their language learning stories, they are also reading published memoirs as well as the writings of literacy researchers and theorists. The examining of personal narratives in this context extends the dialogic experiences within the class to include voices of published authors and theorists. Rosenblatt (1938, 1978) suggests that a new text is constructed from such dialogues. This new poem, which emerges from transacting with a wide range of writers and genres, helps the reader to further reconceptualize theory and practice.

A selection of memoirs, autobiographies, novels, and case studies that focus on language and literacy learning provides teacher learners with diverse and varied social, cultural, historical, and pedagogical perspectives. For instance, in *Hunger of Memory: The Education of Richard Rodriguez*, Rodriguez (1983) describes his experiences growing up Latino American. Rodriguez tells what it was like for him to see himself as a learner in two cultures, what happened to his native language, culture, and family relationships, as he strove for assimilation. Rodriguez's story provides a more complex perspective on TESOL students' assumptions about what it means to be a successful language learner and gives rise to difficult questions: At what costs do we want ESL children to learn English? What strengths—linguistic and otherwise—are lost in the quest to assimilate into U.S. culture? How does one construct one's identity in order to survive in the new culture? What role do teachers and other professionals play in constructing that identity? As a result of contemplating these questions, teacher learners begin to consider how their own language learning stories as well as the stories of ESL students might have been told differently.

Another book read by TESOL students is *Lost in Translation: A Life in a New Language*, Hoffman's (1989) story of her search for self-identity as she journeys from Poland to Canada and to the United States. When reading Hoffman's book, teacher learners tend to be immediately struck by the many tensions and struggles new immigrants face as they enter a new culture. They recognize children they teach as they read Hoffman's description of the school playground as another land where she and her sister stayed in a corner away from everyone else, grasping each other for dear life. Teacher learners vividly respond to Hoffman's account of thinking in two languages or having to Americanize her name, the indignity they find utterly unacceptable, especially because they had begun the semester with telling the stories of their own names.

Opportunities for more in-depth engagement with literature are provided when teacher learners participate in book club dialogues. Students participate in three book clubs around the following themes:

- their own stories of language and literacy development
- language, literacy, and culture
- language, literacy, and schooling

Having been provided with 15 titles related to these themes, book club participants work in small groups to browse through the titles and select a book of their choice. After that, they spend several weeks reading and discussing a chosen text in depth.

Teacher learners value the small-group discussions and often report that they are a highlight of the class. As a culminating experience, each group shares reflections on their book with the class, so that all 15 titles become part of the class conversations. Teacher learners have a choice in terms of the mode of response they might use to present their book to others; tableaux, posters, readers' theater, interviews, and poetry are some of the response forms that have been effective.

As teacher learners listen to what others have to say about the same book, they are often surprised by the divergent responses of their classmates. Sharing the vastly different opinions results in dialogues, which Peterson (1992) identifies as being critical for "understanding, disclosing, and constructing meaning" because of the need for "thoughtful listening and responding" (pp. 103–104) inherent in such exchanges. Thus, new understandings of cultures and of language learning emerge as students read their own stories next to the stories of others.

Reflecting Upon Their Own Learning

TESOL students' reflections upon their own learning suggest that the use of narratives is effective in helping us achieve the programmatic goals. Teacher learners are quick to note new understandings that are constructed as a result of encounters with literature. They point out that narratives help them develop new cultural perspectives and connect to the cultures of their would-be learners. With a sense of urgency and pride, teacher learners speak and write about developing understanding of the cultures of language learners and about the newly found feeling of caring that they experience. This is how Marlene Schippers reflects on her own learning upon reading *My Trouble Is My English,* Fu's (1995) descriptive study of a Laotian family:

> The story of the Savang children. . . . influenced my thoughts this semester in a way different from any other book I have read throughout my time spent at Hofstra. I have read textbooks describing theories, methodologies, strategies, ideas and concepts. However, I have not encountered any textbooks which discuss personal experiences, with detailed descriptions of what ESL children endure.

Perhaps most important, the encounter with literature helps teacher learners develop new ideas regarding their own classroom action. Future teachers become aware of innovative ways of making meaning and fostering literacy development in the ESL classroom. Jennifer Smith wrote about trying book clubs in her own teaching:

> Besides the vast amount of information I learned about literacy from great authors, I also learned how to use book clubs in my own classroom. My children and I love having book clubs in our classroom. . . . They're just great. It's unbelievable how good a first grader can make a book sound if they really like it.

A student's awareness of the capacity of literature to help people understand, connect, contemplate, and commit hitherto unconsidered acts is summarized in the journal entry written by Lisa Abbatiello after reading Hoffman's (1989) *Lost in Translation*:

By reading this book I was able to experience things through Eva that in my life I wouldn't have experienced. . . . I learned a lot about the struggle immigrants face and the frustration they feel when they are unable to share their identity with those who do not speak the same language. . . . This book made me curious if my father felt or faced similar frustrations. When my father was twelve years old he emigrated from Naples, Italy to New York City. After reading this book I struck up a conversation with him about this because I was curious about his life and experiences and if he encountered similar situations. As it turns out, growing up in the United States and barely able to speak English my father felt very much like Eva. . . . His inability to speak his mind and fully communicate his feelings and ideas in English created many social barriers for him. However, he was strong, determined and intelligent like Eva and his perseverance enabled him to succeed in life in a new language. After reading this novel I not only admired Eva but I also admired and respected my father more than I ever had before. I also felt that I understood him more having experienced so many similar things through Eva.

◈ PRACTICAL IDEAS

Use Stories to Help Teacher Learners Construct Their Theories of Language Learning

We suggest the use of story for teacher learners to share and reflect upon their own language learning and to understand how their language learning backgrounds have influenced their theories of literacy and language learning. When set within a larger context of others' texts, students' own stories become dialogic experiences, inviting reexamination and critical analysis. We have found narratives to be helpful tools for opening up the possibilities for understanding the roles that culture, family, and schooling play in language and literacy learning.

Use Literature to Situate Learning Historically

We contend that important elements of ESL teacher learner preparation, such as multicultural education or praxis-oriented education, can be implemented most effectively if the teacher education program incorporates historical fiction or narratives. Stories from the past couched in engaging literary form serve as powerful tools for understanding the present. Instead of being overtly didactic, historical literature is emotionally engaging and thought provoking. By enabling teacher learners to experience (albeit vicariously) instances of nativism or racism, historical literature can serve as a means for engaging teacher learners with the exploration of topics about which they might otherwise feel resistant.

Use an Open-Ended Literature Curriculum

We have come to the realization that the literature component of the teacher education curriculum works best if it is open ended. If you plan to include narratives or fiction in your curriculum, we suggest that the literature component be flexible, amenable to revisions and readjustments. It is crucially important to keep updating the curriculum to provide choices of readings that are not only congruent with the changing interests of the teacher learners but also relevant to current sociopolitical developments.

◈ CONCLUSION

This chapter provides details of some of the literature experiences that teacher learners in a master's degree program in TESOL engage in as they work on building the knowledge base crucial for bridging the disjunctures between cultural minorities and the local communities in which they live and work. As this account suggests, when TESOL students create their own narratives and transact with narratives created by others, they build complex understandings of diverse cultures, connect with their future students, think more critically about the nature of language learning, and become prepared to act more effectively in the classroom.

◈ CONTRIBUTORS

Tatiana Gordon coordinates the TESOL/bilingual master's degree program at Hofstra University, in the United States. Gordon received her EdD in applied linguistics from Teachers College, Columbia University. She has taught EFL in Russia and Poland as well as ESL in the United States. Gordon is a recipient of the 1997 Fulbright Memorial Scholarship.

Joan Zaleski is an associate professor in the Department of Literacy Studies at Hofstra University. She is a director of the master's program and teaches courses in children's literature, teacher research, and literacy teaching and learning. Her research focuses on talk and dialogue as reflective tools for pedagogy and professional development.

Debra Goodman is in the Literacy Studies Department at Hofstra University. She taught in the Detroit Public Schools for 15 years. Her doctoral dissertation explores the social nature of literacy learning. She is author of *The Reading Detective Club* (1999).

CHAPTER 6

Using Enchantment: Children's Literature in an EFL Teacher Education Context

Stuart McNicholls

◈ INTRODUCTION

In this chapter I look at the potential for using children's literature in the teaching of EFL. The focus I adopt is heavily influenced by the context in which I have been working over the past few years, namely a diploma course for teacher learners at the primary school level at the Faculty of Education and Social Work, University of Vigo, in Ourense, Spain. This teaching situation calls for a dual focus that takes into account the needs of both teacher learners and their future primary school charges.

My aim is to teach EFL through juvenile and children's literature to the teacher learners as well as to teach them about children's literature as a vehicle for teaching EFL to future pupils. The semester-long course thus touches on a wide variety of children's literature genres, from nursery rhymes through fairy tales and short stories to novels, and emphasizes adapting the movement from reception to production, typical of communicative approaches, to a more creative context. My aim is to encourage learners not only to appreciate the verbal creativity of others but also to use it as a stimulus for their own productive imagination.

◈ CONTEXT

The English Through Children's Literature course forms part of the curriculum of the specialist diploma in foreign languages at the primary school teacher education centre of the University of Vigo at the Ourense Campus. This is one of many such centres throughout Spain specialising in the preservice training of teachers for the primary stage of education as well as in-service courses for practising teachers and research into all aspects of education.

The Teacher Learners

Traditionally, such centres have offered a means of climbing the social ladder for members of the lower and lower middle classes, predominantly women and people from rural areas, and especially so in a province such as Ourense, where the rural population is nearly as numerous as the urban (see Benso Calvo, 1989). Thus, teacher learners in the course tend to come from families where parents are small businessmen and women, lower level civil servants, primary teachers, farmers, or workers, or are unemployed. Roughly half the teacher learners are from the city of Ourense, whereas most of the rest are from villages and towns in the province.

Teacher learners usually enter the school after completing the Spanish university entrance examinations (*selectividad*), although a minority also join the course having completed other university studies, typically an English language degree. In theory, this implies that all will have had a minimum of 4–7 years of English and should possess a high-intermediate level of English. Practice, however, reveals that few have such a high level; the majority are at an intermediate level and sometimes even lower. At the moment, teacher education for primary school in Spain is carried out through a university diploma course of 3 years, whereas secondary school teachers are required to have a university degree. There are moves to reform the system so that both secondary and primary teachers will be degree holders.

The Curriculum

The Ourense Teacher Training School offers four specialities: infant education, primary education, foreign language education, and special needs education. It has a maximum intake of 354 teacher learners each year, of which 54 are admitted to the foreign languages speciality (English and French), whereas the other three specialities accept 100 teacher learners each (fewer are admitted to the foreign language speciality partly because of the need to keep class sizes lower in the specific context of foreign language teaching).

The English language and training needs of those teacher learners enrolled in the foreign languages speciality can be summed up as follows:

- a knowledge of the English language sufficient for them to pass the competitive state examinations (*oposiciones*) so that they may teach in the primary school system

- a practical preparation for the reality of teaching English in primary education once they have passed *oposiciones*

The curriculum consists of about 50% language and language teaching methodology along with a series of more general teacher education subjects not directly related to language learning (e.g., psychology and pedagogy, sociology, physical education). The 3-year course offers 3–6 hours of English language teaching each week; phonetics (3 hours a week for 1 year); and additional subjects such as English Through Audiovisual Media, An Introduction to English Literature, and English Through Children's Literature, which are all studied for 3 hours a week during one semester. In addition, the teacher learners experience their first contact with the practical reality of teaching through periods of teaching practice, carried out in the city and province of Ourense.

English Through Children's Literature

The subject of English through children's literature was initially introduced into the curriculum to cover a perceived gap: Teacher learners were studying language to help them teach it to the children and also were studying literature that would widen their own linguistic and cultural horizons but without any crossover between the latter and the former. By including a subject that combined both language and literature for children, it was hoped that prospective teachers could be presented with a broad package including an introduction to English children's literature, its potential application in the context of English language teaching, and its use as a vehicle for furthering teacher learners' knowledge of English.

It was also introduced because of the school's belief in the fundamental importance of literature as a reflection of the sociocultural construction of reality. Historically, literature has been one of the means by which society gives meaning to the world and to the lives of individuals within it by creating parallel and virtual worlds whose order and structure reflect a sense of order society might otherwise find lacking. As such, literature represents a psychological imperative for the human being as narrator and spectator. As Applebee (1989) has argued, the role of spectator is one that allows people to confront experiences in a way that fully integrates their representational systems, freed from the necessity for immediate action that characterizes the contrasting role of participant. Children's literature as a social and socializing institution brings out the spectator role in children with a view to integrating the natural values and attitudes of any given society. In addition to this conservative function, literature also offers emancipatory possibilities, because it facilitates not only access to the reproductive imagination that is a sine qua non condition for any society but also access to the creative imagination that is part of the heritage of the whole human race, rather than the exclusive dominion of artists (as the cultural hierarchization of the modern world would have one believe).

Thus, literature in language teaching allows teachers to claim a role for imagination in the language classroom. According to Halliday (1975), one of the seven functions that language performs for children learning their first language is the imaginative function, defined as the use of language to create a world of the imagination. This function, though not ignored, does tend to be granted a position of only secondary supportive importance due to the preeminence in recent methodologies of what has been called the *representational function* or the use of language to communicate information. Children's literature in education, and specifically in the teaching of foreign languages, should not be used exclusively to teach communicative skills or to present learners with perennial favourites of imaginative writing for youngsters. Rather, its use must aim to take advantage of children's innate imaginative potential and playfulness and serve as a springboard for their own creativity, verbal or not, even in the context of the foreign language. This focus is born of a deeper belief in the need for education to prepare future citizens capable both of appreciating the otherness represented (e.g., by a foreign language or culture as a source of richness and stimulus rather than as a threat) and of responding with their own creative and autonomous initiatives to the problems that arise in their lives and their community. This latter emphasis on the use of children's literature, specifically traditional folk and fairy tales, in the fostering of values related to an active and participative citizenship has been explored in depth by Zipes (1995). Such work can play an important role in the context of the native language classroom and can also contribute in the foreign language context, ideally as part of an overall learning situation where storytelling and imaginative writing for and by children constitute a cross-curricular element in learners' language education.

It was these considerations—the aim of helping integrate previously separate areas of language learning and literature studies, the recognition of literature's role in the sociocultural construction of reality, and the desire to incorporate elements of imagination and creativity into the teaching programme—that motivated me to set up the module entitled English Through Children's Literature.

◈ DESCRIPTION

English Through Children's Literature is taught during one semester for 3 hours a week (two classes of 1½ hours), giving a total of 45 hours, or 4.5 Spanish university credits. The syllabus comprises one introductory class and six teaching units dealing with children's and juvenile literature from differing angles, as can be seen in Figure 1. The syllabus is structured in two cycles with the third teaching unit acting as a fulcrum between them. The first cycle, comprising Units 1 and 2 and part of Unit 3, is aimed at exploring young children's literature and its potential for use in the primary classroom. The second cycle (beginning in Unit 3 and continuing to the end of Unit 6) is concerned with older children's literature as a vehicle for furthering teacher learners' own knowledge of English language and as an object of study per se, given its importance in the education and socialization of children and adolescents.

Introduction

Teacher learner group presentations, anticipation of course contents, and presentation of syllabus

---

Unit 1: Nursery Rhymes and Jazz Chants

a. "Incy wincy spider": a nursery rhyme–based teaching unit

b. Using jazz chants in the classroom

c. More on using nursery rhymes

d. Teacher learner presentations

Continuous assessment: nursery rhymes task (group) and teacher learners' poems (individual)

Unit 2: Young Children's Books and Action Stories

a. Action stories and total physical response (TPR)

b. *My Cat Likes to Hide in Boxes* (Sutton & Dodd, 1973): a storybook-based teaching unit

c. Teacher learner presentations

Continuous assessment: presenting storybook teaching unit (group)

Unit 3: Traditional Folk and Fairy Tales

a. "Little Red Riding Hood"

b. "From Tiger to Anansi": Traditional tale–based teaching unit

c. The *meccano* of tales and Propp's (1981) game

d. Teacher learners' fairy tales

Continuous assessment: oral presentation of storytelling in tutorial time (individual) and teacher learners' fairy tales (group)

Continued on p. 75

Unit 4: Children's Verse

a. Poems by children

b. Poems for children

c. Tongue-twisters, limericks, and haikus

Continuous assessment: teacher learners' verse

Unit 5: Short Stories and Modern Fairy Tales

a. Moral stories: "The Green Velvet Dress" (Tucker, 1858/1993) and "The Little Blue Bag" (Mant, 1825/1993)

b. School stories: "Wailing Well" (James, 1928/1993) and "The Caravan Siege" (Massie, 1926/1993)

c. Modern fairy tales: "The Unicorn in the Garden" (Thurber, 1940/1993) and "The Happy Prince" (Wilde, 1888/2003)

d. A contemporary story: "The Convict Box" (Wheatley, 1992/1993)

Continuous assessment: creative rewriting of a story from a different narratorial point of view (individual)

Unit 6: Children's Novels

a–d. Group 1: Dahl's (1989) *Matilda*; Group 2: Rushdie's (1990) *Haroun and the Sea of Stories*

e. Group presentations of respective novels and handout of anthology of teacher learners' own creative writing from the semester's work

Continuous assessment: creative anticipation of storyline (pairs) and presentations of novel (group)

Note. Letters refer to sessions within a unit.

FIGURE 1. Overview of English Through Children's Literature

In the introductory class, the teacher learners get to know each other through an accumulative, alliterative name chain game ("I'm Stuart and I'm studious," "You're Stuart and you're studious; I'm Maria and I'm marvellous," etc.). They are then asked to reflect on definitions of literature, children's literature, genres of children's literature, and the potential usefulness of such material in primary EFL before moving on to look at the proposed course content.

In Unit 1, preservice teachers learn activities for using nursery rhymes, chants, and simple verses in the primary classroom and how to present and practise classroom language associated with these activities. After carrying out the activities, they prepare and carry out their own activities based on a rhyme in microteaching sessions. Teacher learners begin class with a creative writing activity called *spider name poems,* which is illustrated in the following example:

TIM
Toffee
Is
Magic

They end the class exploring ways in which primary pupils can be encouraged to develop their own creativity, moving from subversion of an already learned model (e.g., *eeny meeny mole* instead of *incy wincy spider*) to craftwork and controlled creativity with a combination table that produces name poems (see Figure 2). They also explore the creation of minibooks by pupils so that they may eventually create do-it-yourself libraries.

Further work in the unit draws on that of Graham (1979) to introduce teacher learners to the use of jazz chants in the primary classroom and on activities from the Silent Way (Gattegno, 1996) such as the vanishing rhyme technique (see Rinvolucri, 1984) in which the teacher gradually rubs words out from a poem written on the board and pupils in turn have to remember the whole rhyme.

The aims of Unit 2 include introducing teacher learners to storytelling using total physical response (TPR), presenting them with techniques and suggestions for using authentic storybooks in the EFL classroom, explaining the structure and sequence of a storybook-based teaching unit, giving teacher learners practise in reading EFL resource material, and allowing them to present a teaching unit to their peers on the basis of their reading.

Unit 3 sets out to combine elements of the two cycles (pupil-oriented and teacher learner-oriented) and demonstrate the relevance of children's literature at widely different levels by perfecting teacher learners' storytelling technique, examining ideological implications behind well-known fairy tales, presenting teacher learners with traditional tales from other cultures, demonstrating the potential of traditional stories and fairy tales for use in the EFL classroom, studying theory on story structure, and encouraging teacher learners to produce their own structured fairy tales. The unit begins with an activity based on a subversive fairy tale, "The Practical Princess" (Williams, 1994). In the oral information gap activity, called *combining versions*, teacher learners listen to and correct their respective versions of the same story to come up with one that makes the most sense to them. By allowing teacher learners to choose between a princess who, when confronted with a dragon, shouts "Oh no! Somebody help me!" and one who says "Right! I'll have to deal with this myself!" the class leads naturally to a discussion of the values and ideology represented in children's literature. (The rest of the unit is dealt with in greater detail in the section Model Teaching Unit.)

My spider Meg Mel	Eats	Goo Lemons Lettuce Lions
Ben		Nosh
Ken		Newspapers

Figure 2. Producing Name Poems

Unit 4 provides a change of pace after the more demanding work of the last half of Unit 3 and before the teacher learners confront the difficulties of longer prose works in the next two units. It consists of three classes, whose aims include

- raising teacher learners' awareness of the possibility of literature by (as well as for) children

- providing language input for acquisition for teacher learners

- bringing teacher learners into contact with the cognitive and affective worlds of young people through their creative writing in verse

- studying how rhyme, rhythm, and semantic coherence configurate children's verse

- offering teacher learners the opportunity to write and share their own creative writing in verse

Activities include a cloze dictogloss that demonstrates how literary language can be linguistically applied. The information gap activity is based on an adolescent's poem about parents ("As children we look up to them / We idolize and adore them. . . ."; from "Siân, 16 years," in Curry, 1996, p. 22). In this activity, individual teacher learners, working in small groups, are given copies of the poem with all words except those corresponding to one grammatical category wiped out and must orally reconstruct the original poem (see Figure 3).

Unit 5 covers prose works—short stories from different historical and geographical contexts—that are more difficult than those teacher learners have seen so far in the course. This unit is intended as a stepping-stone to the more demanding task of reading a whole novel in the next unit. The aims for Unit 5 include

- providing input for acquisition for teacher learners to improve their English

- practising extensive reading

- becoming informed about traditional and alternative literary perspectives on the childhood experience

- participating actively and imaginatively in their reading by anticipating and speculating beyond the limits of the words on the page

- learning about the potential of children's literature in the context of a multimedia language laboratory

- expressing their ideas about a text in their own creative writing

Student 1	Nouns and pronouns:		
" children we	them/We	them . . ."	
Student 2	Verbs:		
"	look up / idolize	adore . . ."	
Student 3	Others:		
"As	to /	and . . ."	

FIGURE 3. Example of Reconstructing a Poem

Unit 6 is the most challenging unit and consists of five lessons. The aims for this unit include

- furthering the teacher learners' confidence and enjoyment of extensive reading in English

- providing further input for language acquisition

- raising teacher learners' awareness as to the potential of fantasy and radical imagination for helping young people overcome their existential challenges and problems

- encouraging teacher learners to interact imaginatively with fiction

- developing teacher learners' ability to summarize, synthesize, and simplify story plots so as to present them to others

Model Teaching Unit

To illustrate the kind of work done in this course, Figure 4 offers a compressed version of the salient points of three lesson plans from Unit 3 (Lessons b–d), a transitional unit that sets out to demonstrate the applicability of similar materials adapted for different levels and ages and gives examples of the progression in EFL classroom practice from the receptive to the productive in the field of children's literature and creative writing.

Using videos recorded during fieldwork with primary pupils in a local classroom, teacher learners see how pupils can progress from the reception of a story adapted to their level through language reinforcement and simple story-structuring

Activity Number	Activity Title	Description	Objectives
1	Teacher education video (1): "From Tiger to Anansi"	Teacher learners view video of storytelling with trainer and primary school pupils.	Demonstrate the possibilities of using traditional tales as input in the primary classroom
2	Reinforcement and story structure activities	Teacher learners take part in activities: ordering pictures and sentences, playing whispering story in two teams, and completing story flowcharts.	Familiarize teacher learners with the types of activities that can be used as follow-up from a traditional story input to eventually encourage pupils' own creative response
3	Teacher education video (2): deal a story	Teacher learners view video of productive creative work by primary pupils at the end of the Anansi teaching unit.	Show teacher learners examples of the kind of creative response pupils can be expected to produce
4	Brainstorming and summarizing traditional and fairy tales	Teacher learners as a group brainstorm tales and then work in pairs to prepare a brief oral summary of one of the tales.	Help teacher learners practise telling stories and anticipate stories dealt with when looking at narrative morphology/ typology

Continued on p. 79

Activity Number	Activity Title	Description	Objectives
5	The *meccano* of tales: reading	Trainer reads out loud while teacher learners follow text and match lexical items with translation.	Introduce ideas about narrative morphology to teacher learners
6	The *meccano* of tales: application (trainer)	Trainer relates ideas from text to Cinderella and Snow White.	Demonstrate applicatibility of Paulme's (as referred to in Jean, 1981) typology to stories teacher learners are familiar with
7	The *meccano* of tales: application (teacher learners)	Teacher learners analyse story type and structure of "From Tiger to Anansi"; whole group discusses story in the light of typological and structural analysis.	Enable teacher learners to discover correlations between typology and a traditional tale they have studied in another context
8	Propp's functions: presentation	Teacher learners are introduced to Propp's (1981) functions as they listen to and read definitions while viewing a visually suggestive representation of each one.	Familiarize teacher learners with Propp's narrative building blocks both analytically and imaginatively to prepare them for moving from deconstruction to narrative creativity
9	Propp's functions: practice	Teacher learners analyse and annotate the text of "The End of Baba Yaga" (Grainger, 1997) in light of the presentation on Propp's (1981) functions before sharing their conclusions with the whole group	Give teacher learners further reading practise and to allow them to discover examples of Propp's functions in a Russian folktale
10	Propp's (1981) game	Teacher learners working in groups are given a pack of Propp's cards and asked to select five cards at random; using their cards they write a story incorporating the five functions represented on their chosen cards.	Offer teacher learners the chance to move from aesthetic appreciation and analytical understanding of literary input to their own imaginative production, using functions as a springboard for their own creativity; allow them to experience firsthand the kind of imaginative input-output process that they could later adapt to their own pupils' level
11	Propp's game: feedback	Teacher learners share stories with their peers, reading them out loud as the others follow text.	Allow teacher learners the satisfaction of sharing their creative efforts with their peers and to allow feedback in terms of previously stated objectives

FIGURE 4. Detailed Plan for Unit 3: Traditional Folk and Fairy Tales

activities to simple storytelling arising from a card game called *deal a story* (adapted from ideas in Rodari, 1979, and Palim and Power, 1990). The initial story, "From Tiger to Anansi" (adapted from the version in Briggs, 1974), deals with the way in which an underdog spider eventually outwits the tiger (the king of the jungle) in such a way as to claim stories as his own. Teacher learners explore how primary pupils can then engage in a variety of reinforcement and ordering activities, including a *whispering story* (a competitive variation on Chinese whispers, a popular game in which a message is transmitted along a line of people whispered by one person to the next, usually resulting in comic distortion between its original and final forms) and a *story flowchart* (both based on ideas in Wright, 1995) before watching a video dramatization of how a primary class develops a story from the deal-a-story activity.

Teacher learners next move on to study a text based on the work of Jean (1981), Rodari (1979), Paulme (as referred to in Jean, 1981), and Propp (1981) that deals with the *meccano,* or building blocks, of stories—what the above-mentioned authors have proposed as constituting the basis of many traditional stories. Teacher learners reread a traditional Russian folktale (which they have already read at home), entitled "The End of Baba Yaga," (adapted from Grainger, 1997), and identify Propp's functions in it. For Propp, fairy stories can be defined as tales that start out from an initial misdeed or a lack and pass through intermediate functions or stages to culminate in a marriage or another such successful resolution. Propp concludes that characters are secondary to these functions, which constitute for him the real building blocks of the genre and which he defines in the following way: "the action[s] of a character defined from the point of view of the development of the plot" (p. 33). Thus, the development of the plot could be defined as the result of actions by characters, which give rise to dramatic situations and to successive modifications of those situations.

The Cinderella-like tale of Vasseila in "The End of Baba Yaga" can serve as an example of some of these functions, which are in italics in this paragraph. The typical tale starts out with an *initial situation* (not, Propp emphasizes, in itself a function) in which the protagonist and the members of her or his family are presented. From there a plot might develop in which, for example, an antagonist tries to *trick* the hero in some way. This represents one of the functions that is inevitably succeeded by another; in this case the *complicity* of the hero, who always unwittingly falls into the trap if tricked, as when Vasseila agrees to go in search of fire for her stepsisters. The most famous of the functions is that of the *misdeed* or *lack*—in the case of Vasseila, the *lack* is both material (fire) and emotional (love). Another common function is the *departure of the hero* on a quest to overcome an initial lack (e.g., when Vasseila sets off for Baba Yaga's house). The *donator* is a potential ally for the hero. Provided that the hero responds favourably to the donator's greeting or request, the latter can transmit a magic object or power that will help the hero overcome otherwise insurmountable obstacles or dangers. Thus, Baba Yaga's daughter is befriended by Vasseila and so protects her from the witch by turning her into a pin. The *combat* represents a contest of some sort with the antagonist (in the case of Vasseila, it is a battle of wits with Baba Yaga) that again inevitably leads to *victory* for the protagonist. The hero's return can be jeopardized by the *pursuit* of the antagonist, although this too always results in the hero's *escape*. Finally, the happy ending can involve some sort of *punishment* for the antagonist and for those responsible for the initial misdeed (as in the demise of Baba

Yaga and the stepsisters) and *marriage* or simply a happy ending, as in the case of Vasseila.

Once furnished with a brief theoretical introduction to narrative morphology, teacher learners participate in a game using storying cards, which constitutes a more elaborate version of the deal-a-story activity mentioned previously. The activity is based on ideas from Rodari (1979), Zipes (1995), and Aller Vázquez (1997). Propp's (1981) functions are represented pictorially on 31 playing cards (in my case, specially commissioned from a local artist, Peixe; see Figure 5 for examples) in a way that encourages teacher learners to understand them not only as abstract rational categories but also as imaginative stepping-stones toward a creative goal.

The cards tap into the narrative potential both of fairy tales and also, following Aller Vázquez (1997), of the tarot pack, whereas the mixed collage/drawing technique is suggestive of how the game aims to get teacher learners to mix elements from stories they know with their own innovative ideas. Finally, working in groups, teacher learners elaborate a story based on the five cards randomly dealt to them in what aims to be not only a source of motivating student-centred language work but also an example of the kind of productive creative work they could try out with their future students.

◈ DISTINGUISHING FEATURES

Several features distinguish this course from other approaches to children's literature in the EFL teacher education context.

Dual Focus

The programme was devised to go beyond the study of established classics or the transmission of the history of children's literature with teacher learners. The dual focus—not only on teacher learners but also on the primary learners with whom

FIGURE 5. Sample Cards From the Tarot Pack

they will one day be working—allows a fuller exploration of the potential of children's literature at differing levels.

Broad Definition of Children's Literature

The definition of children's literature underlying the programme is a broad one: "all expressions and activities deriving from the artistic or playful use of the word and which are of interest to children" (Cervera, 1992, p. 11). This means that children's literature can be understood more democratically as consisting not only of the canonically acceptable classics but also of other examples of verbal creativity such as nursery rhymes or limericks that children find so engaging; this also leads into subverting the Anglo-Saxon genitive to extend interest to literature by children as well as for them.

This definition also reflects the interest in the move from reception to production, encouraging pupils and teacher learners to experiment creatively with language and providing them with the valuable experience of having narrative control in their own hands. The emphasis on imagination restores an important linguistic function that communicative syllabuses have perhaps taken for granted to its rightful position; it also opens up possibilities in terms of rebalancing the message/medium equation by allowing learners to discover the patterns underlying literary works—from the phonological regularities of nursery rhymes to the morphological patterns of fairy tales—in a way that enhances their appreciation and bolsters their own creative potential.

Feedback From Teacher Learners

End-of-semester evaluations carried out over the 3 years in which the course has been taught in its present form have shown that, in general, teacher learners appreciate the work done in this course, especially the insights into using children's literature in the primary classroom and the chance to read and enjoy stories and novels in English (although some complain about the amount of reading they have to do in the second half of the course).

When 20 teacher learners were asked whether the course had met its aims of promoting their understanding of the potential for using children's literature in the EFL context and of providing language input for themselves as learners of EFL, the average response was 9.2 out of 10. The teacher learners felt they had learned how to use children's literature in the EFL classroom (average response was 8.7/10). They believed that their listening and reading fluency had improved in the course (average response was 8.2/10) and that the course input had served as a stimulus for their own spoken and written English (average response was 8.4/10). Finally, the teacher learners felt that children's literature has an important role to play in the teaching of EFL at the primary level (average response was 8.9/10). The fact that teacher learners have gone on to incorporate elements of work done in the course into the periods of teaching practice that form part of their training is further encouraging evidence of the positive reactions to the children's literature component of the programme.

◈ PRACTICAL IDEAS

The practical ideas included here, rather than being specific ideas for classroom activities, provide a framework for incorporating children's literature in a syllabus. Although the ideas are presented in terms of children's literature, they can be adapted as a framework for work with other literatures as well.

Decide How Much Children's Literature Is Appropriate for Your Context

Because of circumstantial imperatives (i.e., national curricula, head teachers, set textbooks, parental expectations), some teachers might feel that children's literature can only make a reduced contribution in their syllabus preparation. For others with more leeway, children's literature could become the backbone for a course. For further examples of such all-encompassing approaches, see Vale, Mullaney, and Murphy (1993) and Ellis and Brewster (1991).

Choose Material According to Level

It is best to follow a natural progression when using children's literature in the primary classroom, beginning with simple songs, nursery rhymes, and jazz chants in the early years and only gradually introducing the more demanding stories as the children move up in school.

Incorporate Auditory, Visual, and Kinetic Features

Children's literature is far from being a purely text-based affair. Especially with younger children, it is important that the words are not only read but also heard. If you can use pictures as a visual backup as well as mime and TPR techniques in your treatment of the chosen material, then you will be playing to the strengths of all pupils, be they predominantly of an auditory, visual, or kinetic inclination.

Use Stories Even If They Include Difficult Grammar/Language

Stories are part of the cultural baggage that children bring to school with them, so they possess an acquired story awareness that helps them overcome any initial receptive difficulty presented by the appearance, for example, of past tenses they have not yet studied receptively or productively. Furthermore, because the stories as input are intended purely for receptive purposes and children are clearly not expected to themselves produce anything so complex, past tenses or occasional difficult vocabulary should not be a problem so long as the context, visual aids, and so forth carry the story forward. When pupils come to producing their own stories toward the end of a teaching unit, they can either do so in the present tense or ask for your help to produce appropriate past tense forms.

Do Not Worry About the Abstraction of Stories

As Egan (1990) has recognized, the influence of Jean Piaget has led to a situation where "educational development proceeds . . . from the concrete to the abstract, from the simple to the complex, from the known to the unknown, from active manipulation to symbolic conceptualization" (p. 6), and young children are thus rarely expected to deal with abstractions or situations removed from their everyday circumstances. Nevertheless, fantasy and works of imagination will be a lot closer to most youngsters' everyday concerns than native English speakers, culture, or language and will no doubt be a lot more stimulating as well.

Put Yourself in Your Pupils' Shoes

Teacher education courses that include peer group microteaching, TPR activities, and student creative writing offer an excellent opportunity for teacher learners to remember what it is like to be a pupil. Vale and Feunteun's (1995) *Teaching Children English* is an excellent source of ideas in this respect. Moreover, works of children's literature studied in the course, with stories such as "The Convict Box" (Wheatley, 1992/1993) or novels such as *Matilda* (Dahl, 1989) or *Haroun and the Sea of Stories* (Rushdie, 1990) are in themselves a stimulus for much needed empathy with, and understanding of, children's worlds for teacher learners and practising teachers alike.

Make the Most of Prevailing Favourable Circumstances for Children's Literature

As has been suggested, children are generally favourably disposed to rhymes, chants, stories, and other forms of children's literature because of their upbringing with family anecdotes, bedtime stories, and the like. In addition, there are also commercial and media phenomena and products based on children's literature, such as J. K. Rowling's *Harry Potter* or J. R. R. Tolkien's *The Lord of the Rings,* which can be used to divert attention away from the screen or the supermarket and back to the written word by incorporating work on the books into the syllabus.

◈ CONCLUSION

The experience of working with children's literature in the EFL context over the past few years has proved extremely satisfying, as I have witnessed the pleasure of teacher learners and children not only listening to or reading stories but also working on them and moving toward creating something themselves. I hope other teachers and teacher learners will be encouraged by this necessarily brief survey of the possibilities of children's literature to use such material along the lines suggested so that they may help their students to achieve not only a communicative but also a creative competence in the target language.

In a primary school context, children's literature in English contributes to the wider initiation of youngsters to the world of imagination and creativity, both receptively and productively. By choosing and adapting from this vast pool of authentic material, teachers can provide an input that encourages the motivation and implication of children in the subject by involving them in tasks that entertain as well as educate them. And, in the teacher education context, these benefits dovetail with the potential of children's and juvenile literature for teacher learners, who can explore objectively the exploitation of this kind of material in the primary classroom while experiencing for themselves what in another context Bettelheim (1991) so aptly dubbed *the uses of enchantment.*

◈ CONTRIBUTOR

Stuart McNicholls studied modern languages (French and German) at Exeter College, Oxford University, Great Britain, and subsequently trained as a foreign language teacher at the Metropolitan University of Manchester. Since 1988 he has been teaching at the University of Vigo, in Spain, where he is a lecturer at the Faculty of Educational Science.

CHAPTER 7

Terms of Integration: Educating Primary EFL Teacher Learners

Isabel Martin

◈ INTRODUCTION

In this chapter I describe an innovative module for teaching language and literature to teacher learners who are training to become primary school teachers at the University of Koblenz in Rhineland-Palatinate, a medium-sized federal state to the southwest of the German Republic. Since the Allies divided Germany up into federal states, each state (called *Land*) has had both the freedom and the burden to come up with its own legislation (e.g., in the field of education), and many of the characteristics of the module described here were developed in response to political decrees. The university has a long tradition of educating teachers in Rhineland-Palatinate and is also known for its strong information technology departments; the total number of students is around 5,500.

The hallmark of the module is the integrative approach it takes to language teaching, and I like to think of the module itself as exhibiting five aspects of integration: language and literature, theory and practice, learning and teaching, books and the Internet, and work and fun.

◈ CONTEXT

The innovative character of the module described in this chapter needs to be understood within the context of the different traditional German university degrees for the teaching profession and the most recent political shifts concerning early language learning in German primary schools.

German University Degrees

There are three main types of secondary schools in Germany, all of which start in Grade 5, when the children are 10–11 years old. The *Hauptschule* finishes after Grade 9 and prepares the children for practical jobs; the *Realschule* finishes after Grade 10, leads to a general school-leaving qualification that is equivalent, for example, to the British General Certificate of Secondary Education and may lead to employment as, for example, a bank clerk, medical assistant, tax advisor, or kindergarten teacher; and the *Gymnasium* finishes after Grade 13, when students leave with a qualification called *Abitur*, typically to go on to university. Students wishing to become English teachers traditionally were able to choose between two university degrees: one geared toward teaching English at *Gymnasium* and the other geared toward teaching in *Haupt-* and *Realschule*. Others interested in English choose the *Magister Artium* (MA), a degree without didactic training, with no access to the teaching profession. Another important point is that all students take two different full (major) subjects at the same level for the teaching degrees.

Shifts in Views of Primary School English Teaching

Following the political changes in Europe in the late 1980s and the early 1990s (i.e., the fall of communist regimes and the reunification of Germany), interest in the teaching of English at the primary school level was revived. So, in 1992, a new degree was introduced at Koblenz University: English for *Grundschule* (primary school) and *Hauptschule*, as opposed to English for *Realschule* (now without *Hauptschule*). At the same time, a pilot study of teaching foreign languages (English or French) in an integrative manner was started at several primary schools in Rhineland-Palatinate, and 2-week in-service training courses and local follow-up work groups were quickly established to qualify primary school teachers on a voluntary basis.

When integrated foreign language work for all Rhineland-Palatinate primary schools was officially started in the third grade in 1998 (see Soll, 1999), the shortage of properly qualified teachers soon became evident. Although many dedicated and enthusiastic teachers managed the new task well, many others had not volunteered for the in-service training mentioned previously or felt they had not been trained enough. At the same time, though, the new graduates with the new degree for *Grund-* and *Hauptschule* were not being sent to primary school—they had to go to *Hauptschule* because volunteers for that school type had become extremely scarce. (In Germany, teachers do not have free choice of where to teach but are posted to schools by the government of their *Land*.)

More teachers were required, so in 2000 the ministry introduced the additional possibility of studying Integrated Foreign Language Work in Primary School in Rhineland-Palatinate as a voluntary additional module for students of primary education who were not taking a foreign language as a full (major) subject. The new module was to be tested in a 3-year trial period, and the English department at Koblenz University volunteered for the project and was given a part-time position for the new task.

The Primary English Module

Along the ministry's initial guidelines, I developed a module for primary English IFA (*Integrierte Fremdsprachenarbeit in der Grundschule* [Integrated Language Work at Primary School]) early in 2001. The module consists of 10 courses, each of which runs over one semester of approximately 14 weeks, with one weekly seminar of 90 minutes. The starting point for deciding what kind of courses teacher learners would need to achieve the necessary competencies was to look at the ministry's guidelines for the final 30-minute oral exam (conducted in English) with which the module was to end after a minimum of four semesters. The ministry's guidelines include language skills (with a focus on confidence in oral use of the language, especially appropriate pronunciation and intonation) and professional knowledge, including the aims, basic concepts, and methods of integrated foreign language work at primary level; cultural topics; literary texts; and areas of linguistics and applied linguistics.

To achieve this goal, the module I set up includes four general language practice courses, three didactics courses, one applied linguistics course, and two courses on children's literature and intercultural studies. The last two, Cultural Studies for Primary School and English Children's Literature for Primary School, each require the teacher learners to do Web work, do a presentation in class, and produce handouts and a materials portfolio. Before they can attend the seminar on children's literature or cultural studies, teacher learners are required to complete one didactics course and at least Level 1[1] in language practice.

This module seems to have a number of advantages compared with the regular programme of the degree *Grund-* and *Hauptschule*. First, teacher learners who take the regular degree with English as a full subject can offer two subjects for teaching; teacher learners taking the new module have three subjects to offer—their two main subjects and English. Second, module teacher learners will be qualified to teach in primary school only—where they want to be sent in the first place—and avoid being sent to *Hauptschule* (the regular degree is for *Grund-* and *Hauptschule*). Third, the module includes more on didactics and methodology, and the language courses are designed for the particular needs of these students in oral skills. The teacher learners also attend tailor-made courses in children's literature and intercultural studies that are based on primary school needs and methodology, rather than having to share literature and cultural studies seminars with MA and prospective secondary school teachers, seminars that treat entirely different topics.

An important point about the teacher learners in the IFA module is that only some of them took English as a major at school in Grades 10–13 (the ones that do usually enrol for the regular English degree), and only a few of them have read any English literature apart from the required reading in secondary school.[2] All of them, however, are interested in children's literature, and they have retained a child's enjoyment of picture books, fairy tales, fantasy, songs, games, and rhymes. They have experience in working with small children (they also do practical training at schools in the term breaks) and are familiar with general primary methodology, so their sense of what material is suitable for primary is reliable and their ideas of how to present English children's literature to young learners have proved varied and creative.

Already after 2 years, in 2002, the new foreign language module was made obligatory for all teacher learners of primary education, leading to a sharp increase in student numbers—from 55 in 2001 to 472 in the winter term 2003–2004 and 725 in the summer term 2005. At the same time, the teaching hours in the module were reduced from 20 to 8–12. We assume this was decreed because even though the

---

[1] Level 1 is a general language course in which teacher learners practice oral skills, listening comprehension, pronunciation, grammar, functional language, and vocabulary enlargement.

[2] Indeed, the canon of English literature taught in many secondary schools has proved somewhat resistant to change over the last 30 years and thus may not stimulate reading: Many teachers use the same texts they themselves were given to read as students—George Orwell's *Animal Farm*, William Golding's *Lord of the Flies*, Shakespeare's *Macbeth*, Arthur Miller's *Death of a Salesman*, Tennessee Williams's *Cat on a Hot Tin Roof,* with Doris Lessing's *The Fifth Child* and Todd Strasser's *The Wave* as two recent additions, complete with interpretation guides for the teacher and/or video.

part-time post was turned into a full-time one, there were still not enough teaching hours available to teach such high numbers of teacher learners. Not able or willing to invest in another teaching post, the government instead lowered the number of hours teacher learners were supposed to take.[3] (German universities have been notoriously understaffed for years; also, German students pay no fees. Rhineland-Palatinate has just seen the first student protests against poor study conditions.)

Even before the new module was made obligatory in October 2002, the coalition agreement of August 2001 stated that integrated foreign language work in Rhineland-Palatinate would start in the first grade rather than third in the future. By 2004, about 500 of the 991 primary schools had implemented this policy, and the remaining ones followed in 2005 (see http://www.ganztagsschule.rlp.de/). This new trend in Germany was possibly accelerated by the aftershock of the Organisation of Economic Cooperation and Development Programme for International Student Assessment (PISA), which unexpectedly revealed that German pupils were achieving below the international average (see http://www.pisa.oecd.org/ for information on PISA; see Schock für die Schule [Shock for Schools], 2002, for a German view of the repercussions of the study). This development will obviously double the time designated for language learning in primary schools and will require even more qualified teachers. Our warnings to the ministry that not all teacher learners who would be good primary teachers are gifted enough at languages prompted the following (unofficial) answer: "Not everybody, then, can become a primary school teacher in the future. In the past, teachers had to be able to play the organ. Today, they have to be able to teach a foreign language. The profile has changed because the world has changed." The new module is thus inextricably bound with general educational developments as well as political changes.

DESCRIPTION

Principles Informing the Course

The course on children's literature that I teach is informed by two principles. The first is the way in which young children, in primary school, can learn a foreign language and the methodological direction of integration that the ministry favours. The second principle is that teacher learners are continuously involved in shaping their own learning by helping to design and create the new courses in Children's Literature and Intercultural Studies.

Teaching English to children from the age of 6 or 7 who cannot yet read or write in their own language means approaching the foreign language mainly via oral input for the first 2 years. The children are pretaught new words with the help of drawings or flash cards; listen to stories, rhymes, or songs while watching the teacher perform them; and finally start practising the new words and structures themselves in playful activities once their understanding of them has been secured. (Functional language can be taught more directly, of course.)

---

[3] It took 3 years and a lot of work to convince the university administration that I needed at least one colleague to manage those numbers: A new permanent half-time position was finally granted and will be filled in the winter semester of 2005/2006. Perhaps in 2 years' time we will have managed to turn this into the full-time position that we need.

As I have explained previously, in primary education in Rhineland-Palatinate, integrated language teaching is favoured over a separate language course. Rather than being treated as a new subject, the foreign language is to be presented as another possibility of communication and self-expression, so it should be used flexibly across the curriculum: Saying *good morning* and *good-bye* can be done in English (or any other chosen language), numbers can be practised in English in math, English birthday songs are sung in music, English games can be played in sports, English fairy tales can be told alongside German ones, Halloween costumes are produced in art, and so forth. This means that future primary English teachers in Rhineland-Palatinate have to gain knowledge of children's stories, rhymes, songs, and games as the integrative method precludes the use of a ready-made course book.[4] Therefore, in my Children's Literature and Intercultural Studies course, I have to ensure that teacher learners

- get to know a representative cross-section of children's literature
- learn how to find more material, what to look for, and where to look in the future
- fuel their enjoyment of English children's literature so that they will always continue to want to find more, rather than rely on yellowing notes over the years

The words, linguistic structures, and subject matter used in children's literature are often of the kind that belong to the required vocabulary of primary school teacher learners. The vocabulary for different foods, toys, sports, or holiday activities is important for their future pupils. Logically, one of the course requirements is that only English be spoken at all times, even when teacher learners ask each other for a pencil. This, too, is an integrative principle; it is difficult to establish at first but is very effective later.

The second principle that informs the course is that the classroom is an open classroom in which the teacher learners are involved in deciding about course content and working methods. The combined teaching goals (partly arising from the three course aims listed previously) are to develop self-reliance, responsibility, initiative, and self-confidence and to provide opportunities for presentation practice and language practice. The format most suitable for meeting the various aims and objectives of the course is project work. This means that the teacher learners' research is conducted outside the classroom, and we use contact time to define the goals of the group, define strategies and research methods, discuss the best ways of organising the materials, present the findings, and discuss the presentations.

Project Work

When announcing in the first lesson that the literature course would take the shape of project work, I could see that teacher learners were fairly unfamiliar with this. The first time I taught the course, I sent the teacher learners an e-mail beforehand asking them to brainstorm on this subject in preparation for the first class, which yielded no results. I then distributed a (German) text by one of our leading didactics scholars

---

[4] The first schoolbook publishers have now started publishing teaching materials for the integrative teaching market, so the teachers will not remain dependent on their own creativity only in the future.

informing them about the basis and reasons for more open learning environments, but it was written in didactic jargon that they failed to understand. The second time around, I replaced this text by a much more suitable one, an extract called "Developing a Project" (Fried-Booth, 1986). Fried-Booth lists the ingredients of a good project, beginning with the initial stimulus and definition of the project objectives through the design of written materials, group activities, collation of information, and organisation of materials and culminating with the final presentation (with, obviously, continuous practice of language skills).

After discussing project work, I ask the teacher learners what they think English children's literature or intercultural learning might encompass and which areas they would like or need to learn about. They then brainstorm for ideas in small groups, and, in the end, we collate the results on a transparency. Typical suggestions might include fairy tales, history of children's literature, poets, picture books (series, authors, subjects), nursery rhymes, ideology in children's literature, witches in children's books, how stories portray special events or times (such as birthdays or winter), types of literature for children, culture and nations, images of childhood, finger rhymes and action songs, role-play through children's books, songs and raps, classical stories, literature on the Internet or CD-ROM, puppets and box theatre, and visualization of stories. For the intercultural side of the course, suggestions might include festivals (e.g., Christmas, Guy Fawkes Day, Mother's Day, New Year customs, Thanksgiving), a typical school day and uniforms, British food, American breakfast, Australian musical instruments, schooling in Tanzania, travelling to Britain, party time in English-speaking countries, and so on. With such long lists, we agree that our work in the course has to be selective.

I then announce the course structure and requirements: Week 2 is spent in our university library and in the computer lab doing research on the tentatively chosen subjects, and we finish by finalising the themes and dates of presentations for the work groups (one presentation a week). In Week 3 I do a model presentation. In the following weeks of the term, the teacher learners present their findings on a chosen subject and conduct classroom activities around it. They form work groups, and a schedule is drawn up for each group to see me twice during my office hours for consultation before their presentation date. Right after their presentation, the class gives some feedback and I meet the presenters afterwards for my own feedback and evaluation of the lesson and their oral language skills. The last week is reserved for a roundup and evaluation session and some more discussion of intercultural learning.

Immersion Experiences

I also make sure I provide the teacher learners with a memorable firsthand experience of how hard it can be to learn a language just by hearing it: I show them a short immersion class sequence (storytelling without and with props) in Farsi, tell them an Italian story with the help of flashcards and movements (total physical response) that they then have to reconstruct and retell, and finally teach them classroom language in Russian.

The first time around, the following course plan was agreed:

- poems/*urchin verse* (streetwise poems for modern children, which originated with Rosen's [1974] *Mind Your Own Business*)

- picture books about winter
- Dr. Seuss books and nursery rhymes
- Christmas in children's books (for the session just before Christmas)
- history of children's literature
- Eric Carle and Leo Lionni (famous authors of children's literature)
- storytelling
- witches in stories and witches in history
- action songs and nursery (finger) rhymes
- comics
- roundup/video of notable children's stories (John Cunliffe's "Postman Pat," "Rosie and Jim," and others)

Since then, teacher learners have sometimes chosen the same theme (e.g., storytelling) but often thought of new ones, and there have been no real repetitions so far; every presentation is different. We have also started posting the handouts produced during the module on our homepage (a handout is now part of the course requirement; see *Integrierte Fremdsprachenarbeit* [Integrated Language Work], n.d.-a).

◈ DISTINGUISHING FEATURES

This course is the only one in the programme that does not come with any formal requirement, such as a written or oral test or term paper. It would therefore be all too understandable and easy for teacher learners to use this course as a breather, the consequence of which would be mediocre or even inconsequential lessons. For this reason, offering more help than would normally be given is necessary and justified even while the project character of the course must be maintained. A good working relationship is also required for motivation, but further steps have to be taken to galvanise the teacher learners into wanting to do their best.

Galvanising Teacher Learners

Step 1: The Force of Facts

I raid several of my own children's bookshelves and have collected all the relevant books on children's literature and teaching English at the primary level from the university's library on a few special shelves there. In the first lesson, I enter the room pulling a trolley full of books behind me with some effort, announcing "Children's literature!" After some laughter and bewilderment, the teacher learners jump up to help and spread the books out on the tables for a viewing session later on. The sheer number of books applies a little gentle pressure: They understand there is a lot to do.

Step 2: The Signal of Help

In the second lesson, I direct them to the special children's literature shelves in our library, asking them to browse, and show them the starter *webography* (which includes preselected sites) on children's literature on the module's homepage (*Integrierte Fremdsprachenarbeit* [Integrated Language Work], n.d.-b). Once they realize the ground has been well prepared for them, they feel more comfortable navigating by themselves.

Step 3: The Course Reader

I have created a comprehensive reader with background articles. However, because the two originally separate Children's Literature and Intercultural Studies courses now have to be taught together in half the time, I do not set homework for discussion anymore but leave the choice of articles up to the teacher learners. (They may set for homework what they want the others to read in preparation for their presentation, but this rarely happens now.)

A second reader contains reference material, bibliographies, and so forth. Three further binders now contain the teacher learners' handouts in print. The handout should list all sources used and be comprehensive enough for exam preparation or further research at a later date (though what it obviously cannot contain is the practical part of the lesson, in which the presenters give the class didactic, methodological, or practical tasks to do and the work groups then present their results). All handouts are now posted on the Internet (see *Integrierte Fremdsprachenarbeit* [Integrated Language Work], n.d.-a).

Step 4: Annotated Webographies

Because students are now increasingly suffering from *Googlomania,* I remind the teacher learners that a good presentation is not a random collection of unconnected material and activities and that *Google* (http://www.google.com/) and other commercial search engines do not select sites according to quality. We discuss alternative research options through the town library gateway, which leads to academically prechosen sites (and many directories), and with the help of the new academic search engine (http://www.forschungsportal.net/) that I want them to use alongside *Google* in the future, and with my own annotated webography, they are provided with a list of Web sites and are also advised to use a Web-based bookmark service because they will often collect bookmarks at different computers. Experience so far has shown that they tend to use the shortcut (*Google*). After all, they get no credit for this required course and do not write a final paper.

Step 5: Role Modelling

The final preparatory step is role modelling: I give a presentation. On one occasion I talked about the background to children's poetry, touching on the historical change of the image of childhood, and introduced *urchin verse* as it came to life with Rosen's (1974) *Mind Your Own Business,* using his video *Count to Five and Say I'm Alive!* (Rosen, 1995). I then ended with a discussion about which of those poems could be used in our classrooms and why and how. Another time, I showed the teacher learners how I teach two to three dozen new words and phrases about *English breakfast* in a primary English lesson, using flash cards, rhymes, and a variety of vocabulary games.

Teacher Learner Presentations

The quality of the teacher learners' ensuing presentations and the amount of work invested surpassed all expectations—and still delights me afresh every term. In their first consultation, teacher learners come with a rough idea for a lesson and show some material. Typically, they need advice on the suitability of their material, the necessary variation of activities throughout a 90-minute session, the timing, the working methods and tools, and sometimes on the choice of article to be set as homework for their peers and the kinds of questions to be asked to trigger a discussion. I also have to remind some of them of the presence and importance of books in our library, but they always come back for the second consultation with a much improved lesson plan. Team teaching an entire 90 minutes in English is something they have no experience of, and although they generally know each other well from other courses, almost all the teacher learners show raw nerves when it is their turn to stand up front and be in charge of their classmates' learning.

Typically, the groups start with an outline of the lesson plan (mostly in PowerPoint, sometimes on an overhead transparency) or some leading questions to raise their audience's interest, go on to give a minitalk on the background of their subject, introduce their material, and finish with work-group and classroom activities. Some start with an activity instead (e.g., singing a song, telling a story), but this is left to the individual groups to decide. Trained in primary education and clearly fond of handicrafts, the teacher learners display remarkable creativity in how they present their material visually: They make beautiful displays, flash cards, wallpaper stories, or stick figures; the coloured cardboard for group-work answers comes with matching pen colours; sometimes they prepare typical food (e.g., English tea, American breakfast, hot cross buns, apple pie) and bring it in. Sometimes the room is decorated; other times, the presenters turn up in fancy dress and bring in stickers or role-play costumes for their audience to wear, too, especially when the subject is a festival such as Halloween or Christmas or when it is fairy-tale or storytelling time: It all helps to stimulate their classmates' eagerness to participate and to create a good working atmosphere.

Typical mistakes are occasional loss of contact with the audience; selling oneself short (e.g., "That was perhaps a bit boring, but we'll now come to the fun part"); abrupt transitions; not managing discussions well (being glued to one's questions rather than working with the answers); unclear directives about activities or the length of time allowed for them (some teacher learners still have to learn to be comfortable with the role of being the boss); not looking up the pronunciation of new words or not explaining difficult words to others; and, in one amusing case, not even looking it up beforehand and putting it on the handout: "Lullabies: sung by parents or nurses in order to *intimidate* the child (Twinkle, twinkle)," allegedly a quote from a university Web site that was taken for truth totally uncritically.

Feedback to Teacher Learners

During lessons, I comment on the teacher learners' English when they do group work but only interrupt presenters when they keep mispronouncing their own key words (e.g., *Hogwart, series, archetypes, decade, gestures*). I take notes on the lessons themselves and also on grammar, vocabulary, and pronunciation mistakes. Taking the groups through my notes afterwards—after asking them first about their own impression—gives them information they value. Although their English has improved at the university, most teacher learners still cannot concentrate well on accuracy and pronunciation when in charge of a lesson.

Conversely, it is presentation practice that is needed to reduce the stage fright of speaking English in front of an audience in preparation for their work at school later. To hear teacher learners manage a 90-minute class in English when initially some of them found it hard to speak just for 1 minute is rewarding. To see how they have discovered a liking for English children's books at the same time is also rewarding: It means they are likely to continue to make their own discoveries even after they leave.

Evaluation

The course ends with an evaluation through an anonymous questionnaire, and part of the last session is spent discussing suggestions for improving the course; this also enables teacher learners to hear what their peers think. The course participants are usually glad to have received such a wealth of practical information, both in the lessons themselves and in the handouts, and to have had a chance to see how their peers teach. My feedback after the lessons is also regarded as valuable. When I ask for negative criticism, the discussion usually dries up (similarly, during the course itself, most teacher learners feel unhappy about offering negative criticism to their peers), so it is impossible to say whether or not the following criticisms of the first course were felt to be valid by everybody.

One teacher learner said she had not consulted the books selected for our library shelf because they were "just about children's literature." It transpired that some teacher learners did not wish to learn anything about children's literature as such (the lesson "The History of Children's Literature" as well as information about children's authors was regarded as superfluous by another student) but were interested in practical teaching ideas for primary students only. (I pointed out the obvious: You do not want to be monkey teachers who just copy what they have seen.) Another teacher learner said I should have directed the free choice of subjects for lessons more. (The research tools I had provided, the dozens of children's books in my office for selection, and the help provided during my consultation hours should have been ample for that.)

The criticism probably indicates that I was and still am not always able to convince teacher learners of the need for acquiring theoretical knowledge as a sound basis for future didactic decisions in the classroom; this is perhaps because of the image of the primary school teacher learner at our university and some of the teacher learners' own self-perception and often low self-esteem. As it stands, my second term of integration—theory and practice—was not achieved.

The problem was resolved in the end by mundane pecuniary factors. Having to do children's literature and intercultural learning in one course now, I have dropped the theory but left the material on a shelf in the library for those who are interested in learning more. This way, we now have a new term of integration to substitute for the theory/practice casualty: *literature and culture*.

The written evaluations bring more aspects to light. The answers are usually very positive and detailed, and there is a good deal of agreement. They single out help and feedback by the course leader, extra information given in the course reader, the fact that the course is very informative and helpful for their future careers, the presentations, teacher learners' material for later use in school, comprehensive handouts for later use, the activities and practical parts, the atmosphere, the possibility of seeing such different ways of presenting, team teaching, group work, talking about the authors of children's books and their ideas, and children's books in general. Sometimes they even say that the integration of language and literature, literature and culture, learning and teaching, books and the Internet, and work and fun make this course special and motivating.

◈ PRACTICAL IDEAS

Such an integrative course is a comprehensive project but, once prepared, a great pleasure to teach, and offers many new and enriching learning experiences for both teacher learners and lecturer. The previous sections have illustrated my thinking in detail, with many practical ideas. The following section provides a general overview of points that need to be kept in mind for the success of such a course.

Invest Sufficient Time in Preparation

A course such as this needs to be prepared in advance in great detail: research tools, Internet guide, library shelves, readers, children's books, teaching material from publishers, homepage for handouts, and so on. However, you need not have everything ready the first time around; you can add tools as you go along. The intensive preparation saves time during the term, and the fact that the teacher learners take over the lessons gives you a break from your other teaching commitments as well.

Contact Publishers and Other Educational Institutions

Publishers are usually very interested in providing inspection copies of new material if there is evidence that this material will not disappear into your private shelf at home but will be made available to many teacher learners. I gave a talk on our IFA module at a conference or two and was promptly approached by a few publishers; I then contacted others myself. Such contacts are important in staying immune to cuts in your library budget. We now have an entire office wall full of new material on early language learning.

Conferences are also the best place to meet colleagues in the same field and to find out who would do a good workshop for your teacher learners. There are professionals all over the globe who like working with teacher learners to teach them the tricks of their trade, be they storytelling, games with children, the Internet, or integrative teaching across the curriculum. Such workshops are always great fun and immensely instructive for teacher learners as well as an incentive for them to intensify their English studies. Also, if there is a museum or publisher near where you teach, a visit could be organised. Anything additional relating to the subject happening outside the classroom is motivating to teacher learners—and enjoyable.

Organise the Logistics of the First 3 Weeks

For the first week, bring in as many children's books as you can drag on a trolley, a handout to explain project work (e.g., the extract I use from Fried-Booth, 1986), and a transparency. Start by having a discussion in small groups about what teacher learners think cultural studies is and which English children's literature they already know. Give them time to browse the books. Compare their findings, enrich them, and then either go straight into brainstorming for possible subjects for presentations (in groups, and later collect their suggestions on a transparency) or first give a minilecture on cultural studies and children's literature questions. (Good sources are Doyé, 1999; Gibson, 2000; Tomalin & Stempleski, 1993.) For a rather more difficult discussion on childhood today, I have used Williams (2002), though this is not suitable for an introductory lesson.

For the second week, book a large computer room so teacher learners can surf the Internet for good sources. Bring in the children's books once more and a course plan with dates (of presentations and consultations) on a transparency. Filling in names into the different week slots usually works well simply by hand signal or brief negotiation; when it comes to the penultimate week of term, however, you will need straws—nobody wants to do a presentation in the last 2 exam weeks of the term. Simply pointing out to the unlucky work group that they can prepare their presentation well ahead of time usually sets their minds at rest. A good size for such a course is 30, which means 3 teacher learners per group.

For the third week, pull out all the stops, and do an interesting and entertaining presentation using lots of different media and activities: This lesson is a showcase for the (high) standards you are setting. Make teacher learners sing along to an action song in that lesson—it breaks the ice. Later in the term you may get colleagues checking out your room because of all the noise.

Provide Intensive Counselling During the Term

I allot 2 office hours a week for seeing every group before the group's presentation. I use the consultation sessions to help teacher learners choose from the material they have found, show them material they have not found, help them with varying the activities planned, discuss presentation techniques (reminding them to add visual aids, such as photos from the Internet via beamer, a skeleton checklist on a transparency, a mind map on the blackboard, or practical material to look at), and help them with their time planning (they usually underestimate the time group work and group presentations take). I discuss with them what the best time is to distribute the handout (not the beginning of the lesson!).

All teacher learners need reminding that the particular subject they chose is to be used to teach children the English language; they usually get carried away by the subject itself and forget to think about which language chunks or structures can be taught with the help of their subject. In my experience, the consultations are a good investment and result in well-prepared presentations that are delivered in a lively fashion with background information (this part is not always delivered so well) and a wealth of material to look at and with imaginative, varied classroom activities for practical experience and sheer good fun.

Relinquish Control of What Happens in the Classroom

To feel at ease about relinquishing control requires a little mental openness and flexibility and also a little steadfastness with respect to those teacher learners who feel nervous about having to make their own decisions and try to have me make their decisions. I find it is important not to be pressured into serving up subjects or book choices on a silver platter. Teacher learners manage alone in the end if they have to and because they are given help once they have started organising themselves.

During the presentations, I am treated like all others in the class. I sit with the teacher learners (but near the presenters at the front) and take part in the singing and the games. I interrupt if mistakes occur that would threaten the success of the lesson or if teacher learners have forgotten important details (e.g., telling the work groups how much time they have for a certain activity). Apart from that, I take extensive notes for comprehensive feedback later, and sometimes I take photographs for our homepage. I listen, watch, and enjoy! I thank the presenters and start the applause in the end before asking the other teacher learners for some feedback. I give my own feedback in private once the other teacher learners have left the room: I first ask about their own impression, then give them detailed praise for all that was good and point out the didactic errors they made, and end by thanking them once more.

Find Ways to Motivate Teacher Learners to Perform at the Highest Possible Level

Obviously, it is important to ensure that control over what happens in the classroom is relinquished for a good reason, and it is therefore doubly important to find ways to get the best out of the teacher learners.

One necessary condition is acting as a role model in one's general attitude to work and dedication to the cause—and then by force of one's presentation. Another is giving the teacher learners the feeling that they can deliver excellent work (while keeping a critical distance). Telling them that everybody's English is at their worst when they do the presentation calms their nerves (though only a little). Nobody wants to be the one to present the week after my own presentation, but with the promise that I'll give them extra help, I can quickly persuade the most advanced or most outgoing teacher learners in the group to take the plunge. Their personalities or advanced level of learning, and the help they receive, make for a very good presentation. After that, the pressure is really on to perform well. All else is done by the teacher learners, who, if all goes well, stretch to surpass and surprise themselves.

◈ CONCLUSION

Setting up this new module for teaching language, literature, and intercultural learning (as well as didactics and applied linguistics) to German university teacher learners who are training to become teachers at primary schools has been an interesting task, especially given both the increasingly difficult financial situation and a drastic increase in student numbers. Raising the teacher learners' awareness of the educational importance of their future jobs and of the relevance of learning English well—at a university where the other degrees carry far more prestige—has increased self-esteem and, consequently, effort and diligence on their part. This is especially noticeable in the course described in detail in this chapter, in which the teacher learners are given the responsibility for their own learning, progress, and perform-ance while the lecturer assumes the role of provider of research tools, advisor in questions of teaching, and critic in the evaluation of the final product: the teacher learners' own 90-minute English lesson on children's literature and intercultural learning. If in the Rhineland tired and pale students with a hangover turn up to the last lesson of the winter term for a roundup—this on the very morning after the start of Carnival week, and at 10 a.m.—then I know the course mattered.

◈ ACKNOWLEDGMENTS

I am indebted to my colleagues who run the full English degree, many of whose ideas I was able to remodel for the IFA module. I would also like to thank Heike Baecker, my first IFA student of 2001, who took part in my first Children's Literature and Intercultural Studies class and who now teaches one of the three courses we offer every term as my student assistant.

◈ CONTRIBUTOR

Isabel Martin was born in France and educated in Germany. She is a lecturer at the English department of the University of Koblenz-Landau, Campus Koblenz, Germany; one of the editors of *Primary English* (http://www.oldenbourg.de/osv/zeitschriften /gsm-englisch/); and a teacher educator. Her research interests are English poetry, the education of future teachers, and English in primary schools.

CHAPTER 8

Exploring the Literary Text Through Grammar and the (Re-)Integration of Literature and Language Teaching

Benedict Lin

◈ INTRODUCTION

This chapter describes an initial effort at incorporating a stylistics/linguistics-based approach to teaching reading and interpreting literary texts within an existing Literature in English program in a secondary school in Singapore.

The approach aims at integrating language and literature teaching through close attention to lexical and grammatical features and their consequences for meaning. To illustrate the approach, I describe an actual lesson unit and provide a generic framework for lesson design and a template for lesson planning to help teachers apply a consistent and systematic teaching and learning pattern. I then suggest pedagogical activities that help realize the aims of the approach, give variety within this consistent pattern, and discuss how other agendas of literature teaching may be accommodated within this language-centered approach.

◈ CONTEXT

English in Singapore

English is the medium of instruction in all classes (except for classes that teach the native languages of the students in all schools) in Singapore. However, 70% of Singapore schoolchildren come from non-English-speaking homes. Although out of this 70%, 10–15% manage to get very good results in the language (Lim, 2001), this still means that for the majority of pupils, English is effectively what has been traditionally termed a *second language*. Levels of proficiency in English vary greatly, with academic achievement quite closely co-related: The secondary schools with the best academic performances tend to have a higher percentage of pupils from English-speaking homes, whereas in what are locally termed as *average neighbourhood schools,* the vast majority often do not speak English at home or, possibly, most places outside of school.

Apart from being the medium of instruction for almost all subjects, English is also allocated an average of 3 out of 40 hours each week at the secondary school level. Literature in English is taught as a separate subject, a legacy of British colonialism, and is a compulsory subject at the lower secondary levels (ages 13 and

14), with an average of 1½ hours of instruction each week. At the upper secondary level (ages 15–17), it is optional and is aimed at those who wish to test for the subject at the Singapore-Cambridge General Certificate of Education (GCE) Ordinary (O) Level Examination, the national exit examination for secondary schools set and marked by the University of Cambridge Local Examinations Syndicate in England.

The last decade has seen a sharp decline in the number of pupils taking the subject at the upper secondary level. This, to a large extent, is due to the relative difficulty pupils have had in obtaining good grades in comparison to other subjects at the GCE O-level examination, as well as a general inability on their part to perceive what relevance the subject held for them.

There is therefore a need both to address the difficulties of pupils as well as to reinvent the relevance of literature in Singapore secondary schools. The proposed approach and framework aim to aid this enterprise.

The Literature Syllabus in Singapore and the Place of the Proposed Pedagogical Framework

In part to address these issues, and in part to fill a void, a first-ever formal Literature in English syllabus for all secondary schools in Singapore was introduced in 1999. No such syllabus had existed before, and teaching was largely guided by the agenda of the GCE O-level examination, its assessment objectives, and its prescribed texts. Teachers were expected to make their own decisions regarding what, when, and how to teach, and these decisions were determined by highly varied perceptions of what teaching the subject served and entailed.

The 1999 syllabus, which is still in force, has the following guiding principles:

- response to literature: The personal response of the student is primary. It is the key to making the study of literature "more personally meaningful and enjoyable," with literature providing "opportunities for creative thinking and expression" (Chew & Wong, 1999, p. 92).

- a skills-based approach: There should be an emphasis on close reading skills, with a process-driven orientation rather than a product-driven one. The study of literature thus must also serve the ends of developing general reading and writing skills.

- the text as a resource: Specifically, the text is "primarily a resource for the development of skills of literary appreciation" (Chew & Wong, 1999, p. 92).

- breadth of literary experience: This concerns exposure to all literary genres (prose, poetry, and drama) as well as literature of varied origins, media, and concerns.

The syllabus thus seeks to reassert the relevance of literature by focusing on developing the pupils as individuals and on their personal and aesthetic growth while still being concerned with imparting literary appreciation and experience in their own right. In addition, through its principle of a skills-based approach, it appears to recognize the prior need for close reading skills to enable these aims to be met. To ensure this, unseen texts have been introduced in literature examinations at every level.

Before this, examination syllabuses were dominated by regimes of set texts that allowed or even abetted ready-made readings and interpretations, whether from the teacher or other secondary sources, such as literary critics and guidebooks. To get results, it was safer (and possibly more efficient) to reproduce safe readings from so-called experts, and pupils did not necessarily have to make meaning out of the literary texts themselves. In extreme cases, pupils could get distinctions in the subject without ever having read the set texts themselves, merely relying on secondary interpretations.

The unseen text, however, demands that in the examination hall the pupils address, on their own, a text they have never read before, relying on their own skills of reading and interpretation. This clearly obligates teachers to help the pupils develop these skills, teaching literature as a particular use of language or form of discourse, as well as teaching critical reading and response.

For many teachers, however, this presents a bewildering challenge: How can such skills be taught and learnt in a systematic way? The syllabus, although rich in suggestions for classroom activities for its varied aims, offers no systematic and grounded approach or framework. The approach and framework I describe here hopes to fill this void.

In addition to the Literature in English syllabus, a new English language syllabus was introduced in 2001. Its distinguishing feature is its focus on how generic structures as well as lexical and grammatical features help texts achieve their functions and purposes in discourse in varied contexts. The approach I describe adopts precisely this focus, seeing literary texts as a particular class of texts, to be apprehended in similar ways to other texts. It also seeks to show how texts in general can be more fully read and understood, thus attempting to integrate literature teaching into the larger framework of the language teaching syllabus.

◈ DESCRIPTION

Approach and Rationale

As indicated previously, the approach emphasizes close attention to lexical and grammatical features and their consequences for meaning. The premise is that texts achieve their purposes and create their meanings by managing the lexical and grammatical resources of the language. Comprehension is therefore, in part at least, a matter of attention to these features, whether consciously or implicitly.

The context of the discourse—the context of situation and culture in which the discourse takes place—is, of course, also a powerful contributor to and determinant of comprehension. However, as Widdowson (1975) and Hasan (1985) note, unlike most ordinary uses of language, literature is often read in dissociation from its original context of creation, and the reader is often denied the resources of context in the construction of meaning. Attention to linguistic features thus becomes all the more pressing in reading literature, if comprehension, the foundation for response and appreciation, is to be achieved. Indeed, it might be said that the reader has to recover the context through such attention to language, although students must be encouraged to invoke whatever relevant contextual knowledge they have in their attempts to comprehend and interpret.

In addition, attention to linguistic features leads to awareness of both the constructed nature of a text's meanings and how the construction is achieved. Such awareness enables a grounded critical response and evaluation, surely a valuable aim of literacy and education.

However, mere attention to the management of linguistic features is insufficient, because the very nature of literary discourse distinguishes it from everyday discourse. This relates to the commonsense notion that literary works often have deeper meaning. Literary communication, although related to everyday uses of language and employing its patterns, is distinct from everyday discourse in the nature of both what and how it communicates. Literary discourse distinguishes itself by what Hasan (1996) calls *double articulation,* meaning that it operates through two levels of discourse. The first is the discourse within the text that represents everyday discourse (i.e., the literal or paraphrasable meanings of the text); the second is the discourse between the writer or text and the reader that arises from interpreting the symbolic significance of the represented discourse within the text. It is this second level that gives rise to the deeper meaning, for example, the moral of the story in a fable.

It has been argued that this second level or deeper meaning (often called *theme*) arises out of how linguistic features are artfully patterned so that certain consistencies are foregrounded, thus suggesting a more profound significance (see, e.g., Hasan, 1985; Widdowson, 1975). Thus, teaching the reading of literary discourse involves emphasizing the existence of second-level thematic meaning as well as the need to observe and adduce *patterning of patterns,* to use Hasan's (1985) term, to interpret this second-level meaning.

In summary, the approach described in this chapter involves teaching pupils to

- pay close attention to lexical and grammatical patterns in order to read more precisely what really is happening within the world of the text

- see further patterns in the linguistic patterns and make sense of them in order to interpret the second-level thematic meanings in the discourse between the text and the reader

Pupils can then be encouraged and enabled to respond critically with the awareness that the meanings are constructed by the language and therefore open to question.

The Lesson

The approach can be systematically realised in teaching by selecting and sequencing linguistic features and patterning considerations. The lesson unit described here illustrates how particular lessons in this approach might be taught. It was designed and taught, with my guidance, by a young teacher in her first year of teaching at one of Singapore's top girls' schools.

The 14-year-old girls in her classes gained their places in the school by being among the top achievers at the national Primary School Leaving Examination. Most of them have a very high level of proficiency in English, a far higher percentage than normal coming from English-speaking homes. Nevertheless, the lesson not only illustrates how good pupils can benefit from being taught literature through a greater linguistic focus but also suggests how all pupils may be taught the reading processes necessary to understanding and responding to literature.

The unit focused on the theme of parent-child relationships. As preparation for the lesson, the pupils were asked to read two poems, Thrilling's (1985/1997) "Advice to a Teenage Daughter" and Pastan's (1989) "To a Daughter Leaving Home," both written from the point of view of a mother writing to a daughter. They were also to write freely in their literature journals in response to the poems.

Introduction

The lesson started with the students listening to Aerosmith's "I Don't Want to Miss a Thing" (the theme song from the 1998 movie *Armageddon*) and Bob Carlisle's "Butterfly Kisses." The teacher then led a short discussion about who the persona represented by the singer might be in each case and what feelings are expressed or implied by him. (In both cases, the persona is a father expressing his feelings on missing his child or family; in the former, this is known only from the context of the film, but in the latter, this might be inferred from the language of the song.) The purpose of this introduction was to make the pupils realize that songs and poems often express feelings about relationships, and a good number are about parent-child relationships. The teacher made this explicit by pointing out to pupils that one way they might explore their own relationships with their parents was by reading and thinking about such poems. This, in fact, was what they would be doing in the lesson, and the first poem they would be examining was the poem "Carousel" (Roy, 1993; see the Appendix for text).

The teacher then checked that the pupils knew what a carousel was and elicited predictions as to what the poem might thus be about and reasons it might be so entitled. Responses from the pupils included many predictions that the poem would describe the happy times a child spent at a fairground with his or her mother or father as well as unexpectedly profound statements that the poem might be about the circular nature of life or about life being like a merry-go-round.

First Reading

The teacher then asked the pupils to listen to her reading the poem and see if any of their predictions were right. They were also to identify whether the speaker was a child or a parent, who he or she might be addressing, and what he or she seemed to be thinking most about. (In some classes, copies of the poem were distributed and the pupils asked to read the poem silently, addressing the same questions.)

After the reading, the teacher elicited answers to these questions, requesting justification in terms of clues in what the pupils had heard or read. Most pupils were able to identify the speaker as a daughter addressing her father and recalling the time when he was alive and she was a child, pointing to clues such as the fairground activities and the family members alluded to in the poem.

The teacher also asked the pupils how they would describe the speaker's tone. Many answers focused on notions related to familiarity and intimacy, with some referring to a sense of longing and pain. The teacher also sought intuitive responses as to what the poem might be saying about parent-child relationships (e.g., what lasting impact fathers have on their daughters).

Close Reading: Pronouns

The pupils were then led into a close reading of the poem to confirm or refine their intuitions about its meanings as well as to identify the sources of their intuitions in the grammar. (Copies of the poem were now distributed in classes where initial responses were based on listening to the teacher.) The grammatical focus was on the selection of pronouns and on what experiences the selection of verbs represented.

The pupils were first asked to reread the poem and then underline or highlight all the pronouns, using a different colour each for first-person singulars (e.g., *I, me*), second-person singulars (e.g., *you, yours*), and so on. Collaboration (pair or group work) was encouraged. Their observations were then elicited, and it became apparent that first- and second-person singular pronouns, referring to the speaker and her father respectively, dominated. Teacher-led discussion established that this was where the pupils' perception of a tone of intimacy as well as a preoccupation with a personal relationship emanated from.

The class also noted that the first-person *I* dominated the beginning of clauses, whereas the second-person pronouns tended to be in the latter half of clauses, what in traditional grammatical terms are the subject and object or complement positions, respectively. This led to the conclusion that the starting point of the speaker's concerns had more to do with herself and what her father meant to her than with the father himself.

Close Reading: Verbs

The teacher then asked the pupils to underline all the verbs associated with the speaker (i.e., all the verbs immediately following the first-person *I* or linked to it by conjunction). Following Halliday's (1994) notion that verbs can be said to represent six distinct processes of experience, the pupils were then taught, with examples given, that verbs could be classified as

- action verbs, which refer to someone doing something or something happening (*material action,* in Halliday's [1994] term)

- mental verbs, which refer to thinking, feeling, or perceiving (*mental process*)

- linking verbs, which link someone or something to an identity or attribute (*relational process*)

- saying verbs, which refer to any act of expressing something in words (*verbal process*)

- behaving verbs, which refer to physiological or psychological actions and reactions (*behavioural process*)

- existing verbs, which simply state that something exists (*existential process*)

This activity thus involved the explicit teaching of a new grammatical concept. The pupils had been taught some traditional grammar and were familiar with terms such as nouns and verbs, but were now being introduced to a simple but useful concept from Halliday's functional grammar.

The pupils, working in groups, then had to identify the type for each verb they had underlined and to note any patterns that might arise. Many pupils, drawing on more familiar grammatical knowledge rather than the new concept taught, noted that only the third stanza was in the past tense, whereas the other four stanzas were in the present tense. This helped some pupils realize that the third stanza was a flashback to a time earlier than that of the four outer stanzas. They then also noted the symmetrical structure of the poem.

More saliently, it became immediately apparent to most classes that mental verbs dominated, especially in the first two and last two stanzas (e.g., "I . . . hear" in Line 1, "I feel" in Line 3, "I don't remember" in Line 12). It also became clear that references to the speaker's father in the form of second-person pronouns almost always constituted what followed immediately after the verbs (e.g., "your black arms round me" in Line 3, "your kisses" in Line 12, "you wearing white pyjamas / and waving" in Lines 13–14). This led into a discussion in which it was confirmed or clarified that what preoccupied the speaker about her father (or her relationship with him) were her thoughts, feelings, and perceptions about him; that is, less what he was or did in itself and more what he meant to her or what she treasured about him.

So what was it she treasured about him? To explore this, the teacher pointed out, the reader needed to pay more careful attention to what the speaker thought, felt, and perceived, and this could be found in the *phenomenon* (Halliday, 1994) described immediately after each mental verb. The students were then asked to fill in the worksheet in Figure 1 with direct quotations from the poem, carefully matching each verb with the associated phenomenon. Again, collaborative work was encouraged.

Patterns

Next, the pupils worked in groups to check that they had filled in the worksheet comprehensively and then to scrutinise the right-hand column carefully for any patterns they might observe in the words used to describe the thoughts, feelings, and perceptions (e.g., whether there were common or recurrent images and meanings). Each group filled in the mind map in Figure 2 to consolidate their observations. (The example included in Figure 2 was presented as an illustration.)

When most groups had filled in the worksheet fairly substantially, the teacher elicited their observations and wrote them on the same mind map (either projected through a transparency or drawn on a whiteboard). Many classes noted the emphasis on the colour of the father's arms and hands (black) in contrast to other colours. The recurrence of the image of the father's arms and hands either around or on the speaker, and their size, were also noted. Some classes also made general suggestions about stillness in contrast to movement.

Reminding the pupils that what they had observed represented what the speaker treasured about her father and her relationship with him, the teacher then led a discussion as to what deeper significance the patterns therefore had with regard to

Mental verb associated with speaker	Phenomenon (*what is thought, felt, or perceived*)
Feel	"your black arms round me in a heavy sweep / of closeness, taking me up on notes which fall / like eggs through water." (Lines 3–5)

FIGURE 1. Worksheet 1 for "Carousel"

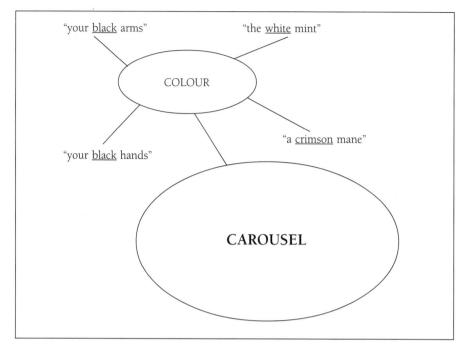

FIGURE 2. Worksheet 2 for "Carousel"

this. She asked questions such as the following to stimulate the discussion: Why the emphasis on skin colour? What significance does it generally have? What do we associate normally with arms and hands, and so why the recurrent images?

The teacher, using the pupils' observations, then demonstrated how it was possible to synthesise the interpretations of the significance of the observed patterns and how, by ascribing symbolic significance to them, it was possible to arrive at an overall interpretation of the poem's theme. For example, using the observations described thus far, skin colour might represent ethnicity and hence basic identity, whereas the large hands and arms around or on the speaker, a child, might suggest security. A possible interpretation might be that what the speaker most treasured was the sense of security as well as the identity her father gave her; one might then arrive at the general point that this is what the poem says about the importance of fathers to their children. The teacher emphasised that this interpretation was not necessarily the only possible or right one: what was important was that it was based on the close reading and observation of patterns done so far.

At this point, the teacher returned to her opening point that reading a poem sensitively could lead people to think more deeply about some facet of their lives, in this case, the significance of parents in our lives. Poems often convey messages, not unlike the moral of a story if one reflects deeply on them. These are often what are called themes. What the lesson had done was to show the pupils how they could approach the reading of a poem and what they could pay close attention to in order to draw more deeply from it.

Reflection

The teacher then asked the pupils to reflect on the stages of reading the lesson had taken them through and to recall what they had done. Working together with the class, these steps were made explicit:

- Begin by thinking what the poem may be about, based on looking at the title.

- Read the poem once or twice, establishing who might be speaking to whom and about what. What deeper messages might the poem be also conveying?

- Read the poem again more carefully, paying close and systematic attention to features of the language. This particular lesson showed that you should pay close attention to

  — the dominant pronouns and where they occur, to establish the answers to questions such as who is speaking and to whom, what the nature of their relationship is, as well as who or what forms the starting point of the speaker's concerns

  — the verbs associated with the main subject indicated by the dominant pronouns observed and whether these verbs are mainly action, mental, linking, saying, behaving, or existing verbs

Based on these observations, you can specify more precisely what the speaker's concerns focus on:

- Observe patterns of word meanings based on the most dominant type of verbs in the poem. This lesson showed that if the verbs are mostly mental verbs, it is important to note very carefully the words describing what is thought, felt, or perceived by the person concerned and see what common patterns there are in this. With action and behaving verbs, it would be important to note patterns in the verb meanings themselves and possibly the circumstances (e.g., when, where, how, and why) in which the actions or behaviours are performed. With saying verbs, it would be important to note what is said.

- Consider what significance the patterns might have. What might each common pattern symbolize or represent? Can your interpretations be consistent with each other?

- Putting all your observations and interpretations together, make a generalization about what the poem might be saying at a deeper level to you.

As a follow-up, the pupils again sat in groups. Each group was given a new poem similar to "Carousel" in theme and style, and the pupils worked on a group interpretation of the new poem using the procedure modelled and outlined previously. These interpretations were then presented and critiqued by the teacher and the rest of the class. The pupils were then asked to write a reflective journal entry on the poems already explored.

◈ DISTINGUISHING FEATURES

Central Perspectives and the Lesson Design Framework

The lesson described illustrates how language and literature teaching are inextricably intertwined in this approach: Literature through language and language through literature are taught simultaneously. This creates far more authentic engagement with both language and literature than other approaches that artificially privilege one over the other, for instance, those that seek to teach language through literature by merely providing sentence-level exercises or cloze-type exercises using literary examples or using literary texts for reading comprehension exercises.

In addition, the pedagogy described involves both implicit learning through the pupils' experiential engagement and explicit teaching of process and linguistic content; one complements the other in meeting the learners' needs. In particular, grammar is seen to be at the heart of both process and content.

Finally and most important, the illustrative lesson is based on a consistent and systematic framework for the stages of every lesson unit, moving from context exploration through textual exploration and explicit teaching to joint construction and independent application. I believe that the routines of such a methodical framework set up expectations that help the pupils understand and work toward the purpose of every part of each lesson, thus maximising learning potential. This framework, based on Derewianka's (1990) and Butt, Fahey, Spinks, and Yallop's (2000) notion of a *curriculum cycle* for language teaching, is presented in Figure 3.

Evaluation of the Approach

Other teachers in Singapore have designed and taught lesson units or cycles similar to the one described but based on other themes such as *women, broken spaces,* and *stopping for death,* and focusing on other specific aspects of grammar. These teachers have reported that the approach has given them greater confidence in ensuring that systematic learning is taking place, because there is a clear learning focus for each lesson as well as consistent methodology. They also felt that the students found reading and interpreting poetry a less formidable and mysterious affair than their previous pupils did. Some of the pupils, too, acknowledged that the lessons benefited them in this way: They knew now what they could or had to do in approaching a poem.

Similar sentiments were expressed by teachers who attended courses and workshops at which the approach has been shared through demonstration lessons. Many said that their experience as students in the demonstration lessons not only helped them to become more conscious and aware of their own implicit reading and response strategies but also clarified how they could focus their teaching to facilitate their students' development in a coherent, systematic way that their own training in traditional approaches via practical criticism could not.

One issue raised by the teachers at these courses and workshops was whether the approach and process would kill natural, affective response from the pupils. The concern was that in being too analytical, one ends up, to echo Wordsworth, murdering to dissect. This reaction has come, in particular, from teachers with strong beliefs in reader response.

However, reader response approaches often assume that comprehension and sensitive attention to details of language are not problematic, which is not always the

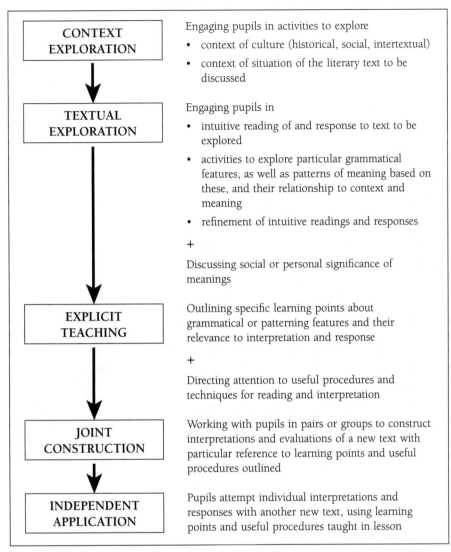

CONTEXT EXPLORATION	Engaging pupils in activities to explore • context of culture (historical, social, intertextual) • context of situation of the literary text to be discussed
TEXTUAL EXPLORATION	Engaging pupils in • intuitive reading of and response to text to be explored • activities to explore particular grammatical features, as well as patterns of meaning based on these, and their relationship to context and meaning • refinement of intuitive readings and responses + Discussing social or personal significance of meanings
EXPLICIT TEACHING	Outlining specific learning points about grammatical or patterning features and their relevance to interpretation and response + Directing attention to useful procedures and techniques for reading and interpretation
JOINT CONSTRUCTION	Working with pupils in pairs or groups to construct interpretations and evaluations of a new text with particular reference to learning points and useful procedures outlined
INDEPENDENT APPLICATION	Pupils attempt individual interpretations and responses with another new text, using learning points and useful procedures taught in lesson

FIGURE 3. Stages in Each Lesson Unit

case. Fundamental attentive reading processes should not be taken for granted, and they involve abilities that often need to be learned or developed: They may be intuitive to some pupils, but not to all. The approach described in this chapter does not aim at teaching literary analysis and dissection but at providing the basis that makes genuine deep response possible. Indeed, less intuitive pupils who have been taught using the approach are more likely to respond to the poems in a more profound and significant way. More intuitive pupils, on the other hand, are more likely to better articulate their responses and their sources.

It is possible that an overzealous focus on linguistic features and reading procedures can turn the reading of literature into a mechanical process. It is, therefore, imperative that other important agendas—personal response, aesthetic appreciation, social or cultural values—be kept in mind (though always with a linguistic focus as the tool and basis for discussion). It is for this reason that the teacher in the lesson described previously included a reflective journal entry.

The results were revealing: The journal entries showed that the close readings of the poems engendered serious reflections by many pupils on their relationships with their own parents. At least a few wrote that they began to realize more acutely some of the more intangible contributions their parents had made to their lives, such as their sense of identity and security. Others began to see difficult parents in a different light. Most interestingly, at least one pupil echoed "Carousel" very strongly in recalling how her most vivid and enduring image of her father was of his large hands enveloping her little hands when she was a small child. Clearly, the approach serves more than a purely language teaching function.

◈ PRACTICAL IDEAS

Figure 4 provides a template for applying the ideas described in this chapter within the framework of a lesson. There can be immense variation of activities and exercises at each stage of the lesson unit, thus avoiding dull predictability. This section presents some of these possibilities.

Explore the Context With the Students

This stage aims to familiarise pupils with the cultural or situational context and to make links to their own experience. Pupils can

- carry out a structured and scaffolded research task (e.g., fill in a worksheet requiring them to look up information in the library or on the Internet)

- review and discuss a lesson in another subject that provides background information (e.g., a history lesson on the particular events influencing the writing of a poem)

- listen to songs or taped material or view videos on similar subject matter or themes (e.g., a documentary about child abuse) and discuss them

- role-play a situation similar to that in the poem and then reflect on and discuss the role play

- read and discuss material from other genres (e.g., newspaper or magazine articles) about the same subject or on the same themes

Provide Activities for Close Textual Exploration

This is a key stage, where pupils look very closely at how language constructs meaning. Pupils can be asked to

- highlight and tabulate selected grammatical features, as in the lesson described in this chapter

- complete worksheets and graphic organizers that draw attention to selected grammatical features

Aims of lesson:

1. Textual (first-level lexicogrammar or second-level patterning/foregrounding) focus:

2. Social/affective response focus:

Sample text for exploration:

Text for joint construction:

Text for individual application:

Lesson procedure:

1. Context exploration:

   Historical, sociocultural, intertextual considerations:

   Situational (field, tenor, mode) considerations:

   Activities:

2. Textual exploration:

   Focus areas: see Aims of lesson

   Activities and techniques:

3. Explicit teaching:

   Points to be made:

4. Joint construction:

   Whole class/group/pair (select)

   Activities:

   Guiding questions, specific tasks, suggested procedures:

5. Individual application:

   Guiding questions, if any:

   Specific instructions and reminders:

   Mode of presentation:

Evaluation of lesson:

FIGURE 4. Lesson Plan Template to Enable Framework Application

- compare the original text with a systematically modified text (e.g., one in which all the adverbials are omitted or altered) and then discuss the consequences of the changes

- rewrite highlighted parts of a text (e.g., replace all the adjectives describing one person with a different set of adjectives) and then discuss the resulting changes in meaning

- reassemble the text from cut-up clauses, lines, or chunks and then discuss possible variations in the reassembly and their differences in meaning and effect

- draw diagrams (e.g., mind maps as in Figure 2) to discern metapatterning

- paraphrase the text and then compare the paraphrased versions with each other and with the original, with special attention to selected grammatical patterns

Teach the Main Points of the Lesson Explicitly

The key learning points about grammatical or patterning features as well as procedures for reading and interpretation should be presented explicitly. Use a variety of modes, for example, oral dictation, printed checklist, and electronic projection (e.g., via a Microsoft PowerPoint presentation).

Encourage Collaborative Learning

This happens during the *joint construction* stage (see Figure 3), in which pupils work with each other to arrive at interpretations and evaluations of a new text using what they have learnt. Vary the following from lesson to lesson:

- groupings: pairs, small groups, larger groups, or the whole class

- tasks: interpretation with a number of guiding questions or with a checklist, in response to two or three general questions, with only a general theme given

- task outcomes: oral presentation, class display on a poster, a Web page, a scaffolded joint essay, written responses to two or three general questions, a joint essay without scaffolding, written responses in some other form (e.g., a letter to a friend or a poem)

Conclude With Independent Application Activities

Pupils should finally attempt interpretation on their own, individually. As with joint construction, vary the tasks and task outcomes for individual work.

Recognize That Literature Teaching May Need to Meet Other Agendas

Literature teaching often has to meet the needs of other agendas, apart from language teaching. In Singapore, for instance, one of the central imperatives of the education system is National Education, which is concerned with building a sense of nationhood and active citizenship. National Education is supposed to be infused into the teaching of all subjects, including literature. How then does the approach incorporate such an agenda?

As the illustrative lesson demonstrates through its concurrent affective aim, the key lies in text selection. Meeting Singapore's need for National Education in teaching literature, for instance, can be achieved by selecting literary texts that have as their themes issues such as those pertinent to national identity and social cohesion. An agenda based on multiculturalism can likewise be met by selecting appropriate texts. The focus on linguistic features to teach fundamental reading and interpretation processes then becomes the key to deepening the meaningfulness of the discussion while encouraging a more critical assessment by raising awareness of language's role in the construction of meaning.

◈ CONCLUSION

In this chapter I have described a preliminary effort at a linguistically based, systematic approach to teaching literature. The outcome thus far appears promising and in line with the expectations of the basic premises of the approach. This approach should therefore find a wider usefulness in varied contexts, whether in a full or modified form, thus contributing to the reintegration of language and literature teaching.

The original proposals (in Lin, 2001) from which the approach emerged have as their informing linguistic theory the systemic functional grammar of Halliday (1994). For those familiar with the theory, this is implied in the description of the illustrative lesson. However, I believe that the approach can be allied with any theoretical perspective, implied or explicit. What is important is that any practitioner following the framework provided have an informed and informing theory as a basis for using the approach. With such a theory, I believe that the approach can be used for building a powerful and effective curriculum for both language and literature teaching.

◈ CONTRIBUTOR

Benedict Lin is currently an associate professor in the Faculty of Foreign Languages and Asian Studies at the Nagoya University of Commerce and Business Administration, in Japan. Before this, he was a language specialist at the Southeast Asian Ministers of Education Organisation Regional Language Centre (SEAMEO RELC) in Singapore, having taught English language and literature for 19 years in secondary schools in Singapore.

◈ APPENDIX: "CAROUSEL" (Roy, 1993)

for Namba Roy, 1910–1961

> I often spin around with you and hear
> the fragile music of a carousel;
> I feel your black arms round me in a heavy sweep
> of closeness, taking me up on notes which fall
> like eggs through water.
>
>   I am older now
> and you have fallen from the garish horse
> a long time since, and I am holding on
> with thin brown fingers. Do you know
> 10 it's been a quarter century since you
> (with your voice like the man who plays God in the movies)
> kissed me? I don't remember your kisses.
> I remember you wearing striped pyjamas

and waving to me from the ward—your great hand
scooping a half-circle out of nothing;
how my brother almost choked on a *Lifesaver*
until a male nurse turned him upside down
and out came the white mint with the hole
that saved him.

20   I dreamed you died, and when I woke
my mother was by the bed. 'How will I light
the fire?' she said. I didn't know.

It was cold in our house; our breath came out
round as balloons and dissolved till we breathed
again. We learned to accommodate spaces
as you must have learned to accommodate . . .
but no. Where there is not place to put things,
no place for your bones or your slippers or my words
there cannot be a place for spaces.

30   It must be fine to know only lack of substance—
the round emptiness in an angel's trumpet—
and still hear music.

              I have the things you made
and she has made me see you in them.
I have the ivory statues and the pictures
telling stories of African ancestors,
a birth, flights into Egypt. In your work
I find the stillness of your eyes and mouth,
the stillness which is always at the centre

40   of the spinning ball which we hurl high and long.

              I often spin around with you and hear
the fragile music of the carousel.
My horse would gallop forward if I let him,
but I prefer the swinging back to where
we were, slow undulations round and back
to identical place. I prefer to see
your black hands with mine on a crimson mane
which will never be swept back by the wind.

CHAPTER 9

Learning and Teaching How a Poem Means: Literary Stylistics for EFL Undergraduates and Language Teachers in Japan

Patrick Rosenkjar

◈ INTRODUCTION

This chapter reports on an approach to teaching literature at Temple University, Japan Campus (TUJ), the branch campus in Japan of Temple University in Philadelphia, Pennsylvania, in the United States. TUJ offers a variety of preacademic and academic programs, with English as the language of instruction. These include the College of Liberal Arts offering associate and bachelor degrees and the College of Education offering master and doctoral degrees in TESOL. Because of TUJ's location in Japan, both the undergraduate and graduate student bodies include many nonnative speakers of English. This fact means that both academic content and issues of English language learning must be addressed at the same time.

This chapter describes two courses taught at TUJ. The first, Introduction to Literature, is for undergraduates in the College of Liberal Arts. This course uses a language-oriented approach in which students work on tasks designed to lead to discovery of the stylistic patterns of literary works and the fashioning of their own interpretations based on this linguistic evidence. The main goal is to develop *literary competence,* students' ability to read and make sense of literature for themselves. In addition, because the tasks focus largely on formal stylistic features, they also facilitate noticing of aspects of language and, therefore, contribute to development of second language competence (Doughty & Williams, 1998). The other literature-based course is Literature in Language Teaching for teacher learners in the TESOL master's program and for doctoral candidates. That course aims at developing teachers' ability to analyze the linguistic features of literary texts and to create lesson plans based on that analysis. It draws heavily on stylistics but addresses more general pedagogical issues as well. These two courses are described in this chapter because they make use of a similar approach and many of the same pedagogical techniques.

This chapter explains how the stylistics-based approach works, provides an extended example of a lesson plan based on a stylistic analysis of a poem, and offers other suggestions for using literary texts with nonnative speakers of English (though a similar approach may be equally useful with native speakers.)

◈ CONTEXT

The undergraduate courses of TUJ are at the same level of academic challenge as those offered in Philadelphia, with academic credits earned at TUJ counting the same as those earned at Temple's main campus. The curriculum is based on a core of course requirements in the arts and sciences, on an upper and a lower division of courses, and on majors and minors in particular disciplines. Some of the core courses are designated as *writing intensive,* which means that they demand numerous academic essays in order to develop writing proficiency as students explore course content. Introduction to Literature is a writing-intensive course.

It is possible for undergraduates to satisfy core distribution requirements without taking literature, and except for freshman composition and two required courses in Intellectual Heritage, no specific courses are required of all undergraduates. (For a description of the Intellectual Heritage courses, see Rosenkjar, 2002.) Because they seem to have had demotivating experiences with the study of literature in the past, many TUJ undergraduates opt to fulfill their humanities requirements with courses other than literature courses. Undergraduates in my course frequently report having found the study of literature in high school boring and difficult, even in their native language. A quote from one student explains why: "I did not like Japanese literature because it was difficult to understand. The class was not interesting to me, either, because tutors only emphasized to memorize important points. So, I did not find Japanese literature interesting and I did not like Japanese literature." Regarding English literature, another student wrote: "Studying English literature in the junior and senior high schools was not much better. We always studied them by translating them into Japanese first, so I never appreciated English literature as they are."

The curriculum of the master's program consists of 10 required courses beyond the bachelor's level. Of these, 5 are core requirements that address issues of linguistics, TESOL methods, and second language acquisition, rather than literature. The remaining 5 courses are electives dealing with areas of specific interest. Literature in Language Teaching is one of these. Though the graduate students who take this course frequently have studied English literature, many even having been literature majors, very few have experience with a stylistic approach or with principles for teaching literature.

Although the undergraduate and graduate literature courses are intended for different student populations, they both center around inductive tasks intended to show how literary writers use the resources of the language to express their meanings. Indeed, many of the same poems are even used in the two courses. However, the graduate course additionally seeks to teach how to create lesson plans based on literary works.

◈ DESCRIPTION

The structure of both of the courses described in this chapter depends on a set of underlying assumptions about the value of literature in the curriculum, about the nature of literary language, and about effective pedagogy.

Widdowson (1992) makes a strong case for including poetry in the curriculum on the basis of its general educational value. He suggests that the study of poetry is worthwhile because it promotes "the reciprocal interests of the individual and society" (p. 83) by developing awareness of two crucial relationships. The first is the relationship between work and the creative leisure essential for regenerating one's energies. Reading poetry is the kind of activity that allows students to refresh themselves intellectually and emotionally by touching the deep sources of their own humanity. The second is the relationship between individual freedom and social constraints. Literary study potentially allows students to experience the freedom to fashion their own interpretations of poems while adhering to the constraint of basing interpretations on evidence actually found in the texts themselves. This is very much in consonance with the basic goal in a liberal arts program of developing students' individual critical faculties.

McKay (2001) argues that literature is valuable for language learners because it makes them aware of formal features of language, promotes integration of the four macroskills, and helps students learn about cultural differences. Her argument mainly concerns the value of literature for language learning, but awareness of how language is used to create meaning and knowledge of cultural differences also contribute to the more general educational goals of the liberal arts.

The second basic principle underlying the two courses is that literary and nonliterary texts are fundamentally different in purpose and in the use of language. Widdowson (1992) argues that the essential nature of literary language is representational, not referential. This means that a poem seeks to re-create, or represent, an experience or feeling through the medium of words. If the medium is skillfully used, the poem provides the illusion of (re)experiencing an event or feeling. Thus, the connection between form and meaning is central to literary texts in a way that is not true of nonliterary writing, and the meaning of a poem is much more than the propositional content of its sentences. For this reason, paraphrases of literary text always involve some loss of meaning. Referential use of language, on the other hand, does not attempt to re-create experiences but only to describe or report them. In referential texts, what is important is propositional content, so paraphrasing the text does not usually result in significant meaning loss.

But how do literary writers use language to create representations of experience? Short (1996) suggests that they do so by manipulating various features of language so that these become "especially noticeable, or perceptually prominent. We call this psychological effect foregrounding" (p. 11). This can be achieved by repetition, parallelism, or deviation, either from a previously established pattern or from the normal way in which language is used.

My third assumption is the principle of discovery learning through tasks. Stylistic analysis is a tool for explicitly describing the foregrounded features of a text and relating them to an interpretation (Short, 1996). Because I wish my students to become adept at practicing stylistic analysis, I do not lecture on the meaning of poems. Rather, I offer tasks by which students can identify and interpret various features for themselves. This, of course, depends on my having thoroughly analyzed the poem before devising the tasks.

Such an approach fits very well with current notions of communicative language pedagogy. For example, Lee (2000) recommends task-based language teaching (TBLT), in which students focus on negotiating meaning with the goal of performing some task with a tangible outcome independent of language practice. Stylistics dovetails with the TBLT approach because a stylistic analysis suggests clear outcomes for activities, such as creating a list or sorting a set of words. Moreover, the tasks are simultaneously both form- and meaning-focused, thus enabling students to discover the evidence upon which to base interpretations of a text. This frees them from the arbitrary imposition of others' authoritative interpretations. Students' critical faculties, therefore, are sharpened as they explore the linguistic form and the meaning of a poem for themselves, and they come to notice not just what a text says but how it creates meaning. Of course, different readers will have different interpretations, but this is entirely acceptable so long as the interpretations are firmly rooted in the actual language of the text.

To illustrate these concepts, I will offer a lesson plan on a poem that I sometimes use in both literature courses, "Woodchucks" (Kumin, 1972/1997; see the Appendix for the full text of the poem). In order to experience the poem as my students would, readers of this chapter are invited to work through the tasks for themselves. As each task is presented, I discuss its objective. At the end of the task sequence, I provide a summary of my analysis and interpretation of the poem with reference to the stylistic evidence highlighted in the tasks.

The lesson plan includes three phases: activities before, during, and after reading. Nuttall (1996) suggests this framework for designing lesson plans, and Maley and Duff (1989) provide a wealth of ideas for all three stages. As in any reading lesson, prereading activities aim at activating students' schemata, providing a reason for reading, and introducing new vocabulary items. The middle phase, in my approach, consists mainly of stylistics-based activities. Postreading activities attempt to exploit the newly acquired knowledge of the poem to build language competence, to transfer to other skills, and to motivate students to engage more deeply with the poem.

The prereading activities for "Woodchucks" are as follows:

Activity 1: Viewing a picture of woodchucks, list facts about these animals (e.g., where they live, what they eat, what problems they may present). If you do not know definite facts, predicting and guessing are acceptable. (If a picture is not available, the same goal can be achieved by brainstorming on the word *woodchucks,* but it may be necessary to look the word up in a dictionary or encyclopedia first.)

Activity 2: Imagine that woodchucks are eating the plants in your garden. List possible solutions to this problem. After you do this, discuss with a partner and then with the whole class the advantages and disadvantages of each suggested solution. Finally, rank the solutions in order of predicted effectiveness.

The two prereading activities are task based, involving the need to produce lists of ideas related to woodchucks. The goal is to prepare to read the poem. This is followed by the literal comprehension activities, which address the need for comprehension and lay the groundwork for later, more stylistics-oriented work:

Activity 3: Now look at the text of the poem in the Appendix. Use two different colors of marking pens and simply highlight all the sentences in alternating colors. Then number the sentences from 1 to 16.

Activity 4: Match the following scrambled paraphrases with the original sentences:

Paraphrase 1 = Sentence #_____: The poison I bought from the local farmers' supply shop was supposed to be painless, and the woodchucks were certainly stealing our food. So, we stopped up their hole and put the poison in, but they escaped.

Paraphrase 2 = Sentence #_____: A single woodchuck is still alive.

Paraphrase 3 = Sentence #_____: The female woodchuck jumped up as she died. She still had a piece of vegetable in her mouth.

Paraphrase 4 = Sentence #_____: He is a clever one, but I have my gun constantly ready to shoot him.

Paraphrase 5 = Sentence #_____: I killed a second young woodchuck.

Paraphrase 6 = Sentence #_____: I wish the woodchucks had simply allowed themselves to be killed by the poison.

Paraphrase 7 = Sentence #_____: While I am in bed, I imagine that I am aiming my gun at the last woodchuck.

Paraphrase 8 = Sentence #_____: I killed the baby woodchuck among the flowers.

Paraphrase 9 = Sentence #_____: My first attempt to exterminate the woodchucks with poison did not work well.

Paraphrase 10 = Sentence #_____: I began to enjoy the feel of the gun's ammunition as I thought about killing the woodchucks for stealing our vegetables.

Paraphrase 11 = Sentence #_____: I shot the female woodchuck a little while afterwards.

Paraphrase 12 = Sentence #_____: A part of me that enjoys hunting and killing began to control my personality.

Paraphrase 13 = Sentence #_____: The woodchucks ruined the flowers and then invaded the vegetables, which they began to destroy as well.

Paraphrase 14 = Sentence #_____: I try to kill the last woodchuck throughout the nighttime.

Paraphrase 15 = Sentence #_____: The woodchucks survived and appeared to be no more harmed by the poison than humans are by the poisons they take.

Paraphrase 16 = Sentence #_____: I used to believe in nonviolence, but as I aimed at the baby woodchuck I was motivated by belief in the survival of the fittest.

Activity 5: Look at the sentences that you highlighted in Activity 3. Which sentences end at the ends of lines, and which sentences consist of only parts of lines or extend across line boundaries? Why is this so?

The point of Activity 3 is to identify the sentences to prepare to match them with the paraphrases in Activity 4 and, thus, to foster literal comprehension. Activity 3 is also a graphic way to see that the close fit between grammatical structure and the lines of the poem established in the first three stanzas breaks down in the last two. This point is taken up in Activity 5. The poem contains five six-line stanzas and 16 grammatical sentences, each beginning with a capital letter and ending with a period. Indeed, the common English poetic convention that every line begins with an uppercase letter is not followed here; only those common nouns that are the first words of sentences are capitalized. In the beginning, there is a tight fit between the sentences and the lines. The length of sentences varies, but in the first three stanzas each sentence consists of one or more full lines. The pattern changes in the fourth and fifth stanzas as the regularity of fit suddenly breaks down and all the sentences (except for the last, which is salient for other reasons) start or end in the middle of a line. Moreover, one sentence in the fourth stanza is elliptical because its subject and verb are missing ("[I shot] [a]nother baby next."). The brevity of this sentence can be interpreted as representing the speaker's swift reaction in killing the baby woodchuck as soon as he sights it. Also, the sentences tend to be much shorter in the last two stanzas. These facts support the interpretation that the speaker is breaking down psychologically in those stanzas.

At this point readers may start looking at the lexical effects found in the poem. The following two activities focus on lexical sets and the effect that these sets have on readers:

Activity 6: Divide the following words into two groups and name the groups. What relationship do the two groups have to one another in this poem?

marigolds	killing	Swiss chard
vegetable patch	food	bomb
.22	drew a bead on	sight along the barrel
bullets' neat noses	dropped	die
broccoli shoots	everbearing roses	gassed
carrots	murderer	Nazi
lapsed pacifist	hawkeye killer	

Activity 7: Divide the following words into three groups and name the groups. Why are these groups of words included in the poem?

merciful	airtight	took over
bomb	righteously	lapsed pacifist
brought down	case	pieties
fallen from grace		

These two activities help the learner realize the richness of "Woodchucks" in terms of lexical sets, defined as groups of words that "have similar collocational ranges" (Cummings & Simmons, 1983, p. 179). This means that words can be grouped together on the basis of sharing a denotative or connotative relationship to a particular domain of experience. At least five lexical sets can be identified, each contributing to the overall communicative purpose. These sets are

- a legal process set: "merciful," "case," and "airtight"
- a warfare/violence set: "bomb," "brought down," "took over," ".22," "bullets' neat noses," "lapsed pacifist," "killing," "drew a bead on," "dropped," "murderer," "hawkeye killer," "hunt," "sight along the barrel," "die," "gassed," and "Nazi"
- a religious set: "merciful," "righteously," "lapsed pacifist," "pieties," and "fallen from grace"
- a plant set: "marigolds," "vegetable patch," "broccoli shoots," "carrots," "food," "everbearing roses," and "leaf of early Swiss chard"
- a sexual excitement set: "rose up hard," "cocked and ready," and "humped-up"

It is especially noteworthy that the warfare/violence set contains so many items; and, if the poem is seen to represent the speaker's psychological change, this is very important for understanding the poem.

Another aspect of these lexical sets is deliberate use of two groups of polysemic items. The first is in Line 4, in which the "airtight case" can mean clear legal evidence or the hoped-for condition of the burrow after the speaker has plugged up its exits. The second is the apparently deliberate use of words that connote sexual feeling, including "rose up hard" in Line 23, "cocked and ready" in Line 26, and "humped-up" in Line 27. The fact that three such references occur at just the point in the poem when the speaker is becoming irrational and agitated suggests the deliberate exploitation of the sexual connotations.

Activity 8 aims for noticing that the poem is rich in two other lexical effects, unusual collocations and the figurative language that makes use of them. Activity 9 looks at the effect created by repeating words.

Activity 8: Look at the following combinations of words. What is unusual about them? What effect does this have?

the case we had against (the woodchucks)—Line 4
(the woodchucks) had a sub-sub-basement—Line 6
beheading the carrots—Line 12
the littlest woodchuck's face—Line 17
(woodchuck) baby—Line 22
murderer (of woodchucks) —Line 23
old wily fellow—Line 25
(the woodchucks) consented—Line 30

Activity 9: Find the one place in the poem in which a phrase is repeated. Explain why it is repeated.

The word "beheading" in Line 12 usually requires a human object, but in this case it is "carrots." The effect is to personify those vegetables. Raising them to human status magnifies the crime of the woodchucks in eating their tops and serves as a justification for the speaker's decision to hunt the animals down. Even more important is the personification of the woodchucks themselves. This is found throughout the poem as terms usually used only of human beings are systematically applied to the woodchucks. These include "the case we had against them" in Line 4, "sub-sub-basement" in Line 6, "the littlest woodchuck's face" in Line 17, "baby" in Line 22, "murderer" in Line 23, "old wily fellow" in Line 25, and "consented" in Line 30. The effect of personifying the animals is to heighten the moral significance of the speaker's violence against them. In Activity 9, the repeated phrase in the fifth stanza "day after day after day" indicates the speaker's full-blown obsession with killing the woodchucks by this point.

"Woodchucks" contains a number of very salient grammatical patterns, so the lesson now turns to examination of pronouns and verb forms:

> *Activity 10:* Circle the personal pronouns in the poem and decide what patterns they make. Then explain why the patterns are found in the poem.

> *Activity 11:* Underline the main verbs in the poem and put them into three groups on the basis of their tense. What patterns do you see? Which sentence and which verb are different from all the others?

> *Activity 12:* If necessary, the teacher will explain the contrary-to-past-fact conditional structure and provide examples. You must complete the last sentence and support your answer with reasons related to the poem's meaning.

The distribution of noun phrases and personal pronouns is suggestive. In Stanzas 1 and 2 the speaker uses the plural first-person pronouns "we" and "our" for humans and either the third-person pronouns "they" and "them" or the plural noun phrase "the woodchucks" for his adversaries. Line 13 begins with a direct quotation of the speaker's words ("The food from our mouths") without the normal punctuation, but this use of "our" is in a quotation and not in the narrative itself. After this point, the speaker uses the pronoun "I" for himself and singular noun phrases or pronouns for the woodchucks: "the littlest woodchuck's face" in Line 17; "he" in Line 18; "the mother" and "she" in Line 19; "another baby" in Line 22; "one chuck," "old wily fellow," and "he" in Line 25. This supports the interpretation that, in the speaker's view, the situation has changed from an impersonal collective contest to a more personal and individual struggle.

Analysis of verb forms reveals that all of the verbs in the first four stanzas are in the simple past tense, consistent with the fact that the speaker is narrating a sequence of past events. In Stanza 5, however, there are two important changes in verb morphology. The verbs in Lines 25 to 28 suddenly shift to the simple present, and this is consistent with the idea that the speaker is now telling about a current situation of repeated or habitual action. Indeed, at this point the speaker is obsessed with killing the last surviving woodchuck; his obsession is further indicated by the highly prominent repetition of "day after day after day" in Line 26. Secondly and quite significantly, the last two lines of Stanza 5 consist of an incomplete contrary-to-past-fact conditional ("If only they'd all consented to die unseen / gassed underground the quiet Nazi way."). This seems to express the regretful wish that things had turned out differently, but we do not know how the conditional structure is completed because the poem ends at this point. Does the speaker regret that killing the woodchucks was so messy and difficult? If so, the sentence would end with "it wouldn't have been so troublesome to exterminate them." Does he regret that he has been forced to confront the violence in his own nature? If so, the sentence would end with "I wouldn't have had to face my own fascination with violence." The choice of these alternatives depends on the individual reader's interpretation of the poem.

The foregoing activities should serve to illuminate the way language is used in this poem to represent the gradual change in the speaker from dispassionate rationality to obsession with violence for its own sake. Having worked through the activities, learners are at this point able to evaluate a coherent interpretation of the poem. I would claim that this poem represents the changes that take place in the personality of the speaker as he tries to solve the problem of pests in his garden.

The opening sentence is the speaker's regretful summary of the failure of his first attempt to eradicate the woodchucks. He is a rational and educated man who initially desires to exterminate the animals in a quick, painless, and impersonal way by stopping up their burrow and injecting cyanide gas into it. He speaks of this killing almost as an execution decided upon through dispassionate judicial process. However, he discovers that the gassing is unsuccessful because the animals have tunneled deeper than the gas could penetrate. The conflict between human and woodchucks now takes on the character of a just war to protect innocent personified flowers and vegetables from the depredations of a marauding army. Soon it becomes a righteous crusade in which the true character of the speaker's deep emotional involvement is only partially masked by his rationalization that he is acting properly for the good of his family by shooting the woodchucks one at a time. The woodchucks are no longer a collective animal enemy; they have become individualized and personified. The speaker justifies the killing in both quasi-religious and scientific terms that reveal awareness of his own growing fascination with violence. He begins to feel a thrill of power from dispatching the woodchucks one by one. His diction starts to include cavalier colloquial terms related to killing. He becomes much less rational and is obsessed with killing the last remaining woodchuck. He even feels a sexual thrill from the hunt. In the end, the speaker's personality is taken over by his obsession, but he retains enough self-awareness to wish wistfully that the cyanide had worked. He seems to yearn for the impersonal efficiency of gassing the woodchucks in the Nazi manner. Thus, the last sentence of the poem echoes the tone and word choice of the first, providing an evaluative frame for the narrative.

Though the poem is a carefully crafted linguistic artifact employing many of the standard conventions of English poetry, it gives the impression of ordinary conversational speech. This commonplace register supports the interpretation that a consuming obsession with violence potentially lies within the heart of any person, even one who is rational, educated, and humane. What makes this a good poem is the fact that the gradual change in the speaker is demonstrated by the way language is used as well as reported in the propositional content of what is said. The poet has subtly used the expressive resources of English to re-create the speaker's personality change, not just to refer to it.

The final stage of the lesson plan is to explore how the poem functions as discourse by imagining its propositional content from different perspectives and in different contexts. This is the objective of Activity 13.

> *Activity 13:* As a follow-up, you must either rewrite the poem as a newspaper article for *The Gardener's Gazette*, a weekly publication with tips on gardening, or as an article for *Animals Are People, Too*, a newsletter for the animal rights activist community. Then compare the tone, word choice, discourse structure, and viewpoint of the two articles. Also analyze how both articles are different from the original poem.

The point of this activity is to induce the students to explore how the poem functions as a whole piece of discourse. This involves various aspects of context and viewpoint. Fowler (1996) elaborates three types of context important for understanding how a literary text works as discourse: context of utterance, of culture, and of reference. *Context of utterance* means the immediate setting in which the speakers are conversing, their location in relation to one another, and the mode and channel by which they are communicating. The *context of culture* is the whole network of social conventions that influence the form that discourse may have. *Context of reference* means "the topic or subject-matter of a text" (p. 114). In "Woodchucks" the whole poem is structured as a first-person narrative told by a fictional persona. This persona appears to be an educated man familiar with the law (e.g., "the case we had against them was airtight"), academic vocabulary (e.g., "Darwinian"), and religion (e.g., "righteously," "lapsed," "pieties," and "fallen from grace"). Yet, as he becomes more fascinated with killing, he begins to use colloquial terms related to hunting (e.g., "drew a bead on" and "dropped") and the sexual slang terms previously discussed. The switch in register reflects the psychological change that occurs in him. Note, though, that there is no definitive evidence for the speaker's gender. That it is possible to assume the speaker to be a female is an example of the legitimacy of multiple, and even conflicting, interpretations.

The speech act that the speaker in the poem is performing may be viewed either as self-justification, as expressing annoyance, or as expressing regret. In this connection, how the last sentence is completed is important. In my interpretation, the speaker is expressing regret and dismay at his newly acquired awareness of himself as a "murderer" and "hawkeye killer."

Unlike some poems, "Woodchucks" does not suggest a definite context of utterance; the reader cannot infer from the text where the speaker is telling his story or to whom. Therefore, this aspect of the analysis allows scope for a range of possibilities. For example, the persona may be speaking to his spouse, to his best friend, to his therapist, to his spiritual advisor, or to a number of other people. The lack of limitation on the context of utterance influences the context of culture because discourse form is usually constrained by the social relationships existing between interlocutors. However, the context of reference is clear, and this is true on two levels at once. Most obviously, the speaker is talking about the topic of exterminating garden pests. In discussing this topic, the speaker presents a narrative containing a situation-problem-solution-evaluation pattern (McCarthy, 1991). At a deeper level, however, the topic is the capacity of ordinary humans for violence, or the *banality of evil* as Arendt (1963) famously termed it.

It should be noted that not all of the stylistic features discovered in the original analysis were made into the focus of a learning activity. The teacher chooses those that are most clearly relatable to an interpretation of the poem and that the students are likely to be able to discover. Also, not all of the students need to do all of the activities given previously. It is quite possible to allow different groups to work on different tasks and then to share their findings with the rest of the class. This both saves time and builds in a greater measure of choice for the students.

An example of a feature that was not used in the lesson is the nonce word "chuck" in Line 25. It is very prominent because it is a deviation from the normal use of the language. It seems to be a shortened form of *woodchuck*, but this abbreviation is not part of standard English. It does follow a common English pattern, though, in which terms are shortened to indicate intimacy or familiarity. The implication is that the speaker has so personified and individualized his adversary, the "old wily fellow," that he even has a familiar name for him. It is quite significant that this form occurs in the last stanza rather than earlier.

Moreover, because students often find it boring to look for rhyme and meter, this lesson plan does not attempt to make use of phonological analysis even though the poem contains several forms of sound patterning. First, the number of stressed syllables per line is fairly regular until the fourth stanza. Stanzas 4 and 5 both violate the stress pattern established in the first three stanzas. There is also a very consistent end-rhyme scheme, with each stanza following a pattern of *abcacb*. Some lines make not true rhymes but consonance (Lines 7 and 10 and Lines 20 and 24), and some pairs are parallel through assonance (Lines 25 and 28 and Lines 27 and 29). However, if we allow these minor variations, the sound pattern of the words at the ends of lines is consistent across all stanzas. It is noteworthy that most of these variations occur in the final two stanzas, the fifth stanza being especially rich in deviations from the norm established earlier. I would argue that the reason for this is that the speaker has become obsessed and psychologically unbalanced by this point.

◈ DISTINGUISHING FEATURES

Multiple Interpretations Accepted

The focus of this approach is the combination of study of specific features of language with an interpretation of the value of those features for creating meaning. Students often report that understanding poems is mystifying and difficult. The stylistic approach asks them first to look at readily discoverable objective evidence in the text and then to interpret its value. Thus, they have solid grounds upon which to base their interpretations, making the process comprehensible and practicable.

In addition, so long as their interpretations are consistent with the evidence and logically argued, they are acceptable, even if they do not agree with those of the teacher. So, students also learn that, if they formulate logical opinions based on facts, their understanding is as valid as that of authority figures. This makes poetry exciting and interesting for most students.

Poetry Read With Pleasure

The main goal of my literature courses is that students should be able to read and understand poetry for themselves. In this way, I hope that they will learn to like poems and even read them for pleasure. Anecdotal evidence that this has succeeded is available in journal entries written by the undergraduates in Introduction to Literature after about 7 weeks of studying poetry through this approach in the fall term of 2001.

Of course, this evidence is not conclusive because students may have merely written what they knew I wanted to read; however, I hope that their eloquence is some indication of sincerity. Of the nine students enrolled in that course, eight wrote that they had come to have a new way of understanding poetry. (One student chose not to submit a journal entry on this topic.) One student wrote:

> Now that I have finished studying about poems in this course, my fixed idea that poems are plain and shallow literature works compared to other long pieces of literature such as essays or fictions has reversed completely. I used to think that the pleasure of reading English poems was just to enjoy the rhythm, or the feelings you get from reading them. Surely, feelings are important, but how nice it is to be able to present a logical reason for having those feelings. From being able to do that, I found that I could strengthen my feelings or confirm my ideas on the poem.

Another student expressed a similar idea:

> Before taking this course, poetry was not so attractive to me because I often did not comprehend what poems expressed. Now, I know the reason why I did not understand poems, and that was because I did not know how to read them well. I just read a poem once or twice, and I quitted reading it even when I did not get its meaning. My way of reading a poem by just following words was not effective to understand what the poems represent and it was natural that I did not have fun. I learned how to read and understand poetry in this course, and now I know that poetry is enjoyable.

◈ PRACTICAL IDEAS

Choose Poems That Are Appropriate for Your Students

Some of the criteria by which the appropriateness of poems for your own students can be judged are as follows:

- Be sure that the work chosen is at an appropriate level of linguistic complexity. Will the students be able to understand the poem at the basic literal level?

- Carefully consider appropriateness of theme. Is the theme too sophisticated for your students?

- Think about the length of the poem. In general, short works are less daunting to students than longer poems.

- Choose poems on the basis of richness and transparency of stylistic features. Does the poem contain many instances of linguistic foregrounding that can be readily found by students?

- Ask yourself how familiar the content and context will be to students. Do students have the schemata necessary to understand the poem?

- Evaluate the extent of deviation from the standard language. Are there so many deviant features that second language learners are likely to be confused by them?

- Consider the probability that the students will be interested in the topic or theme. Is the poem about a topic that students are likely to care about?

- Occasionally allow students the chance to select poems themselves. Have the students had the opportunity to choose the works they want to deal with? Giving them the chance to do so, after adequate preparation, is both motivating for students and enlightening for teachers.

- Look for poems that are exploitable. Does the poem facilitate further learning, either of language points or of related themes?

After Choosing a Poem to Teach, Perform a Stylistic Analysis for Yourself

Carrying out a thorough stylistic analysis means that you will have an inventory of the prominent features and a notion of what meaning they may represent. You will almost certainly not use all of them in your lesson plan, but completing a systematic analysis is the best way to decide which features to choose to focus on in your lesson.

Note that in the lesson plan on "Woodchucks," many features discussed in the analysis are not included in the tasks. The reasons for omitting some features of the analysis from the lesson plan may be that they are too difficult for your students (e.g., close analysis of meter or rhyme scheme), that it may be unsuitable for some groups to highlight certain features (e.g., sexually suggestive language), or that the features may not be readily relatable to an interpretation (e.g., alliteration).

Think About What Your Students Will Need to Understand in Order to Approach the Poem

This includes bottom-up vocabulary and structures and top-down schemata. It is almost always useful to think first in terms of basic *literal* understanding and to move from there to *literary* understanding because it is difficult for students to identify and interpret stylistic features unless they first understand the propositional content of the poem. Therefore, your first task is to devise ways for them to comprehend at the literal level. For ESL/EFL students, this is especially vital and may include preteaching of vocabulary. Note that in the present lesson plan, the function of the paraphrase matching activity is to ensure that students understand the poem at the literal level.

Create Exercises Relating to a Set of Stylistic Features

Choose a set of salient stylistic features that your students can identify and that can be related to an interpretation, and create exercises that ask students to recognize these features and interpret how they contribute to the experience that the poem is trying to represent. Develop a large repertoire of such exercises because it is useful to vary the tasks you set for students. Several valuable resources for this exist, including Duff and Maley (1990), Short (1996), and Widdowson (1975).

**Devise Follow-Up Exercises to Exploit the Theme,
Content, and Language of the Poem in Motivating Ways**

Good follow-up exercises may either be listening to or reading poems or other types of texts on a similar theme or writing or discussion activities that use the study of the poem as a springboard for students to explore their own ideas while producing language output. Maley and Duff (1989) offer many good suggestions for this type of exercise.

❖ CONCLUSION

This chapter has discussed an undergraduate course in literature and a graduate course in teaching literature to demonstrate how stylistics, the analysis of the language patterns of literary texts, may be useful to ESL/EFL teachers who wish to use poems in their classrooms. It has advocated a language-based view of literature in the belief that students can find the foregrounded features present in a text if they are shown what to look for. Having found the salient language patterns, students have an objective basis for their own interpretations. This approach has been successful in developing literary competence in both undergraduate and graduate students in my courses. Because it focuses students' attention on language forms within a primarily meaning-focused environment, it can also be theorized to contribute to second language acquisition.

❖ ACKNOWLEDGMENTS

I would like to thank all my literature students, both graduate and undergraduate, past and present, for their insights and creativity in applying the concepts discussed in this paper to the project of increasing the literary understanding of us all. I would also like to thank Ken Schaefer, Sandy McKay, Pat Porter, and Stephen Browning for their comments on earlier drafts of this chapter.

❖ CONTRIBUTOR

Patrick Rosenkjar is a faculty member of Temple University, Japan Campus, where he is a professor of English education and assistant dean for English language education in the College of Liberal Arts, an adjunct professor in the College of Education, and the director of the Academic Preparation Program. He has taught undergraduate courses in literature, history, humanities, linguistics, and American studies and various graduate courses in TESOL methodology.

❖ APPENDIX: "WOODCHUCKS" (Kumin, 1972/1997, p. 80)

> Gassing the woodchucks didn't turn out right.
> The knockout bomb from the Feed and Grain Exchange
> was featured as merciful, quick at the bone
> and the case we had against them was airtight,
> 5   both exits shoehorned shut with puddingstone,
> but they had a sub-sub-basement out of range.

Next morning they turned up again, no worse
for the cyanide than we for our cigarettes
and state-store Scotch, all of us up to scratch.
10   They brought down the marigolds as a matter of course
and then took over the vegetable patch
nipping the broccoli shoots, beheading the carrots.

The food from our mouths, I said, righteously thrilling
to the feel of the .22, the bullets' neat noses.
15   I, a lapsed pacifist fallen from grace
puffed with Darwinian pieties for killing,
now drew a bead on the littlest woodchuck's face.
He died down in the everbearing roses.

Ten minutes later I dropped the mother. She
20   flipflopped in the air and fell, her needle teeth
still hooked in a leaf of early Swiss chard.
Another baby next. O one-two-three
the murderer inside me rose up hard,
the hawkeye killer came on stage forthwith.

25   There's one chuck left. Old wily fellow, he keeps
me cocked and ready day after day after day.
All night I hunt his humped-up form. I dream
I sight along the barrel in my sleep.
If only they'd all consented to die unseen
30   gassed underground the quiet Nazi way.

CHAPTER 10

Theory Into Practice: Teaching and Responding to Literature Aesthetically

Nazan Tutaş

◈ INTRODUCTION

In this chapter I examine issues in literature teaching in EFL situations, particularly in Turkey, arguing for the use of the transactional reader response approach developed by Rosenblatt (1938) as an alternative way of teaching literature. I also present an empirical study, which investigated the applicability of transactional reader response theory in an EFL context and which examined the possible effects of approaching literature aesthetically or efferently on students' responses. Finally, I suggest some practical ideas for teachers who would like to implement the transactional reader response approach in the teaching of literature in their own context.

◈ CONTEXT

Education in Turkey

The education system in Turkey is centralised, and education is compulsory and free. The present structure of the Turkish education system includes a basic education programme, which is compulsory and lasts 8 years, and high school education (called *Lycee*), which includes general, vocational, technical, and private high schools. It provides a minimum of 3 years of schooling. General high schools mainly train students for higher educational institutions. In their second year, pupils have a choice of attending science or literature branches; pupils in the literature branch concentrate on Turkish language and literature and social sciences. In state schools, foreign language education starts in the fourth year of basic education and is compulsory. The foreign languages available are English, German, and French. Around 95% of pupils choose English, and in many schools it is the only foreign language taught.

Teaching Literature in Turkey

At Selçuk University in Konya, Turkey, as in other Turkish universities, the students in the English literature department are selected by means of a highly competitive Central University Entrance Examination, which tests their competence in English. About 50% of the students who enter literature departments are graduates of private schools where, for example, out of 10 hours of English lessons per week, 4 are in English literature. The other students come from state schools and have studied literature only in Turkish. Not all have listed English as their first choice: For example, of the 36 students in the study described here, 10 students selected the English department as their first choice, 8 included it as one of their first 8 choices, and the others ranked it even lower amongst their choices.

English literature is a main 4-year degree course subject, consisting of eight semesters of 15 weeks each. The students are expected to pass midterm and final examinations for all the courses offered. In the first years of these programmes, students study grammar, composition, translation, and introductory courses dealing with different genres. Various periods of English literature are also taught, starting from the second year. Literature courses taught in the department include history of English literature, different periods of fiction, English and American drama, poetry and prose appreciation, English and American poetry, Shakespeare, Chaucer, and literary criticism. In their final year, the students are required to write a short dissertation on literature or on teaching methods. In addition, those who want to qualify as teachers are expected to fulfil the requirements for teaching practice in the final semester of the programme.

Literature teaching at the primary and secondary level is usually teacher centred, and this traditional approach is still the main practice at university level as well. This approach includes lecturing as well as having detailed question-and-answer sessions. This is a teacher-centred process, a common variation of which involves the teacher in working through the text and asking a long series of questions, and is associated with explaining the text. In most literature classes, the teacher preaches while the students become passive recipients, improving their skills in note-taking.

The biggest weakness in the traditional approach is its indifference to the reader's role in the reading process. This is shown by the questions set in exams, which consist of the analysis of texts and aim at attaining the so-called correct interpretation. The exams usually test the students' ability to memorize rather than to appreciate what they have read.

The reason for using the traditional method is often a fear that students may miss some vitally important or interesting detail. However, because all decision taking is in the hands of the teacher and the students themselves are not actively or emotionally engaged in literary texts, this kind of student-teacher relationship does not encourage the development of the students' thinking skills. More important, it may diminish the motivation and interest in the literature class, especially among EFL students who already are finding it difficult to read in a foreign language.

Because most students who enrol in English language and literature departments in Turkey become teachers, it is important for them to be encouraged into a way of learning that might contribute to their own effective teaching of literature. The present traditional approach, focusing on the correct interpretation, does not seem to encourage creative thinking. A better approach would be one that allowed more exploration of the literary text by the learners themselves and invited learners to develop their own responses. I believe that student-centred approaches that are appropriately controlled and monitored by the teacher are most likely to create enjoyment of literature learning and teaching.

Students' Views on Literature

In a study to understand the students' views of literature and the teaching of literature, I interviewed 36 students and asked them to talk about their previous literary experience (Tutaş, 1996). The interview results revealed that the majority of the students had experienced traditional ways of literature teaching, analysing, and explaining the literary works, concentrating on the literary elements such as plot, characterization, theme, style, and author's intention.

This experience contrasted quite strongly with what students considered an ideal literature class: one that includes active discussions as well as projects and assignments. When asked to give a profile of an ideal literature teacher, one student stated that she should be like the one Robin Williams plays in the movie *Dead Poets Society*: "We need a literature teacher like him who would make us live and feel whatever we read. I really would like to be a teacher like him." Other students thought that the teachers must be in "close interaction with the students" and "should not make the lesson monotonous." Most of the students said that they would like to be given opportunities to express what they think and complained that, unfortunately, they became accustomed to accepting whatever their teacher says: "We always think that the teacher is always right. Whatever she says we write them down."

The Transactional Reader Response

The undesirable effects of the traditional approach on students in the English language and literature departments in Turkey argue strongly for an alternative approach. After reviewing the research literature, I realised that the kind of approach that requires interaction between the literary texts and the reader comes from reader response theory, a view pioneered by Rosenblatt (1978). The theory and its distinction between aesthetic and efferent reading seemed to offer the neatest way of describing the existing situation in Turkey and contrasting it with the desirable situation.

In her transactional theory of reader response, Rosenblatt (1978) describes two possible stances, aesthetic and efferent, that readers may take while reading, depending on their purposes for reading. An *efferent stance* focuses readers' attention on the information to be carried away from reading, and readers select common, public referents of words and ideas evoked during reading. When reading informative texts such as textbooks, newspapers, and reference materials, a reader's focus is on the information to be learnt from the text, which results in a study of the text. According to Rosenblatt (1993), "the efferent stance is involved primarily with analysing, abstracting, and accumulating what will be retained after the reading" (p. 383).

Certain ways of teaching literature may encourage pupils to adopt an efferent stance while reading, because they know that the teacher usually quizzes them on factual aspects of a text, even if the text is called a poem or a story. Students know that they will be successful and rewarded if they focus on factual information in the text rather than on the experience of reading. Efferent tasks in literature include analyses of character, setting, and plot; assignments that ask students to extract information; and activities that use literature to teach reading skills (Rosenblatt, 1991). They also include directing the students' attention to the structure of language and the analysis of literary elements in a *school criticism* manner (Cox & Many, 1992) as well as identifying characters and setting, style, rhyme pattern, and genre (Zarillo & Cox, 1992).

The *aesthetic stance*, on the other hand, focuses the reader's attention on the lived-through experience of reading. Readers concentrate on their personal thoughts, images, feelings, and associations evoked during reading. When students respond aesthetically to literature, they actively live "the experience created through the personal transaction of the text" (Many & Cox, 1992, p. 252). Students who read aesthetically repeatedly make associations with their own life experiences and the experiences of others in other stories such as books, stories, films, television shows, and media events. Rosenblatt (1956) states that for most literature, especially poetry, novels, and stories, the teacher's primary responsibility must be to encourage the aesthetic stance. She believes most teaching with literature is misdirected and leads students to adopt efferent stances. Instead, she suggests that after students read, teachers should help them to relive the experience. She argues that using literature to illustrate the sophisticated use of symbolism or irony results in turning students away from the experience of life and literature: "Surely the purpose of reading literature is more than the acquisition of a get-quick rich knowledge of literature" (p. 74).

With this theoretical framework in mind, combined with my findings about the views of the students in the interviews discussed previously, I decided to put the transactional reader response theory into practice in my EFL context. I thought that although Rosenblatt and other reader response theorists dealt with native speakers, their conceptualisation of the reading of literature might still be applicable to EFL situations. The Description section details the study I conducted to find this out.

◈ DESCRIPTION

The study compared the possible effects of approaching literature aesthetically or efferently on students' responses in an EFL context (i.e., a situation where students need to deal with literary texts written in a foreign language). The study also investigated whether the teaching approach affected students' responses to a subsequent reading task. A further purpose was to investigate the students' and their teachers' attitudes toward efferent and aesthetic teaching.

For the study, I randomly divided 36 students into two groups: the efferent group and the aesthetic group. The themes, topics, and texts of the two classes were similar, but one class was introduced to the literary works aesthetically, focusing on associations, feelings, and images, and the other class efferently, focusing on literary analysis of characters, events, problems and solutions, and definition of genres. The teaching took 14 weeks (for 4 hours a week). Both teachers used the same general type of activities and materials in their teaching: The students in both groups were involved in written and oral activities and worked in groups and pairs but with different tasks. For example, the students in the efferent group would be asked to write about their knowledge of the author and 18th-century life, whereas the students in the aesthetic group would write a letter to the author of the novel.

At the beginning of the study, I provided students in both classes with notebooks and asked them to keep logs to write their responses to the novels they were studying. They were also given some general guidelines on what to include in the logs and on how to approach the novels. Logs were checked twice during the study to make sure that the students continued keeping them. They were collected at the end of the study, photocopied, and returned to the students with written feedback.

I also asked the students to write an essay before the study to determine their initial stance when responding to a short story. I asked them to write another essay at the end of the semester to determine whether the teaching approach would affect not only their reactions to the literary works being studied but also their manner of responding to subsequent works. The students in both groups were asked to write anything they wanted about the short stories they read at the beginning and at the end of the study, namely, Hemingway's (1925/1987) "Cat in the Rain" and (1927/1987) "Hills Like White Elephants," respectively. In addition, I interviewed the students and the teachers both at the beginning and at the end of the study.

I collected the written responses to the novels and short stories and coded them as being aesthetic or efferent. Aesthetic responses were defined as those that focused on the associations, emotions, and feelings evoked while reading and on identifying with story characters as well as on predicting possible outcomes. The responses classified as efferent were those that noted the author's development of characterization, setting, theme, language, and literary devices. To identify a response as efferent or aesthetic, I developed a key word list. Figure 1 shows the categories of efferent and aesthetic responses together with the key words that helped categorise each response.

◈ DISTINGUISHING FEATURES
Efferent Versus Aesthetic Teaching

The course the teachers were teaching in the groups was entitled The 18th-Century English Novel (the students had already been introduced to aspects of the novel in their second year). In the semester researched they were working on *Pride and Prejudice* (Austen, 1813/1996) and *Moll Flanders* (Defoe, 1722/1996). The objectives of the course, which were spelled out by the teachers, were introducing students to the subject matter of the 18th-century novel, such as the class-conscious hero, individualism, and the status of women in a newly developing society. In addition, the objectives included providing information about 18th-century society and forming a fuller awareness of 18th-century social life and values. At the end of the course, the students were expected to be able to capture the fictive world a novel presents, make criticisms, and present different views on the novels they read.

The two teachers participating in the study were chosen because one of them was predominantly efferent in her approach, whereas the other was predominantly aesthetic. During the study, I discussed with the teachers ways of ensuring that they were consistent and that they maintained the distinguishing features of their two different approaches, although both teachers taught in a mixture of aesthetic and efferent teaching. The discussions included suggestions as to activities and questions that would encourage students to respond.

In the efferent group, the teacher tended to use more efferent prompts than aesthetic ones. Much of the teaching consisted of reading significant passages aloud, rephrasing and explaining them, and often translating them into Turkish. Although she occasionally presented students with questions or prompts that encouraged

Efferent Responses	*Aesthetic Responses*
Responding to the structure of language	**Making associations**
difficult/easy/complicated/fluent/clear	remind/remember/resemble
language/dialogues/conversation/phrases	culture/book/film
sentences/structures	
	Relating feelings
Identifying the characters	we/you/reader
characters/hero/heroine	I (like/liked, feel/felt, think/believe/love)
Identifying the setting	(disappointed/affected/influenced) me
setting/hotel/station/place	
	Hypothesizing and extending
Identifying the plot	will/won't may/might future/next
theme/topic/subject/events/tells/told/	seems/maybe/perhaps/probably
says/said	
	Imagining and picturing
Evaluating literary devices	if (I were/would/could)
title/style/paragraphs/describe	imagine/picture/dream
description/characterization/repetitions/	
successful/effective/writer/narrator/	**Making judgements**
Hemingway/Defoe/Austen/story/novel/	right/wrong/good/bad
book	agree/not agree/because
	in my opinion/according to me/for me/I mean
	must/never/should
	sensitive/insensitive/indifferent/selfish
	proud/prejudiced/thoughtful

Figure 1. Key Words for Coding Efferent Versus Aesthetic Responses

aesthetic responses, she mostly asked questions about characters and events in the novel, questions that required simple recall to answer or that required analysis and interpretation. She also focused her questions on literary techniques such as style, theme, setting, characterization, and writer's intention. Interestingly, she also tended to stand by the table and often did most of the talking.

In the aesthetic group, on the other hand, the teacher was more interactive. Most of her teaching consisted of group work and whole-class discussion. The teacher asked different groups to present chapters or scenes in the novels being studied. In her questions, she tended to use more aesthetic prompts than the efferent teacher, thus facilitating personal responses to the two novels. She asked questions to focus students' attention on the experience of the story and to encourage them to make links between their own personal experience and the novels they were reading. Typical questions included the following:

- What is your first reaction to this chapter?
- What would you do if you were the character in the novel?

- What feelings do you have as you read the novel?
- What would happen next in the story?
- Did this novel remind you of any other novels or films?

From time to time, however, the teacher did analyse the books based on the literary elements (especially character and setting).

My observations in the classrooms showed that in both classes, when students were asked to say anything they wanted about the novels they were reading, there was a tendency to retell the plot. This is consistent with the research on the developmental aspect of response. In the aesthetic group, however, the teacher provided opportunities after the retelling for the students to respond aesthetically. She asked questions that encouraged students to shift from retelling to using their experience while they were reading.

Students' Reactions to Aesthetic and Efferent Teaching

The feedback from the students and observations in class supported the argument of Rosenblatt (1991) and Protherough (1983) that reading and responding aesthetically can facilitate students' enjoyment and engagement in literature.

Observations in the aesthetic class showed that group work was very enjoyable both for the teacher and for the students. Students responded not only to the teacher's questions but also to the comments of their classmates as well. When one student recalled an experience while reading a part of the novel, other students would recall the same episode and express their reactions. Responses in these group discussions and presentations sometimes went beyond words: They laughed, nodded in agreement or disagreement, and made facial expressions of joy or distaste, evidence that they were personally involved in the novels they were studying. The discussions, especially at the end of the presentations, were very stimulating. But occasionally, there were still moments of silence, probably because the students wanted approval from the teacher or wanted the teacher to summarise what they had said so far to make sure that they were on the right track. The students came from a traditional classroom, where the teacher had the final say, and this could not be unlearned so easily. There therefore had to be times when the teacher intervened in the discussions to help bring up a relevant point or an interesting thought. Herein lies the teacher's role as a "facilitator of response rather than as teacher of the correct response" (Ali, 1995, p. 22).

After the study, I interviewed the students to learn their feelings and views about the aesthetic and efferent teaching they experienced. Interview results revealed that most of the students who were taught aesthetically enjoyed the experience (although there were still some students who did not like to talk about their feelings and complained that what they did in the classroom was not useful in the exams).

When the students were asked to talk about the things they liked and disliked about the teaching they experienced, the majority in the aesthetic group said that they liked it. They stated that they enjoyed talking about their opinions and enjoyed listening to their peers' reactions, as noted in the following excerpts from their interviews:

> It is very important for people to express their opinions freely. Everybody has different opinions and they should be able to discuss them without hesitation.

In the classroom, we were asked to talk about our opinions and this was very nice.

The advantage of this kind of teaching is that we develop our speaking and thinking skills. For example, even if I don't speak, I think and try to judge what my friends say. We usually expect our teachers to think for us and even to put it into words in English for us to copy. But here the teacher created a friendly atmosphere that we were not afraid to say what we think.

When we normally read a novel we just read it in order to finish it. But in this course, I learnt how to read a novel properly not as a literature student but also as a normal reader. I learnt to judge what I read. Ask questions like why are they doing this or what would happen if they didn't do this. You begin to question everything.

I think the writers write because they want people to find something in it for themselves. But what we usually do is to read it and for the exams we study the criticisms of it written by the critics, we are not used to think deeply, we don't even try. In this lesson we understood that we must not just read a novel or a poem and leave it like that. We must learn a lesson from it and apply it in our real lives.

Some students in the aesthetic group said that they had expected the course to be boring and monotonous but that it turned out to be very enjoyable and interesting:

The lessons were above my expectations. I wasn't expecting that I was going to enjoy it this much. I am very pleased with the outcome.

I was surprised that in this class even I myself who had a very limited literature background could talk about the novels and make comments. The teacher liked my comments and I felt better.

In the efferent group, on the other hand, approximately half of the students stated that they liked the lesson as it is:

The teacher asks questions and gives us her answers to the questions. This is very good because we write it down and before the exams we revise these notes.

This quotation suggests that the students in this group felt safe with a teacher who provides them with ready-made interpretations or, as they say, "the right answers." Because the exams that their teachers set for them usually tested not their ability to analyse, synthesize, or evaluate but how well they reproduced the teacher's interpretations, they felt insecure and dependent on the teacher and happiest when answers were provided.

Moving From an Efferent Stance to an Aesthetic Stance

In the responses to prestudy essays, there was no significant difference between the aesthetic group and the efferent group: About 35–40% of the responses of the two groups were aesthetic, and 60–65% were efferent. This, however, changed during the teaching, and the written responses in the students' logs revealed differences in the nature of responses according to the teaching approach that students experienced. Most of the students who experienced the aesthetic approach moved to a more clearly aesthetic stance, focusing on associations, relating emotions and feelings, making judgements, hypothesizing and extending, and imaging and picturing when responding to the two novels they studied. On the other hand, approaching the novels efferently resulted in a more detached literary experience in which most of the students held back their personal opinions and instead focused on analysis of literary terms, identification of the characters, plot and setting, and analysis of structure of language and style.

In the log entries in the efferent group, the percentage of efferent responses was very clearly higher than that of aesthetic ones, with nearly 75% of responses falling into the efferent category. For the aesthetic group, there was an equal number of aesthetic (50%) and efferent responses (49.5%). This was probably because in the early stages of the study (the first 6 weeks), most of the students were still writing significantly more text-centred responses; in the second half of the course, having experienced aesthetic teaching for some time, they began to write significantly more aesthetically. The results may be interpreted as showing that as the students experienced aesthetic teaching they learned to share their feelings and reactions.

This interpretation is strengthened by the students' responses on the poststudy essay. There, the students' responses in the aesthetic group were predominantly aesthetic (approximately 75%), whereas the responses of the efferent group were predominantly efferent (again, approximately 75%). The presence of efferent responses in the aesthetic group and of aesthetic responses in the efferent group shows that the reading process of the students in this study lies on a continuum between efferent and aesthetic poles. However, whereas the aesthetic teaching successfully brought out the aesthetic stance in the learners, efferent teaching similarly strengthened the frequency of efferent responses. This indicates the extent to which these responses are learned responses that are capable of being transformed by the type of teaching learners experience.

Qualitative analysis of the written responses showed that the primary concern of those responses analysed as efferent was to critique work in the manner of *school criticism*. Students focused on story content or analysis of the story through the study of literary elements such as plot, character development, or structure of the work; they criticized the author's style; and they held back personal opinions regarding the story. Most of the students' written responses coded as efferent were the repetition of what their teacher said in the classroom, as students believed that she was providing the correct interpretation. These interpretations were often memorised by the students and presented in their writings. It was obvious in some logs that some students copied the interpretations from literary critics. The students seemed to assume that their personal opinion was not valued and that there was only one correct answer that they were expected to reach.

Responses coded as aesthetic tended to be very personal and emotional. Students were more likely to apply their experiences with literature to life and generalize or create new possibilities. The students generated relationships with real life or identified similar events or characters in their own lives. The aesthetic responses showed that the aesthetic approach elicited more personal responses and reactions and provided students with opportunities to explain how they felt about the literary works.

In the aesthetic responses, students often focused on imagining themselves in the character's place, picturing the scenes described, making associations, and relating feelings evoked while reading. Students also hypothesized about why certain events occurred in the story or even extended the story line beyond what actually occurred, doing what Iser (1978) has described as filling in the gaps of the text.

Pre- and Poststudy Responses

Results also showed a marked difference between the pre- and poststudy responses, within each group, in terms of the response type. The students in the aesthetic group were able to respond from a more aesthetic focus, and the students in the efferent group responded from a more efferent focus.

This suggests that the students applied what they had experienced from the teaching they received to a later literary reading task. I emphasise that, as it was impossible to teach purely aesthetically or efferently, the students in both groups had been exposed to the efferent and aesthetic teaching and had opportunities to respond efferently or aesthetically. Nevertheless, it was the group who experienced the aesthetic teaching that had a majority of students who chose to respond aesthetically to the subsequent short story. In the aesthetic group, students' responses to the poststudy short story were filled with feelings, attitudes, images, and ideas evoked in them and upon which they have reflected. This shows that aesthetic teaching encouraged the students to respond at a more mature level.

Teachers' Reactions to Aesthetic Teaching

One notable outcome of this study was that both teachers who participated in the study noted that they were inspired by the experience and have now a better understanding of the need to facilitate students' engagement in literature even more. In the interviews, they not only talked about their feelings about the experience but also suggested some more activities and materials that would encourage the students to respond more genuinely.

In the interview, the aesthetic-group teacher stated that she enjoyed the experience and was pleased to discover that when the students were allowed to respond freely, they were able to produce different types of responses. She noted that her weakest students were also more excited about the novels than in previous years. She noted that all of the students were noticeably more involved in the lesson and the novels and was very pleased to see them talk and discuss their feelings and ideas. In addition, she was amazed to see them work in groups and present their work in a talented way.

Both teachers stated that they would definitely include the reader response prompts in their teaching to encourage students to produce personal responses. They said that their focus would be on encouraging affective and imaginative responses and creating an atmosphere where students can discuss relationships between literature and personal experience or the world outside the literary text.

◈ PRACTICAL IDEAS

In this section, I offer some practical suggestions for teachers who would like to implement the aesthetic approach in the teaching of literature in their own context (adapted from Cox & Many, 1992; Hancock, 1993; Langer, 1994; Zarrillo, 1991).

Always Begin With the Initial Impressions

Inviting initial impressions is always a good way to break the ice, because all the students can have something to say. They may at the very least say whether they liked what they have read or not. This also helps the students to voice their initial understandings; they can then begin to construct and refine meaning.

Provide Opportunities for Students to Talk

Students should talk to each other, to the whole class, and to teachers who genuinely want to know what they think. In this study, the aesthetic-group teacher used a great deal of group work and group presentations in her teaching. In addition, she talked less in class than the efferent-group teacher. By providing these opportunities, you encourage students to develop their own well-formed interpretations and gain vision from others.

Act as Listener, Responder, and Helper
Rather Than as Provider of Information

Open-ended prompts and questions are particularly conducive to aesthetic reading.

Encourage Students to Make Personal and Intertextual Connections

This can be done with questions such as

- Have you ever experienced what a character in the story, play, or book experienced, or have you ever known anyone like a character in the story, play, or book?
- Have you ever read a story (or seen a TV show or movie) where the event in the book, play, or story happened? Relate it to your own experiences, and share similar moments from your life or from books you have read in the past.
- Talk to the characters as you begin to know them. Give them advice to help them. Put yourself in their place, and share how you would act in a similar situation. Approve or disapprove of their values, actions, or behaviour. Try to figure out what makes them react the way they do.

Students should also be encouraged to consider why they respond as they do as well as encouraged to develop a sense of tolerance for responses that differ.

Create an Environment Where Literature Is
Appreciated for Its Artistic Value

Literature can amuse, sadden, thrill, frighten, and inspire. You can encourage students to feel this by asking questions that will identify vivid episodes, such as

- Write about what seemed wrong, annoying, weird, funny, or sad.
- Talk about the things that caught your interest most or things that pleased, frightened, surprised, or troubled you.

By doing this, you act as a facilitator to the interaction between the text and the reader.

Pose Questions and Prompts That Encourage Students to Relive the Reading Experience

This can be done by imagining, visualising, and hypothesising, for example:

- If you could be any character in the story, who would you be?
- What would it feel like to be a character in the story, play, or book or participate in an event in the story, play, or book?

This can also be done by expressing preferences (e.g., Write about your favorite or least favorite scenes in the story, play, or book) or by asking for summative opinions (e.g., Did you like the title of the book? What about the book led to your judgement?).

Encourage Students to Respond in Writing

In the study, the teacher of the aesthetic group noted that it was very useful to ask students to keep logs. She noted that "responding in writing could establish a habit of thinking deeply and personally about what they read."

Pose Questions and Prompts That Ask for Interpretation Through Speculation

This can be done through questions such as

- Make predictions about what you think will happen as the plot unfolds. Validate, invalidate, or change those predictions as you proceed in the text.
- Make predictions about what will happen to the characters in the book, play, or story in the future.

Provide Students With Opportunities to Engage in a Variety of Activities

Different types of activities may be readings involving books, plays, poems, dramatic interludes; role-playing; one-to-one conversations with peers (in small groups or in whole-class discussion); writing, both private (journal writing, logs) and public; project work ranging from drawing the mental images created while reading a text to rewriting the text; responding to the film adaptations of the work; filmmaking; and dramatizations of the text.

◈ CONCLUSION

As this chapter has shown, the teaching approach affects the stance the students take toward the texts they read and their response to subsequent literary works. Interviews with the teachers and the students, as well as the observations, revealed that aesthetic teaching has the potential to create interesting discussions and exchanges. It also can create a desirable atmosphere that is pleasant for both the teachers and the students.

The use of an aesthetic teaching approach also helped to extend students' growth not only as readers but also as individuals. Through the classroom interactions, the students were able to get to know their classmates and to realise that there were alternative perspectives to life. This might have reassured them that there were many ways of solving problems and that they were not alone in their feelings.

As literature teachers, we reached a better understanding of the ability of our students as readers and responders. When given opportunities, they were able to express their feelings and ideas about the literary work they study as well as make criticisms and interpretations. Responses of the students in my research showed the possibilities for change from an older, traditional model of a text-centred literature approach to a more reader-centred and response-centred one.

◈ CONTRIBUTOR

Nazan Tutaş is an assistant professor in the Department of English Language and Literature at Ankara University, in Turkey. Previously she was head of the Linguistics Unit at the Department of English Language and Literature, Selçuk University, in Konya. Her primary interests are the teaching of literature in EFL contexts, reader response approach to literature teaching, and genre analysis.

CHAPTER 11

Stepping Into the Shoes of Romeo and Juliet

Milena Vodičková

❖ INTRODUCTION

This chapter demonstrates how a British literature course provided teacher learners in the Czech Republic with an introduction to Shakespeare's play *Romeo and Juliet* and, at the same time, gave them opportunities to use the English language. The approach used is an example of how classical literature, which frequently frightens young people or to which they have a hostile attitude, can be brought alive and made appealing because it deals with problems that all people encounter and understand. As the students are involved in a teacher education programme, this approach to literature can also serve as inspiration in their future teaching careers.

❖ CONTEXT

November 1989 transformed the political scene in the Czech Republic, and this transformation was reflected in the attitude toward foreign languages. The desire of Czechs to be part of Europe launched new educational programmes, especially in foreign language teaching. English has become the main foreign language and has been introduced in schools instead of Russian, starting at the age of 10. There are still more ambitious plans to start with a foreign language at primary schools, which are attended by pupils from the age of 6 up to the age of 10. (Primary schools are the lower stage of 9-year basic schools, which go up to the age of 15. Pupils then move on to 4-year secondary schools.)

To start with a foreign language so early is not an easy task, mainly because of the lack of qualified teachers in the Czech Republic. To fill the need for language teachers, which schools have been facing since the early 1990s, new university programmes were started, ranging from the requalification of teachers to new fast-track programmes. Most of these programmes did not rely on the previous, rather academic, approaches to language teaching but brought new ideas and expertise, provided to a great extent by the British Council.

As the aim currently is to start teaching a first foreign language in the primary school, in 1996 the Pedagogical Faculty of the Palacký University in Olomouc launched a 5-year programme (consisting of 10 terms) to train foreign language teachers for primary school. Its curriculum contains general subjects that the primary teachers must master in traditional programmes within 4 years as well as an additional foreign language component. In the 5th year, the teacher learners concentrate purely on foreign language courses and final exams. After graduation they become fully qualified general primary school teachers as well as foreign language teachers entitled to teach the foreign language at the primary level (Grades 1–4). However, in reality, they frequently teach the foreign language even in higher grades, regardless of their qualification. It is in this way that many schools tackle the lack of foreign language teachers. The curriculum for this initial foreign language teacher education programme includes the four following components:

- language development
- linguistics (phonetics and phonology, morphology, syntax, lexicology, text analysis, and psycholinguistics)
- background studies (British and U.S. studies, British and U.S. literature, and children's literature)
- methodology (with teaching practice as an integral part)

In addition to the new programme for primary training, the university runs a traditional 4-year programme for double-subject training, which provides teacher learners with a qualification to teach English and another subject to pupils from the age of 11 up to the age of 15. While the double-subject students have on average 10–12 lessons a week in the Department of English Language and a similar amount of lessons in the department of the other subject they are taking, the primary teacher learners have an extensive programme in the Department of Primary Education. For this reason, in the first 4 years they can attend only six to eight 45-minute lessons a week at the Department of English Language, which is why their English language curriculum has been considerably modified. In the first year the emphasis is on language development, phonetics, and phonology. In later terms, the courses comprise language development; a linguistic-discipline background studies; and, after the fifth term, methodology.

Because of the lack of qualified teachers, the Department of English Language also offers courses for distance teacher learners who already teach English without a proper qualification. Although the distance programme relies on many assignments that the teacher learners complete on their own, twice a month they attend regular classes that provide them with instruction in all the subjects mentioned previously. The Department of English Language thus provides teacher education for three groups: double-subject, primary education, and distance education teacher learners.

◈ DESCRIPTION

Literature in the Programmes

In general, all teacher learners study literature; however, each programme is specific and requires different approaches respecting the needs and abilities of the teacher learners. The literature component is much stronger in the curriculum of the double-subject courses than in the curriculum for future primary teachers. Double-subject teacher learners start with literature seminars in the first year, and literature features in the curriculum in every term. The emphasis is mainly on adult British and U.S. literature, and children's literature is studied only in one term. In contrast, the primary teacher learners embark on literature studies only in the fourth term, when a 45-minute seminar called Introduction to Literature provides them with the basic literary theory, terminology, and skills that enable them to discuss works of literature. Every week the teacher learners are assigned texts in various genres, and, it is hoped, they develop regular reading habits.

In line with the professional needs of the teacher learners, children's literature is covered later in two terms, thus assuming an important place in the curriculum. In comparison, the same number of lessons is allocated to the courses on adult British and U.S. literature together. There is therefore very little time devoted to the two survey courses, especially taking into account that the aim is to provide teacher learners not only with a survey of British and U.S. literature but also to expose them to texts they must interact with in the lessons—all in a weekly 90 minute seminar over two terms. Consequently, the chosen texts must be representative of the chosen period, be motivating and challenging in terms of both literary and language difficulty, and should relate to the teacher learners' experience and promote their interest.

Structured Drama Approach

When introducing Shakespeare, we chose *Romeo and Juliet* (Shakespeare, 1597/ 1993) because of the theme of this play—love—which is universal and close to young people, so teacher learners can identify with the main characters and their life dilemma. However, dealing with the text in English brings about many linguistic difficulties, which is why only double-subject teacher learners, who are more proficient, analysed this play in a traditional academic way. To primary and distance teacher learners, *Romeo and Juliet* was presented as a structured drama, making their experience of interacting with the play more enjoyable as well as bringing out the dramatic quality of the play in a comprehensible way. At the same time, this type of presentation enabled the teacher learners to respond to the key scenes, understand the dramatic structure and the development of the characters, and focus on the language of love. The inspiration came from the course ELT and Drama Education, run by the British Council in the Czech Republic and led by Gaffen and Svobodová (1998), who pioneered structured drama in the Czech Republic. Originally, it came into existence in Great Britain and was introduced to Czech drama schools by British drama teachers, mainly Jonothan Neelands.

The advantage of using a structured drama approach is the way in which it involves both intellect and emotions. The definitions of theatre and dramatic conventions within this approach result from the assumption that the theatre interprets as well as expresses human behaviour and meanings. As Neelands (1999) states,

> the experience of theatre is distinguished from real-life experience by the conscious application of form to meaning in order to engage both the intellect and the emotions in a representation of meaning. In the theatre, meanings, social codes and interactions are presented, shaped and crafted through the conventions of dramatic activity. (p. 3)

Theatre is a learning medium where creative imagination is stimulated through the experience of people imagining that they are somebody else in a different place at a different time. In the theatre, a mirror reflects people's own behaviour and their reactions to others. This can be exploited in the seminars when teacher learners are expected to interpret human behaviour and be involved both intellectually and emotionally. As structured drama leads to an active exploration of a text and its meaning, its effectiveness depends directly on the dynamic structuring of drama activities prepared by the teacher beforehand. Figure 1 shows the drama activities chosen for *Romeo and Juliet* mapped onto a diagram of the action as an arch, starting with an exposition with the tension rising through complications (or crisis) to a climax, which is followed by a falling action and a resolution. As the aim of structured drama is not to retell the whole story but to have insight into human behaviour with both emotions and intellect involved, the choice of activities is limited only to those that can contribute to the active exploration of the text.

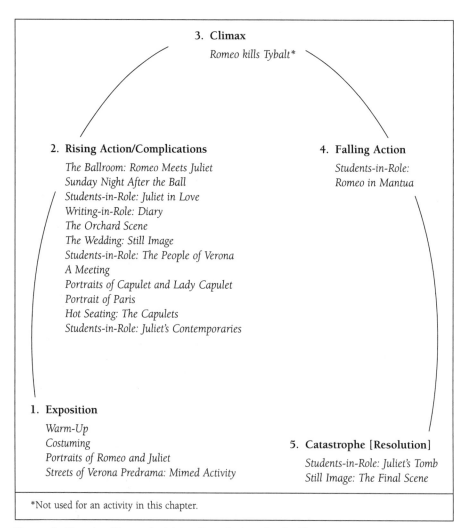

3. Climax
Romeo kills Tybalt*

2. Rising Action/Complications
The Ballroom: Romeo Meets Juliet
Sunday Night After the Ball
Students-in-Role: Juliet in Love
Writing-in-Role: Diary
The Orchard Scene
The Wedding: Still Image
Students-in-Role: The People of Verona
A Meeting
Portraits of Capulet and Lady Capulet
Portrait of Paris
Hot Seating: The Capulets
Students-in-Role: Juliet's Contemporaries

4. Falling Action
Students-in-Role:
Romeo in Mantua

1. Exposition
Warm-Up
Costuming
Portraits of Romeo and Juliet
Streets of Verona Predrama: Mimed Activity

5. Catastrophe [Resolution]
Students-in-Role: Juliet's Tomb
Still Image: The Final Scene

*Not used for an activity in this chapter.

FIGURE 1. Mapping Drama Activities Onto Actions in the Play

The responsibility of the teacher is to structure all drama activities, but the teacher learners must be prepared for them. They must especially be familiar with drama conventions, which can be seen as "a bridge between spontaneous and innate uses of theatre and the more poetic conventions of performance act" (Neelands, 1999, p. 5). Drama conventions represent approaches used in the exploration and creation of character and can emphasise various qualities in the theatrical possibilities of time, space, and human behaviour. Some of the conventions, such as *portraits*, *costuming*, *diaries*, and *still image*, can set the scene or add some information to the context of the story. Other conventions, such as *meetings*, *hot seating*, *a day in the life*, and *teacher-in-role*, contribute to narrating the action and can create and promote an interest in the drama. Yet other conventions can provide visual images (e.g., *still image* or *mimed activity)*, whereas others emphasise verbal communication (e.g., *role-play* or *teacher-in-role)*. I discuss these drama conventions, which are at the core of our approach, in the Distinguishing Features section.

◈ DISTINGUISHING FEATURES

Planned Sequence of Activities

Using a play in the structured drama approach requires a planned sequence of activities that are structured according to the story line and that focus on key scenes. The variety of conventions, their timing, and their pacing provide the possibility of emphasising the important aspects of the action and the personalities of the characters and make the presentation more interesting and dynamic. The week before the seminar, the teacher learners were assigned several sections from the original drama where the language of love is in the forefront and were asked to read them carefully to get the flavour and beauty of Shakespeare's text. The focus is on the following scenes:

- 1.1.176–193: Romeo is expressing his fickle feelings for Rosaline
- 1.5.45–57: Romeo declares his true and deep love for Juliet
- 2.2.1–140: the orchard scene

Warm-Up

In general, it is helpful to set up scenes not only in words but also in pictures, which is why the class started with Renaissance music evoking the play's atmosphere. The convention used here was *portraits*, in which pictures or photographs of characters provide teacher learners with a visual representation of the characters and with an opportunity to speculate about their human characteristics and their behaviour. The teacher learners are usually guided by the teacher's questions, which lead to a deeper understanding of the complexity of the characters.

In this case, Renaissance paintings provided suitable representations of the main characters (Romeo, Juliet, Capulet, Lady Capulet, and Paris). Portraits of a young man and a young woman displayed on the board served as portraits of Romeo and Juliet. The teacher learners were asked to speculate on what it would have been like to be young and live during the Renaissance period, what young people enjoyed and longed for, and what was expected from them by their parents and society. Based on this, they worked in groups to establish the personalities of the main protagonists, speculating on their wishes, dreams, and expectations (and their parents' expectations). They thus developed an understanding of the protagonists' behaviour and how they were influenced by the social conventions of their time. In this respect, they also looked at the similarities and differences between themselves and their Renaissance counterparts.

At this stage I used another convention: *costuming*. Neelands (1999) suggests that articles of clothing or other significant cultural objects can be considered as a useful introduction to a character or a culture. If possible, it is advisable to bring a bundle of clothes and ask teacher learners to establish the costumes for the main characters. When teacher learners are matching costumes to characters, so-called *sign costumes,* they reflect on the artefacts and clothes as symbols for cultural beliefs and attitudes. They deepen their understanding of cultural differences, and the costumes become an expression of the identity of the characters. If there is not enough time (as in the case of our seminars), the teacher should determine the costuming and introduce the sign costumes him- or herself.

At this point in the lesson, I thus introduced the sign costumes. As the characters were acted either by the teacher or the teacher learners, it was agreed that anyone who was wearing a sign costume would personify the particular character. It helped identify the individual characters and helped teacher learners believe in their roles. (We used the following sign costumes: a wreath of white flowers for Juliet, a brocade waistcoat for Romeo, a big headscarf for the nurse, a shawl for Lady Capulet, and a hat for Capulet.) The visual presentation of some scenes was enlivened by props, for example, a dagger and a small bottle of poison. Finally, music is always a good means of evoking atmosphere and enhancing the action.

Streets of Verona Predrama: Mimed Activity

The teacher learners walked in the classroom, imagining that they were in the streets of Verona, meeting first their friends and later their enemies. (The scene was enhanced by background music.) Their feelings were demonstrated by their facial expressions and by body language that indicated Renaissance conventions and courtesy. Later, in pairs, they described their feelings, and the activity established the framework for the whole drama.

The Ballroom

Once again, the music set the scene, first in a discotheque and then in a ballroom in Verona. The teacher learners danced with their beloved, and, as a result, they experienced happiness, which then vanished because of their beloved's indifference. They mimed their emotions and expressed them by confiding in a good friend. With a partner, they described their anguish using the contemporary language of unhappy lovers, embodying Romeo, whose love for Rosaline is unrequited. As the focus was on the language, the teacher learners compared their declaration of love and suffering with Shakespeare's text (1.1.176–93). Romeo speaks about his feelings using exaggerated images based mainly on contradictions, whereas contemporary lovers do not want to be too affectionate and prefer to hide their feelings. Romeo's flowery speech made the teacher learners realise that he represents a typical stereotype of a Petrarchan lover, who abounds in affection.

The Ballroom Later

In my class, one teacher learner who represented Juliet (wearing her wreath) appeared in a circle and danced while the other teacher learners were instructed to portray Romeo madly in love at first sight with Juliet. In pairs, they tried to express their genuine and deep feelings.

Their confessions were then compared with Shakespeare's text (1.5.45–53), which showed the seriousness of Romeo's emotions. It was evident that, unlike his infatuation with Rosaline, his love for Juliet was genuine, and, consequently, his declaration was more convincing. The comparison of emotions that young people nowadays experience with those of Renaissance lovers demonstrates that the feelings of people have not changed over centuries. It is only the way of talking about love that has changed: The language is much simpler, less emotional, and less poetic than that of Shakespeare's protagonists.

Students-in-Role: Juliet in Love

Teacher learners imagined that they were Juliet and were in love for the first time. They walked in the garden and focused on their feelings, which sensitised them for the next activity.

Writing-in-Role: Diary

In this convention, teacher learners assume the role of a character and write a diary entry in which they reflect on the character's experience. In this case, teacher learners in the role of Juliet focused on her feelings. They worked in groups of four or five and wrote an entry about the ball, each contributing a sentence in turn. This provided an opportunity for them to gain insight into Juliet's character and explore her emotional inner life. In terms of language production, the teacher learners had to think not only about the content but also about the appropriate register.

The Orchard Scene

First, the teacher learners read an extract from the orchard scene. The focus was on the different attitudes of Romeo and Juliet to the dangerous situation, which reveals the difference in their personalities. Although this activity was mainly text based, the teacher learners were encouraged to prepare a conversation depicting the meeting of the two lovers. They were also asked to predict whether, on a first date, their peers would react differently from Shakespeare's protagonists.

The Wedding: Still Image

Still image is a convention in which participants, working together, express the main concept in the form of an image, using their bodies like a sculpture. This crystallises a moment, an idea, or a theme and represents the most important elements of the story at a particular moment. It has the same function as an illustration in a book, which usually focuses on the key moments of the story. While the students are preparing the still image, they must negotiate, which encourages a lot of speaking in the target language. As Neelands (1999) states, it is

> a very economical and controlled form of expression as well as a sign to be interpreted or read by observers . . . it simplifies complex content into easily

managed and understandable form, requires reflection and analysis in the making and observing of images. (p. 19)

In this case, four teacher learners were asked to prepare a still image that represented the wedding.

Students-in-Role: The People of Verona

The remaining teacher learners were requested to take on the role of the people of Verona; the still image of the wedding provided a stimulus for their reactions. What comments would the citizens of the Renaissance Verona make about these lovers who disobeyed their parents? Would they sympathise with them, or would they disapprove of them? Each teacher learner expressed his or her judgement of Romeo and Juliet respecting the social conventions and morality of the time. This scene is vital for teacher learners' understanding as they must realise that the protagonists did not make any errors for which they should be punished and that should consequently result in tragic death, as is typical of the great tragedies. Still, the critical judgement of their contemporaries made teacher learners realise that Romeo and Juliet were guilty in the eyes of Elizabethan society as they did not obey their parents and married without their consent.

A Meeting

The *meeting* convention gets students to meet within the drama, make collective decisions, and suggest strategies to solve problems, which moves the action forward. All the teacher learners met at this point to discuss what would be the best solution to the lovers' problem. They listed all the possibilities and their consequences. They asked questions such as: Should Romeo leave or stay? What would happen if he stayed? Should Juliet go with him? Which problems would they have to face? Should Juliet tell her parents about her marriage? How might they react to this news?

Portraits of Capulet and Lady Capulet

The teacher learners worked together and speculated about the characters of Capulet and Lady Capulet. The portraits of a young Lady Capulet, who is hardly 30, and her considerably older husband were utilised to stimulate the teacher learners' ideas about the nature of this marriage. Consequently, they generated questions as to why Lady Capulet married this man and discussed the dependence of children on the decisions of their parents. This was also reflected in the relationship between Juliet and her parents, who, while loving their daughter, expected her to be obedient.

Portrait of Paris

The portrait of a young and handsome nobleman representing Paris provided some hints about him. The teacher learners realised that he was chosen by Juliet's father because he wanted his daughter to be happy.

Hot Seating: The Capulets

Neelands (1999) describes the *hot seating* convention as an interview in which a group of students question a role player who remains in character. It provides insights into the personality, motivation, and behaviour of the character. At this point, two teacher learners representing the Capulets were seated in the front of the class while the others interviewed them to find out their opinion of marriage in general and their intentions toward their own daughter.

Students-in-Role: Juliet's Contemporaries

One teacher learner, playing the role of Juliet, came into the middle of a circle and was requested to ask her contemporaries what they would do if they were in her shoes. All the other teacher learners tried to come up with advice. The teacher learners were told to express the opinions of the Elizabethan audience.

Students-in-Role: Romeo in Mantua

All teacher learners imagined that they were Romeo in Mantua and had just received a letter about Juliet's death. They walked about, reading the letter, and each of them thought of a sentence that would typically depict Romeo in that situation. Later, they worked in groups of four and put together a plan of what Romeo could possibly do.

Students-in-Role: Juliet's Tomb

To better prepare teacher learners for the upcoming task, they watched a scene showing the death of Romeo and Juliet, which was mimed by two fellow teacher learners who were wearing the sign costumes and using props (a small bottle of poison and a dagger). The teacher learners reacted to the death of the protagonists as if they were the people of Verona. Each of them approached the dead couple and spoke a sentence that expressed either their emotions or their judgements. Four teacher learners in the roles of the Capulets and the Montagues delivered messages to their dead children, indicating that they realised how foolish their feud had been and that they had reconciled.

Still Image: The Final Scene

This still image was the catharsis of the play. In groups of six, teacher learners presented the final scene as a still image. This portrayed the reconciliation of the hostile families and suggested some of the optimism that ends the play.

This sequence of activities was followed by activities in which teacher learners discussed their overall conception of the play (see the Practical Ideas section).

The Experience

As stated in the Context section, this project was carried out not only with full-time teacher learners but also with distance teacher learners who were at the time teaching English to 11- to 15-year-olds. We felt that literature seminars with these teacher learners should be related to their teaching experience and provide them with models of how to exploit literary texts in language lessons. For this reason, the structured drama seemed an appropriate methodology for this group.

Teacher Learner Perspectives

The whole lesson itself was very playful, and the teacher learners' involvement and their eager participation was a source of motivation and energy for the teacher. Even teacher learners who are usually very quiet and reluctant to join a discussion in literature seminars contributed to the presentation, and it seemed that this lesson helped create a more positive attitude toward literature.

All teacher learners were asked to reflect on the activities and write an evaluation of the way in which the drama was presented. The distance teacher learners were encouraged to think about whether this approach could be modified into activities that would be suitable for their learners. Their comments were mostly very positive: All of them welcomed this approach to the drama and found the lessons enjoyable. After academically oriented lessons, this type of seminar was characterised as "a pleasant surprise." Some of them (who described themselves as introverts), however, expressed their reservations about the activities because of shyness. They felt inhibited when asked to act in front of others. Such worries indicate that this type of project requires a very sensitive approach and that some previous preparation is needed so that teacher learners learn to respond to similar tasks and how to act. (The importance of this becomes apparent, as their future profession of teachers involves a great deal of acting.) It is important that the teacher learners become familiar with the basic conventions beforehand so that the atmosphere can become more relaxed.

Teacher learners appreciated their active participation in the lesson, and even the shy ones admitted that they gradually managed to overcome their inhibitions. They commented very positively on the fact that their teacher acted with them, which helped them to relax. On the whole, they asked for more lessons of this kind because they felt that active involvement could reinforce their memory and help them recall material more easily than if it were presented in a traditional seminar.

The distance teacher learners were able to relate this project to their own teaching experience and to evaluate all activities in terms of a model that could be adapted to their own lessons. They commented mainly on the amount of time. They felt that their students could remain attentive for only a short time span, and some of them suggested that the drama should be split into a series of shorter activities exploited over the course of several lessons. Some of them worried about maintaining discipline during acting, and some expressed their doubts whether adolescents would be interested in similar activities. It was, however, encouraging to see that only very few of them found drama activities unsuitable. Nearly all of them thought that they could present simple stories in the form of drama. They were also aware that such a lesson requires a lot of preparation on the part of the teacher. I fully agreed, but, for me, their positive responses were the greatest reward.

As the double-subject teacher learners analysed *Romeo and Juliet* in a traditional teacher-centred seminar, it was interesting to compare them with the other groups. In the literature class, the double-subject teacher learners were asked questions that were meant to stimulate discussion, but only those who liked literature responded, whereas the others remained passive. In addition, the majority of the lesson was dominated by the teacher, which does not occur in the case of structured drama. At the end of the term, teacher learners were given a test that included questions concerning certain issues from *Romeo and Juliet*. The primary and distance teacher learners were more successful on the test than the double-subject ones, which proves that they had better insight into the play and that people remember material better when it can be related to personal experiences.

Teacher Perspectives

From the teacher's point of view, the preparation was quite time-consuming but, on the whole, very enjoyable. The planning of all activities had to be very thorough and detailed, and it was especially necessary to match the content and conventions in such a way that the whole structure led to a development of understanding and experience.

Looking critically at structured drama, I point out that the lesson, too, is time-consuming. Although the main issues of the play can be discussed in one seminar, their presentation through structured drama requires two sessions. On the other hand, the time spent on structured drama is not wasted time because of students' involvement in the areas of literature and language production. An additional issue might be the size of the group. Whereas in a traditional seminar, it is advantageous to work with a maximum of 15 teacher learners, structured drama, being a collective and social activity, requires a larger group of participants. (I found a group of 15–25 teacher learners quite satisfactory.)

✥ PRACTICAL IDEAS

In this section, I focus on issues that have to do with the teacher's preparation for using structured drama. Preparation not only requires thoughtful planning of activities but also, because the drama is like telling a story and sets another world, requires the teacher to create the dramatic context, draw the students into the story, and encourage them to cooperate.

Ensure That There Is an Atmosphere of Trust and Cooperation

Teacher learners must lose all fear of ridicule and be prepared to take risks with words and actions. This can be achieved gradually over the course of lessons that make teacher learners familiar with the drama conventions. The teacher learners I worked with practised *hot seating* and *writing-in-role* during a preceding class focusing on the description of the main character in the short story "Eveline" (Joyce, 1914/1967). The convention *meetings* was successfully exploited when teacher learners were looking for the best solution to Eveline's dilemma whether to leave her home or to stay. (See chapter 3 of this volume for an extended discussion of this story, including writing-in-role activities.) Although teachers are responsible for introducing teacher learners to the activities and leading them through the whole process, because they must "ensure that the work is controlled, purposeful and effective" (Neelands, 1999, p. 63), they should take a rather informal position as facilitator and monitor.

Vary the Time Allocated to the Session According to Language Proficiency

Because of syllabus constraints, originally only a 90-minute class was allocated to *Romeo and Juliet*. The experience showed that, for less proficient teacher learners who were not familiar with most of the drama conventions, it was necessary to allow for two 90-minute seminars. This created a more relaxed atmosphere, provided enough time to focus more on the language in the drama, and allowed time for the dramatic activities to be enjoyed more by the teacher learners. At the same time, it enabled the teacher learners to use English in situations where they felt a need to communicate.

Consider Asking the Teacher Learners to Read the Play in Their First Language (L1)

Especially when teacher learners' second language proficiency is not high, it may be useful for them to read in their L1 in order to understand the story and its characters.

Change the Modality of Activities

The activity presented here as a diary activity could also be done as an oral activity if time presses. Oral activities can easily be made into diary entries, and other activities can be modified as well.

Close by Shifting the Focus From Emotions to Intellect

At the closure of the drama, a calming-down activity should stimulate teacher learners to reflect on important issues in the drama. In this case, they speculated about all the circumstances that contributed to the tragic ending.

From the story it is obvious that the main protagonists are not surrounded by bloodthirsty villains who are attempting their destruction but, instead, by well-intentioned people. Romeo and Juliet are driven by their romantic love, do not follow the advice of their friends, and act without thinking about the consequences. Overall, it is clear that in this play Shakespeare has a simple conception of tragedy, in which the young people are victims of fate. They are doomed, and they have to die.

To make teacher learners aware of this, it was helpful to look at the inevitability of the tragic ending and to speculate about what led to it. The most significant element that contributed to the destruction of Romeo and Juliet was the feud, and teacher learners speculated by generating structures such as "Romeo and Juliet would not have died if their families would not have hated each other, if they had not been so impatient and had not got married so quickly, if Romeo had not killed Tybalt, if Romeo had not been banished, if Capulet had not suddenly insisted on Juliet's marriage to Paris, if Friar Lawrence's letter had been delivered in time, if Romeo had not killed himself before Juliet awoke." The teacher learners worked in pairs and listed all circumstances that contributed to the tragic outcome of the play. Whereas advanced teacher learners created a number of similar structures very quickly, slower teacher learners (the primary group) were only provided with an example and were asked to finish this task for homework.

When the teacher learners had listed the major extraordinary coincidences, so improbable in real life, and added the fact that Paris's appearance on the scene had hastened the tragedy, it was important to point out the time scale. So many events had happened at great speed within a few days, and we looked at the various references to lightning in the play. These activities thus take the teacher learners away from the high involvement of the previous activities and move them to an intellectual consideration of the play.

Analyse the Activities From a Methodological Point of View

With teacher learners at the Pedagogical Faculty, who might use these classes not only as a way of interpreting the play but also as guidance for their own lessons, we also looked at the activities from a methodological point of view as a way of approaching literature and developing language skills.

◈ CONCLUSION

This chapter has focused on an example of a British literature seminar in a teacher education programme, where Shakespeare's *Romeo and Juliet* was presented as a structured drama. This way of dealing with literature, based on a dynamic structuring of drama activities, requires teacher learners to become involved in an active exploration of the text. Teacher learners, guided by the teacher's instructions, follow the selected conventions and, as a result, are drawn into the story through identification with the main protagonists and an interpretation of the behaviour of the other characters; thus both their emotions and intellect are engaged.

In the course of the seminar, teacher learners are provided with many opportunities to express their opinions and use English in a natural way. Evaluating the seminar, teacher learners appreciated their active participation in all activities, which they found enjoyable, and even the shy ones, who approached some activities with some apprehension, admitted that the atmosphere of trust and cooperation helped them overcome their inhibitions. The teacher learners with teaching experience thought about possible modifications to this approach that could, in turn, be used in their own lessons. The positive comments were very encouraging and, in light of the careful preparation needed, also highly rewarding.

◈ CONTRIBUTOR

Milena Vodičková is a teacher educator at the Pedagogical Faculty, Palacký University, in the Czech Republic. Her special interests include British literature, drama, and children's literature.

CHAPTER 12

Collaborative Producing of Digital Learning Objects for Language and Literature Instruction in the Netherlands

Frits Schulte

◈ INTRODUCTION

In this chapter I discuss the way in which the language departments of the teacher education institute of Fontys Universities in the Netherlands try to contribute to solving the Dutch problem of *digital children and analogous schools*. I begin with a brief sketch of the origins and context of the SABEMA project (an acronym for *collaboration with Maasland and Bekkers* and a Dutch household expression for *icing on the cake*) in which teacher educators, teacher learners, and practising teachers collaborate in the production of digitally enriched materials for language instruction, including literary instruction. I continue with a description of the principles of the digital methodology adopted by the project, a description of the production process in general, and a sample product for language/literary instruction. I conclude with a few comments on the achievements and impact of the project so far.

◈ CONTEXT

ICT in Dutch Secondary Schools

Since 1998, Dutch secondary education has been going through a series of rapid and fundamental changes, prompted by the dropout rate of approximately 45% of first-year students in tertiary education and by the alarming increase of the shortage of teachers. Within the context of these changes, information and communication technology (ICT) is used (or abused) to accelerate innovations at all levels: methodological, managerial/financial, and curricular (e.g., new national curricula and exam requirements for secondary education and the introduction of the bachelor-master system in tertiary education).

A few examples illustrate the spread of ICT within Dutch secondary education. Most schools and teacher education institutes now have fairly adequate hardware and network facilities and standard software applications at their disposal. Dutch providers are in fierce competition to offer schools more advantageous rates for their broadband connections. Almost all teacher learners and students, as well as 75% of practising teachers, command basic ICT competencies (*Voortgangsrapportage* [Progress Report], 2004). Managers in all types of educational institutions are buying and installing expensive electronic learning management systems. There is an over-whelming amount of educational material for all subjects (and all levels) available on the Internet, which more and more teachers know how to find.

And yet, in spite of all the facilities, resources, in-service training, available examples of good practice, government subsidies, and European funding of international educational ICT-projects, a 2004 survey showed that the actual use of ICT had not really progressed beyond the level that had been reached in the mid-1990s (*Voortgangsrapportage* [Progress Report], 2004). Even more alarmingly, this contrasts with an explosion in the use of ICT in the home environment since the mid-1990s, which has made the Dutch school-going population the most computer literate and digitally active in all countries of the European Community. Clearly, Moore's law of exponential ICT-growth is working for the home environment but not for the educational environment. The resulting problem is commonly referred to as the problem of *digital children in analogous schools*:

> Of the more than one thousand pupils questioned in May 2001, 97% had a computer at home, 84% had Internet access at home, 80% had their own e-mail address and 22% said that they had their own Web site. . . . In secondary schools, more than 25% of the teachers have either no basic ICT skills or have minimal skills (6% and 21% respectively), and almost 60% have either no skills or minimal skills with respect to the pedagogic uses of ICT (25% and 31% respectively). Fifty-one percent of the Dutch schoolgoing population never use the PC in the school environment. (*ICT in Cijfers* [ICT in Numbers], 2002, p. 30; my translation)

The SABEMA Project

Educational Partnership (EPS), a large, government-funded project, was a belated attempt to address the problem. The overall aim of this huge national project was to promote collaboration among staff, developers, and researchers in teacher education institutes; teacher learners; practising teachers; and developers of educational and commercial software in stimulating regional and often local projects for the digital enrichment of secondary education. The idea was to promote awareness of and expertise in digital methodology (as distinct from digital competency) of teacher educators, teacher learners, and practising teachers. EPS wanted them to work together in developing, adapting, and actually implementing digitally enriched teaching materials and approaches (e.g., online courses and modules, classroom activities, WebQuests, thinkquests, action mazes). When EPS financing had run its course by the end of the 2002–2003 school year, it was hoped that this form of partnership would have been so firmly embedded in the way schools and teacher education colleges run their joint-school practice and other related activities that EPS activities would be continued without specific government funding.

Under the aegis and financing of EPS, Fontys Teacher Training Institute in Tilburg (http://www.fontys.nl/) ran a large number of projects in which Fontys staff and students worked together with schools in the southern part of the Netherlands to promote and implement the digital enrichment of secondary education. One of these Fontys/EPS projects was the SABEMA project. In this project, teacher educators, teacher learners, and practising teachers worked together to produce materials for the digital enrichment of foreign language teaching (including literary

instruction) in the participating schools: Maasland College in Oss (http://www
.maaslandcollege.nl/), Bisschop Bekkers College in Eindhoven (http://www.bbekkers
.nl/), and Roncalli College in Bergen op Zoom (http://www.roncalli-boz.nl/). The
project started in January 2001 and ended in July 2003. The project group consisted
of 5 Fontys staff members, 20 teacher learners, and 10 teachers in each of the
participating schools. The scope of the project can be understood by the time
commitment expected of members: All project members were expected to contribute
200 hours to the project, with the Fontys project leader contributing 400 hours.

The three participating schools wanted to use ICT as a catalyst for methodological and professional innovation in preparation for the schools' plans to build schools
for the future. In view of the traditional, central role of foreign language teaching in
Dutch secondary education, the schools decided to take language teaching as the
starting point for the methodological and digital innovation of teaching in all
subjects.

The materials developed were tested in the participating schools, fed back into
the Fontys teacher education courses (and could then be tried out by teacher learners
all over the southern parts of the Netherlands), and evaluated and commented on by
teachers and experts in the so-called contact schools of Fontys (schools that Fontys
teacher educators and publishing companies collaborate with in the testing of
materials and in conducting methodological experiments) and of the participating
publishing companies. Two students in a Fontys master's research programme
conducted action research projects related to various aspects of the actual implementation of the ICT-materials, in particular the pupils' experience. The definitive and
tested materials, the samples of good practice, were disseminated all over the
Netherlands and Europe by incorporation into the ELISE project (*ELISE Web Site,*
n.d.), a Brussels-funded project for online, in-service courses for teacher educators
and teachers interested in implementing e-learning technologies and digital methodology. The project has reached its conclusion, and by September 2005 six in-service
courses were expected to be available online: one on e-coaching/e-learning in
general, three on the digital methodology of teaching EFL, one on the digital
methodology of teaching history, and one on the digital methodology of teaching
science.

DESCRIPTION

The aim of the SABEMA project was the production of digital learning objects for
language and literary instruction. A digital learning object can be defined as follows:

> A modular, free-standing unit of instruction that is able to satisfy a single
> learning objective, is coherent and unitary within a predetermined schema, is
> transportable among applications and environments, independent of format-
> ting and non-sequential. (Fox & Harris, 2003, p. 5)

For the project group, this meant that all of its digital learning objects would
have to meet the following criteria:

1. have the overall objective of offering language and literary/cultural
    instruction for Dutch 16- to 18-year-olds at the secondary school level

2. have a well-defined set of subobjectives, specifying the skills and subskills to be trained and competencies to be mastered and giving each object coherence and unity

3. have a specified study load (e.g., 40 hours)

4. be stand-alone (i.e., course book–independent)

5. be platform independent (i.e., HTML-based and requiring only standard or consumer plug-ins and applications)

6. be capable of integration into electronic learning management systems (e.g., Blackboard, http://www.blackboard.com/; WebCT, http://www.webct.com/; or N@Tschool!, http://fontys.nl/natschool/, the most popular commercial e-learning environment in Dutch secondary education)

7. must be nonsequential (i.e., pupils must be able to work through the objects in an order of their own choosing, depending on their learning styles and preferences)

In addition, the digital learning objects would have to meet the criteria for the methodology of digital language instruction, the so-called five commandments:

1. Pupils are exposed to authentic and contemporary input of English in use in a multimedia context (text, audio, video, pictures).

2. Pupils are asked to process that input (spoken language; reports, essays, and articles; reader responses; minisummaries; main summary; rewrites) in terms of content (main points, minor points, memorable phrases).

3. Pupils are asked to process that input in terms of form (formats, grammatical correctness, spelling, appropriate vocabulary).

4. Pupils are asked to produce output (reports, reader responses, minisummaries, main summary, captions, brochures, presentations) and are supplied with appropriate models (both mental and visual) and mind tools (diagrams, grids, concept maps).

5. Pupils are trained in strategies while completing their digital assignments (e.g., skimming, scanning, summarising, compensatory strategies, effective use of pictures and quotes).

Both sets of criteria could be met by restricting the production process to the development of a specific type of digital learning object: the *WebQuest*. The methodology of the WebQuest was first developed by Dodge (n.d.) and his team at San Diego State University as "an inquiry-oriented activity in which some or all of the information that learners interact with comes from resources on the Internet" (n.p.).

The WebQuest is a digital learning object that combines digital methodology and a constructivist, task-based approach to learning. As such, the WebQuest fits very well into the social-constructivist orientation of Dutch education in general. All WebQuests, regardless of subject, use the following framework:

- introduction (introducing the topic or subject of the WebQuest)

- task (specifying the task and subtasks or assignments for the WebQuest)

- process (outlining the steps pupils have to take to complete the task)

- evaluation (criteria for the successful completion the tasks and subtasks)
- credits

The concrete aim of the project then became the production of new WebQuests or adaptation of existing ones for language instruction, including literary instruction, in Dutch, English, French, German, and Spanish in the upper forms of the participating schools while meeting the central curricular and exam requirements as laid down in the laws of the Dutch Ministry of Education on the *Tweede Fase* (school-leaving curriculum).

❖ DISTINGUISHING FEATURES

The necessity to comply with the intricacies and peculiarities of the Dutch exam requirements led the project group to adapt the standard WebQuest methodology and give the SABEMA WebQuests the distinguishing features described here.

Knowledge-Building Community

The SABEMA WebQuests are based on a combination of collaborative and individual learning. Pupils have to negotiate and agree on a division of subtasks. They also have to work together in combining their individual products into joint products (e.g., presentations, brochures, essays) with a uniform layout. The group task encourages pupils to share information, knowledge, and expertise. The subtasks are done individually and are set up in such a way that they can be marked individually. Marks can then be given for the individual efforts (stored in separate documents), but these marks can be upgraded on the basis of the merits of the group products.

In other words, a pupil's results need not be negatively affected by a failure and correspondingly mediocre results of the group process. On the other hand, pupils cannot mask their individual shortcomings and lack of effort by jumping on the bandwagon of the work of the other group members. The group effort may be adequate, but a teacher can still assess an individual effort as insufficient and insist on revision of the work or set additional, remedial tasks. However, a teacher may also upgrade the mark for individual effort because of the strength of the group effort (and the individual's contribution to that group effort).

The Learning Environment and the Role of the Teacher

The SABEMA WebQuests are completely self-supporting in the sense that pupils have all the necessary helpdesk elements and supporting materials at their disposal (i.e., formats, examples of good practice, structured vocabulary and grammar materials/exercises, URLs, guides, and manuals). The pupils can therefore work independently of the teacher and, to a large extent, regulate their own learning process. As the WebQuests will be made available online or on CD-ROM, pupils can work on the individual subtasks at any time or place. However, the built-in group assignments necessitate face-to-face interaction with fellow pupils within the school environment.

The main role of teachers is that of coach and facilitator. They set the parameters for the WebQuests (deadlines) and can design and digitally publish an accompanying study guide within an e-learning environment (e.g., the Blackboard environment).

Teachers can also point pupils to supplementary and alternative materials (e.g., URLs, movies, documentaries, books, newspapers, songs) and design (and digitally publish) new subtasks.

One of the teacher's main responsibilities is to supervise the formation of groups and to ensure that in each group there is a productive balance and chemistry of learner types and learning styles. Teachers monitor the individual and group process, get it started (e.g., by providing a stimulating kickoff for the project), and keep it going or get it restarted. For this, they can also utilise a project-learning environment (e.g., *Viadesk,* http://www.viadesk.com/) or the Moodle environment (http://moodle .org/), a free, open-source learning and project environment. During the face-to-face group sessions, teachers encourage the pupils to use the target language in their group discussions and occasionally participate to keep a discussion going or provide language input on the spot. Teachers then mark and assess the individual and group effort, though peer assessment of the group effort is also possible and, to a certain extent, preferable.

Curricular WebQuest

In the standard San Diego WebQuest approach (Dodge, n.d.), pupils follow more or less individual and ostensibly random learning paths. It is impossible to predict and control exactly what nooks and crannies of the Internet the pupils will end up exploring and which texts, words, phrases, or grammatical constructions they will encounter and master. Indeed, pupils pick up all kinds and bits of knowledge and will practise their skills, but the teacher no longer has complete control over the process and over the exact nature and content of the knowledge and skills that pupils acquire. The teacher can no longer set final tests for all pupils at the end of a series of activities but has to judge individual performances. In short, standard WebQuests offer mainly episodic knowledge, gathered by the pupils in their increasingly independent and unpredictable exploration of Internet resources while completing their quests, rather than codified knowledge supplied and controlled by the designer of the WebQuest.

For all kinds of reasons, teachers, parents, school inspectors, and quality controllers in the Netherlands are not ready for that (yet). It was decided, therefore, that the main distinguishing feature of the SABEMA WebQuests would be their *curricular* character; that is, they would take pupils through a combination of teacher-controlled, codified and fixed knowledge and skills (which all pupils would have to acquire) and of episodic and flexible pupil-controlled, individualised knowledge and skills. In this way, the curricular WebQuests combine the best of the traditional teacher/exam-centred approach and the constructivist pupil/portfolio-centred approach. (For more information on the curricular WebQuest, see Fontys Teacher Training Institute, 2004.)

Collaborative Production

All SABEMA WebQuests are the result of collaborative efforts of Fontys staff, Fontys teacher learners, and the practising teachers in the participating schools. In this way all WebQuests are based on an up-to-date implementation of ICT technologies and on recent insights into digital methodology (supplied by the Fontys experts and the Fontys-trained teacher learners) and on an integration of this somewhat abstract expertise with the grassroots needs and practical expertise of the practising teachers. Collaborative production also guarantees that the materials developed will actually find their way into the classrooms and will be used and tested out by pupils. Classroom implementation will then be used to fine-tune the finished products and to provide the online dissemination through the *ELISE Web Site* (n.d.) with comments and reflections based on actual classroom experiences.

New Exam Requirements and Their Effect on Literary Studies

The new exam requirements (in place from 1998–1999 onward) drastically reduced the amount of time available for literary instruction, thus forcing language departments in secondary schools all over the Netherlands to work together, if only to prevent overlap and save precious time. The new exams also caused a shift in emphasis, from cognitive/analytical competencies to creative and evaluative/appreciative competencies, thus encouraging reader response and thematic approaches to literature at the expense of the traditional emphasis on literary history and analysis of works belonging to the official canon. The new exam requirements specifically insist on digitally researched, documented, and published personal reading reports and reading autobiographies or portfolios. Finally, the exam requirements also include the competency to compare and contrast novels and their movie versions in the list of literary competencies to be acquired.

In an effort to meet the new exam requirements and to create somewhat more time for literary activities, the English teachers in the SABEMA schools wanted to develop a number of online, literary WebQuests, which would also contain elements of language skills training and elements of cultural aspects of the English-speaking world. Part of the literary work could then be listed under the heading *language/ cultural studies,* for which there is much more time available.

Screening and Publication of WebQuests

The editorial board of the overall project group screens and corrects the final version of the WebQuests. The Web editors then decide on the appropriate manner of publication of the WebQuest. For technical and copyright reasons, WebQuests are published on the project Web site without the heavy resource files (audio and video) if the WebQuest makes sense without them. Pupils can then work with the online version whenever they want and access the complete version, including the audio and video materials, on CD-ROM, either at their schools (through the schools' CD-ROM jukeboxes) or at home with private copies of the CD-ROM version. If the WebQuest does not make sense without the heavy resource files, it is published only on CD-ROM. The CD-ROMs are made available to the pupils through the schools' jukeboxes or through copies for private use.

WebQuests Produced So Far

A large number of WebQuests have been developed so far for Dutch, Spanish, German, French, and English. Topics range from quality papers and tabloids in the Netherlands and formal and informal writing (Dutch), to cosmetic surgery and Dutch-German relationships and prejudices (German), to calligrammes and Breton music/*chansons* (French), to *Dido and Aeneas,* Emily Brontë's *Wuthering Heights,* James

Joyce's *Ulysses, Macbeth* and Shakespeare's theatre, debating, the environment, soccer fans, and J. R. R. Tolkien's *Lord of the Rings* (English).

The CD-ROM WebQuests (i.e., not available through the Internet) include assignments for F. Scott Fitzgerald's *The Great Gatsby* (with a substantial excursion into the history of blues and jazz, illustrated with numerous audio and video fragments); a WebQuest on the Arthur legend (illustrated with movie excerpts from *Excalibur*, *First Knight*, *Lancelot du Lac* [Lancelot of the Lake], and *Merlin*); a WebQuest on Joseph Conrad's *The Heart of Darkness* (with a comparison of the novel and Francis Ford Coppola's film *Apocalypse Now*, illustrated with excerpts from the movie and the soundtrack); and a WebQuest on Nathaniel Hawthorne's *The Scarlet Letter* (using the movie version and excerpts from Arthur Miller's *The Crucible*).

Of the material produced so far, the project's most innovative product is the CD-ROM on tyranny. This CD-ROM contains a number of WebQuests that are all centred on manifestations of tyranny and are heavily and functionally illustrated with audio and video fragments. The CD-ROM is also an example of integrated literary instruction, in which the various languages work together and pool resources (and time) for literary instruction. The menu for the CD-ROM appears in Figure 1.

Tyranny in Dutch, English, French, and German Literature

A. Literature and the world we live in (Dutch)

Assignments addressing the following issues:

What is literature?

Working with the concepts of first reality (= actual reality), second reality (= writer's re-creation of the first reality), and third reality (= reader's creation of the second reality of the author).

Tyranny and satire (assignments based on authentic footage of Adolf Hitler juxtaposed with excerpts from Chaplin's *The Great Dictator*).

B. Tyranny in education (English)

A webquest with assignments on Bronte's *Jane Eyre*, Dickens's *Hard Times*, Spark's *The Prime of Miss Jean Brodie*, Eco's *The Name of the Rose*, and Winterson's *Oranges Are Not the Only Fruit*.

C. Tyranny in the family (Dutch)

A webquest with assignments on novels and poems by various Dutch masters (Bordewijk, Couperus, Wolkers, 't Hart).

D. Tyranny of the environment (German)

A webquest with assignments on Remarque's *All Quiet on the Western Front*, Prose's *The Blue Angel,* and Böll's *The Lost Honour of Katarina Blum*.

E. Tyranny of obsession (French)

A webquest with assignments on Molière's *L'Avare*.

F. Integration

A webquest with assignments that encourage pupils to discover the elements that some of these key works in Dutch, English, French, and German have in common and to discern the relevance of these works to the post-September 11 world they live in.

Figure 1. Menu for the CD-ROM on Tyranny

◈ PRACTICAL IDEAS

The practical ideas in this section take as their basis the production process of a curricular WebQuest for English, the New York WebQuest, which combines instruction in language skills, cultural studies, and literature. The choice for New York as the thematic pivot for this WebQuest was prompted by the events of September 11, 2001, which had rendered most of the New York materials in the schools' course books out of date. The project group strongly believes that the production process and adaptation of the WebQuest methodology described in this section can serve as a model for collaborative producing of ICT materials for foreign language teaching all over Europe (or, indeed, in other regions) and can easily be adapted by teachers, teacher educators, and teacher learners to serve their specific needs. (For more guidance, consult the *ELISE Web site,* n.d. Since September 2004 it has also included online in-service courses.)

Choose the Right Subject for a Curricular WebQuest

Developing WebQuests can be a time-consuming activity. Make sure that your WebQuest is reusable by having a subject or theme that will retain a contemporary interest and that will appeal to pupils in the future. Also choose a subject that can be linked to both skills-related activities and to cultural or literary studies. In this way, the WebQuest becomes a multipurpose one, which can be used for skills training and for the teaching of literature. In short, the subject should be one that is regularly featured in radio, television, movies, and magazines and generates a lot of recent multimedia content for language training as well as content for cultural/literary studies. The New York WebQuest is an example of such a subject.

Ensure That the WebQuest Is Truly a Collaborative Project

All members of the English team looked for and handed in reading texts, audio materials, and other such materials, and developed assignments and digital exercises or quizzes once the team had decided on which texts to use. Whenever the opportunity presented itself, some of the materials, in particular the reading texts and the audio segments, were tried out in class. Most materials were first developed in word-processed format, thus enabling all members of the team, regardless of their specific ICT competencies, to make a contribution to the project. The webmasters then digitised all the materials (text, audio, video); incorporated them into the adapted WebQuest template, using Microsoft FrontPage 2000 as the HTML editor; and uploaded the whole to the SABEMA server (Fontys Teacher Training Institute, 2004).

Exploit the Full Multimedia Potential of a WebQuest Subject

The New York WebQuest uses the standard WebQuest methodology and the standard framework: introduction, task, process, evaluation, and credits. An innovation, however, is the subdivision of the process part into two parts: *basics* and *projects*.

Process: Basics

This part, which requires a study load of 20 hours, constitutes the codified or fixed part of the WebQuest and is obligatory for all pupils. In this part, pupils acquire basic knowledge of New York and its boroughs (mainly through exploring online materials on New York), read a number of prescribed texts, listen to a number of audio segments, acquire some 300 words, and complete various exercises (in grammar, reading, listening, writing) based on the materials offered. Some of the exercises are digital exercises (designed with the software Hot Potatoes 6); others depend on pupils recording answers and assignments in their personal question-and-answer document and maintaining their own digital vocabulary file (using a shareware tool known as Overhoor [Cramming]; see EFKA-Soft, 2005).

Process: Projects

After completing the obligatory basics, pupils can then move on to the projects. This part has a study load of 20 hours and constitutes the episodic or flexible knowledge part of the overall New York curricular WebQuest. It consists of a number of Internet assignments (some also in the form of WebQuests) from which pupils can choose two or three, depending on their own preference, as long as the combined total adds up to a study load of 20 hours. The following Internet assignments and WebQuests have been completed to date: graffiti, Ellis Island, New York bohemians, New York in movies, skyscrapers, and New York food. With each assignment, pupils can follow their own preferences or explore parts and aspects of New York they have developed an interest in on the basis of their work on the obligatory basics component.

Identify the Literary Components That Can Be Worked Into the WebQuest

Each Internet assignment/WebQuest also contains tasks that have a specifically literary component and that can be further developed by pupils in the reading reports on a minimum of three English novels (or three collections of poems or three plays) that they have to include in their overall, school-leaving literary portfolio. The assignments on New York bohemians, for instance, encourage pupils to explore the Beats; the assignments on Ellis Island lead pupils to explore various immigrant novels and memoirs; the assignments on New York movies take pupils from crime movies set in New York to crime novels such as Mario Puzo's *The Godfather* or E. L. Doctorow's *Billy Bathgate*. Working through and on the two process parts (obligatory themes and optional projects) of the New York WebQuest gives pupils the background knowledge, language skills, and literary skills to include a full reading report on at least one New York item (a novel, poem, or play) in their personal literary portfolio. To provide an idea of the nature of the projects assignments, Figure 2 shows the process part from the New York in Movies Internet assignment/ WebQuest (Fontys Teacher Training Institute, 2004).

The other steps in the process section help the pupils narrow down their provisional list of five movies to their favourite New York–borough movie. Groups of four pupils then combine their individual researches and efforts into putting together a New York Movie Night, which features their favourite movies, and write the programme and brochure for that movie night.

The last step in the process section gives pupils a list of typical New York–borough novels, plays, or poems. They have to choose one of those texts to accompany their favourite borough movie and to write a reading report on that text, which they can include in their literary portfolio. They have to use the standard

Process: New York in Movies

Group Work

Step 1: Getting to know the boroughs of the city and selecting your borough

- Go to the Web sites given below and study the characteristics (geography, population, neighbourhoods, places of interest) of each of New York's main movie boroughs: Manhattan, Brooklyn, or the Bronx/Queens.

    http://www.nationmaster.com/encyclopedia/Manhattan
    http://www.nationmaster.com/encyclopedia/Brooklyn,-New-York
    http://www.nationmaster.com/encyclopedia/The-Bronx
    http://www.nationmaster.com/encyclopedia/Queens

    Listen to the audio fragments below to get an idea of life in the movie boroughs, and do the exercises to make sure you have understood the audio fragments. You can also watch the fragments (click on video fragments). While listening and or watching, pay attention to the locations, people, and buildings you see and the street noises you hear. All this will help you to get an idea of life in the boroughs.

    Manhattan: audio/video exercises—Clips from *Manhattan, The Devil's Advocate, Midnight Cowboy, Wall Street, Hester Street, Ghostbusters, The Cotton Club, The Godfather, Fisher King, Tootsie, Carlito's Way, Hoodlum, Men in Black, Vanilla Sky*

    Brooklyn: audio/video exercises—Clips from *Do the Right Thing, Good Fellas, Smoke, Summer of Sam, Saturday Night Fever, Prizzi's Honor, Donnie Brasco, Little Odessa, Radio Days, A Tree Grows in Brooklyn*

    The Bronx/Queens: audio/video exercises—Clips from *Beat Street, A Bronx Tale, Bonfire of the Vanities, Quiz Show, Someone to Watch Over Me, Maid in Manhattan, Once Upon a Time in America, The Chosen*

- Choose the borough that you would like to concentrate on in this WebQuest. Once you have chosen your borough, you will limit yourself to studying and exploring movies set in and/or about this borough.

Step 2: Finding and selecting movies about your borough

- First read this <u>article</u> about Martin Scorsese's favourite New York movies and do the accompanying exercises (<u>Exercise 1</u> and <u>Exercise 2</u>) so that you get an idea of the kind of movies you may deal with in this WebQuest.

- Each of you will go to the international movie database (<u>http://www.imdb.com/</u>). Go to the search engine of this site and choose "plots" as the category of your search (you can use the pull-down menu to make this choice). Type in the name of your borough, activate the search, and you will get a list of movies in which your borough plays a central part. Click on the title of the movie, and you will get a brief description of its plot, contents, and other marked features. These databases can also be reached by going to Moviedatabases in the WebQuest menu bar.

- Put together a list of five movies that you personally would like to see or find out more about and that also gives information about your borough (people or ethnic groups living there, places of interest, streets and neighbourhoods, social life in the borough, crime in the borough, history of the borough, etc.).

- Make sure that your provisional list contains at least one sample of each of the main movie genres (comedy, action/crime/adventure, and drama) and that there is at least one movie from the period 1930–1980.

Note. Underlined text denotes links that students would use in their research.

FIGURE 2. The Process Part of the New York in Movies WebQuest

format for reading reports (e.g., character analysis, comments on the theme, comments on the use of symbols, personal response) that is currently used in their school. However, they also have to add a section to the reading report in which they link their analysis of and response to the text to the movie(s) they have studied in the course of the New York in Movies WebQuest. Suggested combinations include

- Manhattan: Puzo's *The Godfather* (movie and novel), Jay McInerney's *Bright Lights, Big City* (movie and novel)

- The Bronx: Tom Wolfe's *The Bonfire of the Vanities* (movie and novel), Doctorow's *Billy Bathgate* (movie and novel), Stan Lathan's *Beat Street* (movie), Richard Price's *Clockers* (novel and movie, though set in New Jersey)

- Brooklyn: Betty Smith's *A Tree Grows in Brooklyn* (movie and novel), Chaim Potok's *The Chosen* (movie and novel).

In their specific New York section of their reading report, pupils have to answer questions such as these:

- Which of the two New York products appealed to you more: the text or the movie? Account for your answer.

- Which of the two would you recommend to a fellow pupil who is interested in finding out about life in the borough of your choice? Why?

- What, to you, would be the best order for getting the most out of both the text and the movie: read the text first and then watch the movie or vice versa? Account for your answer.

- List your two favourite scenes in the movie and your two favourite passages from the text. Explain your choice.

◈ CONCLUSION

The project has achieved its objectives, and teacher educators, teacher learners, and practising teachers have collaborated in producing digital learning objects that are tailor-made for the participating schools and, consequently, are actually being used by them. Teachers, teacher educators, and teacher learners have benefited considerably from participating in the project: They have refined their digital skills; become aware of and proficient in some of the basic principles of digital methodology; and gained experience in acting as coaches for pupils who are engaged, individually or in small groups, in digital assignments.

The project has accelerated the methodological and ICT-related innovation of the Fontys curricula for the teacher education courses. Other departments, both within Fontys and within the participating schools, have taken an interest in the project and have copied parts of the production process, particularly the involvement of teacher learners. Some departments (e.g., the geography, science, and history departments) are now in the process of adopting and adapting the WebQuest methodology.

Teachers in the participating schools have become more actively involved in formulating the schools' long-term ICT objectives and overall strategic planning. Above all, the *digital children* can now learn their languages in a truly multicultural, multidisciplinary, and multimedia learning environment that manages to bridge the gap between the analogous and the digital teaching worlds.

At the time of writing, the project continues under its own financial steam, provided by the participating schools, because EPS funding has expired. Through presentations, demonstrations, and articles, the project members try to disseminate the results of the project and to encourage colleagues, both at home and abroad, to join the production process. So far, 17 more schools from the area have joined the project and the process of collaborative producing and are now working on producing curricular language/literary WebQuests. From the school year 2004–2005 onward, three of the participating schools began offering their language and literary instruction for 16- to 18-years-olds in Dutch, English, French, German, and Spanish in a course book–independent, digital format. The others were to follow suit from 2005–2006 onward.

Comments by others are more than welcome, as are contributions (provided they conform to the methodology and standards of the project as outlined previously): The members of the project group are more than willing to turn their schools into knowledge-sharing as well as knowledge-building communities and can be reached via e-mail to the overall project leader at f.schulte@fontys.nl.

◈ CONTRIBUTOR

From 1992 Frits Schulte has been employed as a senior lecturer in the methodology of teaching the language and culture of the English-speaking world by Fontys Universities, in the Netherlands. He has been the project leader of various national and international projects for the ICT enrichment of (language) teaching and e-learning.

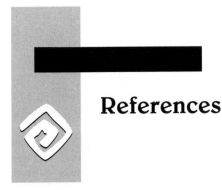

References

Abbs, P. (1974). *Autobiography in education*. London: Heinemann.

Achebe, C. (1958). *Things fall apart*. London: Heinemann.

Achebe, C. (1960). *No longer at ease*. London: Heinemann.

Ali, S. (1995). *The applicability of the transactive reader-response theory to the teaching and reading of literature in a second language*. Unpublished doctoral thesis, Cambridge University.

Aller Vázquez, M. (1997, March). Un tarot para inventar historias [A tarot for storymaking]. *Cuadernos de Literatura Infantil y Juvenil, 30*–36.

Applebee, A. N. (1989). *The child's concept of story*. Chicago: University of Chicago Press.

Arendt, H. (1963). *Eichmann in Jerusalem: A report on the banality of evil*. New York: Viking Press.

Atkins, S. B. (1993). *Voices from the fields: Children of migrant farmworkers tell their stories*. Boston: Little, Brown and Company.

Austen, J. (1996). *Pride and prejudice*. London: Penguin Books. (Original work published 1813)

Bal, M. (1997). *Narratology: Introduction to the theory of narrative* (2nd ed.). Toronto, Canada: University of Toronto Press.

Ball, A. (1998). The value of recounting narratives: Memorable learning experiences in the lives of inner-city students and teachers. *Narrative Inquiry, 8*(1), 151–180.

Banjo, A. (1985). Issues in the teaching English literature in Nigeria. In R. Quirk & H. Widdowson (Eds.), *English in the world: Teaching and learning the language and literatures* (pp. 200–206). Cambridge: Cambridge University Press.

Barnes J. (1991). *Talking it over*. London: Picador.

Bassnett, S., & Grundy, P. (1993). *Language through literature*. Harlow, England: Longman.

Bates, M. (Ed.). (1999). *Chalk face muse: Poetry as a foreign language*. East Linton, Scotland: White Adder Press.

Beck, R. (1995). *Macbeth, Animal Farm* und kein Ende! Was haben studienanfänger in der Anglistik gelesen? [*Macbeth, Animal Farm* and no end! What have first-year English majors read?]. *Neusprachliche Mitteilungen, 48,* 31–38.

Belcher, D., & Hirvela, A. (2000). Literature and L2 composition: Revisiting the debate. *Journal of Second Language Writing, 9*(1), 21–39.

Benso Calvo, Mª C. (1989). Escolarización e sociedade: Modalidades, niveis, e funcións da escolarización na sociedade ourensá franquista [Schooling and society: Modalities, levels, and functions of schooling in Ourense society during the Franco regime]. In A. Requejo Osorio & X. M. Cid Fernández (Eds.), *Educación e sociedade en Ourense* (pp. 69–112). A Coruña, Spain: Ediciós do Castro.

Bettelheim, B. (1991). *The uses of enchantment: The meaning and importance of fairy tales*. London: Penguin Books.

Bouman, L. (1983). Who's afraid of poetry? *Modern English Teacher, 10*(3), 14.

Bredella, L., & Delanoy, W. (1996). Introduction. In L. Bredella & W. Delanoy (Eds.), *Challenges of literary texts in the foreign language classroom* (pp. vii–xxviii). Tübingen, Germany: Gunter Narr Verlag.

Briggs, R. (1974). *The fairy tale treasury*. London: Puffin.

British Council. (2000). *Crazy world*. Retrieved August 9, 2005, from http://www .learnenglish.org.uk/crazyworld/

Britton, J. (1982). Response to literature. In G. M. Pradl (Ed.), *Prospect and retrospect: Selected essays of James Britton*. Montclair, NJ: Boynton/Cook.

Brody, C., Witherell, C., Donald, K., & Lunblad, R. (1991). Story and voice in the education of professionals. In C. Witherell & N. Noddings (Eds.), *Stories lives tell: Narrative and dialogue in education* (pp. 257–278). New York: Teachers College, Columbia University.

Browner, S., Pulsford, S., & Sears, R. (2000). *Literature and the Internet: A guide for students, teachers and scholars*. New York: Garland.

Brumfit, C. J., & Carter, R. A. (1986). *Literature and language teaching*. Oxford: Oxford University Press.

Bruner, E. M. (1986). Ethnography as narrative. In E. M. Bruner & V. Turner (Eds.), *The anthropology of experience* (pp. 139–155). Urbana: University of Illinois Press.

Bruner, J. (1994). Life as narrative. In A. H. Dyson & C. Genishi (Eds.), *The need for story: Cultural diversity in classroom and community* (pp. 28–37). Urbana, IL: National Council of Teachers of English.

Brunner, D. (1994). *Inquiry and reflection: Framing narrative practice*. Albany: State University of New York.

Buchman, M. (1988). Argument and contemplation in teaching. *Oxford Review of Education, 14,* 201–214.

Butler, R. O. (1992a). Crickets. In *A good scent from a strange mountain: Stories* (pp. 59–64). New York: Henry Holt.

Butler, R. O. (1992b). The trip back. In *A good scent from a strange mountain: Stories* (pp. 29–44). New York: Henry Holt.

Butt, D., Fahey, R., Spinks, S., & Yallop, C. (2000). *Using functional grammar: An explorer's guide* (2nd ed.). Sydney, Australia: National Centre for English Language Teaching.

Byatt, A. (1995). The Chinese lobster. In *The Matisse stories* (pp. 91–132). New York: Random House.

Carter, R., & Long, M. N. (1987). *The web of words: Exploring literature through language*. Cambridge: Cambridge University Press.

Carter, R., & Long, M. N. (1991). *Teaching literature*. Harlow, England: Longman.

Carter, R., & Nunan, D. (Eds.). (2000). *The Cambridge guide to teaching English to speakers of other languages*. Cambridge: Cambridge University Press.

Carter, R., & Tomlinson, B. (1985, March). Language through literature and literature through language. *EFL Gazette,* p. 9.

Celce-Murcia, M. (Ed.). (2001). *Teaching English as a second or foreign language* (3rd ed.) Boston: Heinle & Heinle.

Cervera, J. (1992). *Teoría de la literatura infantil* [Theory of children's literature]. Bilbao, Spain: Mensajero.

Chan, P. (1999). Literature, language awareness and EFL. *Language Awareness, 8*(1), 38–50.

Chew, K., & Wong, M. W. (1999.) A literature syllabus for Singapore secondary schools. In S. H. Chua & W. P. Chin (Eds.), *Localising pedagogy: Teaching literature in Singapore* (pp. 90–95). Singapore: National Institute of Education, National Technological University.

Clandinin, D. J. (1986). *Classroom practice: Teacher images in action*. London: Falmer Press.

Collie, J., & Porter Ladousse, G. (1991). *Paths into poetry*. Oxford: Oxford University Press.

Collie, J., & Slater, S. (1987). *Literature in the language classroom: A resource book of ideas and activities*. Cambridge: Cambridge University Press.

Cox, C., & Many, J. E. (1992). Toward an understanding of the aesthetic response to literature. *Language Arts, 69,* 32–33.

Cummings, M., & Simmons, R. (1983). *The language of literature.* Oxford: Pergamon Press.

Curry, J. (Ed.). (1996). *Wondercrump poetry!* London: Random House.

Dahl, R. (1989). *Matilda.* London: Penguin Books.

Dahl, R. (2002). Lamb to the slaughter. In *Skin and other stories* (pp. 22–34). New York: Puffin Books. (Original work published 1953)

Defoe, D. (1996). *Moll Flanders.* London: Penguin Books. (Original work published 1722)

Derewianka, B. (1990). *Exploring how texts work.* Newtown, New South Wales: Primary English Teaching Association.

De Ruiz, D., & Larios, R. (1993). *La Causa: The migrant farmworkers' story.* Austin, TX: Raintree Steck-Vaughn.

Dewey, J. (1933). *How we think.* Carbondale: Southern Illinois University Press.

Dodge, B. (n.d.). Site overview. *The WebQuest page.* Retrieved May 3, 2005, from San Diego State University, Educational Technology Department Web site: http://webquest.sdsu.edu/overview.htm

Doughty, C., & Williams, J. (Eds.). (1998). *Focus on form in classroom second language acquisition.* Cambridge: Cambridge University Press.

Doyé, P. (1999). *The intercultural dimension: Foreign language education in the primary school.* Berlin, Germany: Cornelsen.

Drew, J. (2001). An Anglo-Hungarian poetry empire. *IATEFL Literature and Cultural Studies SIG Newsletter, 21,* 8–11.

Duff, A., & Maley, A. (1990). *Literature.* Oxford: Oxford University Press.

Eagleton, T. (1983). *Literary theory: An introduction.* Minneapolis: University of Minnesota Press.

Edmondson, W. (1997). The role of literature in foreign language learning and teaching: Some valid assumptions and invalid arguments. In A. Mauranen & K. Sajavaara (Eds.), *AILA Review Vol. 12, 1995–1996: Applied linguistics across disciplines* (pp. 42–55). Milton Keynes, England: Open University Press.

EFKA-Soft. (2005). Overhoor [Cramming] [Computer software]. Retrieved July 8, 2005, from http://home.wxs.nl/~efkasoft/overhoor/overhoor.html

Egan, K. (1990). *Teaching as storytelling.* London: Routledge.

Eliot, T. S. (1963). Journey of the Magi. In *Collected Poems, 1909–1962* (pp. 99–100). New York: Harcourt. (Original work published 1927)

ELISE Web Site. (n.d.). Retrieved July 7, 2005, from http://filolog.uni.lodz.pl/elise/

Elliott, R. (1990). Encouraging reader-response to literature in ESL situations, *ELT Journal, 44*(3), 191–198.

Ellis, G., & Brewster, J. (1991). *The storytelling handbook for primary teachers.* London: Penguin Books.

Endo, E. (2001, May 23). Surge in LI's Asians. *Newsday.* Retrieved July 28, 2005, from http://www.newsday.com/news/local/longisland/ny-census-asians,0,3104793.story

Engku Haliza, E. I. (1995). Summary of the brief survey of the current literature teaching practice in the UK. *IATEFL Literature and Cultural Studies SIG Newsletter, 11,* 8–12.

Ferradas Moi, C. (2003). Hyperfiction: Explorations in texture. In B. Tomlinson (Ed.), *Developing materials for language teaching* (pp. 221–233). London: Continuum.

Fontys Teacher Training Institute Tilburg, Department of English. (2004). *New York, zet je tanden erin* [New York, take a bite]. Retrieved July 8, 2005, from http://www.fontys.nl/lerarenopleiding/Tilburg/Engels/currwebquest2/NewYorkNewYork/index.htm

Fowler, R. (1996). *Linguistic criticism* (2nd ed.). Oxford: Oxford University Press.

Fox, M., & Harris, J. (2003). *Reusable learning objects: Content and context.* Brighton, England: Epic White Papers.

Freire, P. (1997). *Pedagogy of the heart* (D. Macedo & A. Oliveira, Trans.). New York: Continuum.

Fried-Booth, D. L. (1986). *Project work.* Oxford: Oxford University Press.

Fu, D. (1995). *My trouble is my English.* Portsmouth, NH: Heinemann-Boynton/Cook.

Fugard, A. (1980). *Boesman and Lena and other plays.* London: Oxford University Press.

Gattegno, S. (1996, February). The Silent Way: An approach that humanizes teaching. *The Science of Education in Questions* (No. 13). Retrieved August 23, 2005, from http://assoc.wanadoo.fr/une.education.pour.demain/articlesrrr/sw/shaktie.htm

Gibson, R. (2000). *Intercultural business communication.* Berlin, Germany: Cornelsen and Oxford University Press.

Gilroy, M., & Parkinson, B. (1996). Teaching literature in a foreign language. *Language Teaching, 29*(4), 213–225.

Giroux, H. (1988). Culture, power, and transformation in the work of Paolo Freire: Towards a politics of education. In H. Giroux (Ed.), *Teachers as intellectuals: Toward a critical pedagogy of learning* (pp. 108–120). Granby, MA: Bergin and Garvey.

Giroux, H., Shumway, D., Smith, P., & Sosnoski, J. (1988). The need for cultural studies. In H. Giroux (Ed.), *Teachers as intellectuals: Toward a critical pedagogy of learning* (pp. 143–157). Granby, MA: Bergin and Garvey.

Goodman, D. (1999). *The reading detective club.* Portsmouth, NH: Heinemann.

Goodman, Y. (1997). Multiple roads to literacy. In D. Taylor (Ed.), *Many families, many literacies.* Portsmouth, NH: Heinemann.

Gower, R. (1986). Can stylistic analysis help the EFL learner to read literature? *ELT Journal, 40*(2), 125–130.

Graham, C. (1979). *Jazz chants for children* (Teacher's ed.). New York: Oxford University Press.

Grainger, T. (1997). *Traditional storytelling in the primary classroom.* Leamington Spa, England: Scholastic.

Greene, M. (1978). *Landscapes of learning.* New York: Teachers College Press.

Greene, M. (1994). Multiculturalism, community, and the arts. In A. H. Dyson & C. Genishi (Eds.), *The need for story: Cultural diversity in classroom and community* (pp. 11–27). Urbana, IL: National Council of Teachers of English.

Haggan, M. (1999). A linguist's view: The English department re-visited. *English Teaching Forum, 37*(1), 22–25.

Hall, G. (2003). Poetry, pleasure and second language learning classrooms. *Applied Linguistics, 24*(3), 395–399.

Halliday, M. A. K. (1975). *Learning how to mean: Explorations in the functions of language.* London: Edward Arnold.

Halliday, M. A. K. (1994). *An introduction to functional grammar* (2nd ed.). London: Edward Arnold.

Hanauer, D. (2001). The task of poetry reading and second language learning. *Applied Linguistics, 22*(3), 295–323.

Hancock, M. R. (1993). Exploring and extending personal response through literature journals. *The Reading Teacher, 46*(6), 472.

Harmer, J. (2001). *The practice of English language teaching* (3rd ed.). Harlow, England: Pearson Education.

Hasan, R. (1985). *Linguistics, language and verbal art.* Victoria, Australia: Deakin University Press.

Hasan, R. (1996). On teaching literature across cultural distances. In J. James (Ed.), *The language-culture connection: Selected papers from the RELC Regional Seminar on Exploring Language, Culture and Literature in Language Learning.* Singapore: SEAMEO Regional Language Centre.

Heath, S. B. (1996). Re-creating literature in the ESL classroom. *TESOL Quarterly, 30,* 776–779.

Hedge, T. (2000). *Teaching and learning in the language classroom.* Oxford: Oxford University Press.

Hemingway, E. (1987). Cat in the rain. In *The complete short stories of Ernest Hemingway* (Finca Vigía ed., pp. 127–132). New York: Simon & Schuster. (Original work published 1925)

Hemingway, E. (1987). Hills like white elephants. In *The complete short stories of Ernest Hemingway* (Finca Vigía ed., pp. 211–214). New York: Simon & Schuster. (Original work published 1927)

Henkes, K. (1991). *Chrysanthemum*. New York: Greenwillow.

Hermes, L. (1995). Learning logs als Instrument der Selbstkontrolle und als Evaluation in literaturwissenschaftlichen Proseminaren [Learning logs as self-monitoring tools and as evaluation in literature classes]. In W. Börner. & K. Vogel (Eds.), *Der Text im Fremdsprachunterricht* (pp. 85–98). Bochum, Germany: AKS Verlag.

Hirvela, A. (1990). ESP and literature: A reassessment. *English for Specific Purposes, 9,* 237–252.

Hoffman, E. (1989). *Lost in translation: A life in a new language*. New York: Penguin Books.

Holzmann, C. (1997). More of the same or something completely different: Some observations on the reading development of EFL students. *IATEFL Literature and Cultural Studies SIG Newsletter, 14,* 16–20.

Horowitz, D. (1990). Fiction and nonfiction in the ESL/EFL classroom: Does the difference make a difference? *English for Specific Purposes, 9,* 161–168.

ICT in cijfers: ICT-onderwijsmonitor schooljaar 2001–2002 [ICT in numbers: ICT education monitor 2001–2002]. (2002). Radboud University Nijmegen, The Netherlands: Instituut voor Toegepaste Statistiek. Retrieved April 27, 2005, from http://www.minocw.nl /brief2k/2002/doc/11303c.pdf

Immigration and Naturalization Service. (1996). *Immigrants admitted by state and the metropolitan area of intended residence* [Online]. Retrieved August 15, 2005, from http:// uscis.gov/graphics/shared/aboutus/statistics/annual/fy96/997.htm

Inada, L. (1992). Rayford's song. In *Legends from camp* (pp. 43–45). Minneapolis, MN: Coffee House Press.

Integrierte Fremdsprachenarbeit [Integrated Language Work]. (n.d.-a). *Handouts.* Retrieved July 15, 2005, from the University of Koblenz Web site: http://www.uni-koblenz.de/~ifaangl/handouts.htm

Integrierte Fremdsprachenarbeit [Integrated Language Work]. (n.d.-b). *IFA links.* Retrieved July 15, 2005, from the University of Koblenz Web site: http://www.uni-koblenz.de /~ifaangl/handouts.htm

Isaac, A. (2002). "Opening up" literary cloze. *Language and Education, 16*(1), 18–36.

Iser, W. (1978). *The act of reading: A theory of aesthetic response*. Baltimore, MD: Johns Hopkins University Press.

Ishiguro, K. (1989). *The remains of the day.* London: Faber and Faber.

James, M. R. (1993). Wailing well. In J. Mark (Ed.), *The Oxford book of children's stories* (pp. 304–314). Oxford: Oxford University Press. (Original work published 1928)

James, P. D. (1986). *A taste for death.* New York: Ballantine Books.

Jean, G. (1981). *Le pouvoir des contes* [The power of stories]. Paris: Casterman.

Jennings, A. (1996). "Viewer, I married him": Literature on video. In R. Carter & J. McRae (Eds.), *Language, literature and the learner* (pp. 185–203). Harlow, England: Longman.

John, J. (1986). Language vs. literature in university English departments. *English Teaching Forum, 24*(4), 18–22.

Jones, B. (2001, May 23). Island's little El Salvador. *Newsday.* Retrieved July 28, 2005, from http://www.newsday.com/news/local/longisland/ny-census-salvadoran2,0,4684641.story

Jooste, P. (1998). *Dance with a poor man's daughter.* London: Black Swan.

Joyce, J. (1914/1967). Eveline. In *Dubliners* (pp. 25–29). Oxford: Oxford University Press.

Joyce, J. (2002). *Ulysses.* Mineola, New York: Dover. (Original work published 1922)

Kachru, B. B. (1985). Standards, codification and sociolinguistic realism: The English language in the outer circle. In R. Quirk & H. Widdowson (Eds.), *English in the world:*

Teaching and learning the language and literatures (pp. 11–30). Cambridge: Cambridge University Press.

Karolides, N. (1999). The transactional theory of literature. In N. Karolides (Ed.), *Reader response in secondary and college classroom*. Mahwah, NJ: Lawrence Erlbaum Associates.

Kelly, R. K., & Krishnan, L. A. (1995). "Fiction talk" in the ESP classroom. *English for Specific Purposes, 14*(1), 77–86.

Kim, M. (2004). Literature discussions in adult L2 learning. *Language and Education, 18*(2), 145–166.

Kramsch, C. (1993). *Context and culture in language teaching*. Oxford: Oxford University Press.

Kramsch, C. (1996, January 11). De l'explication de texte à l'analyse de discours [From *explication de texte* to discourse analysis]. Talk given at the Ecole Centrale, Nantes, France.

Krashen, S. (1981). *Second language acquisition and second language learning*. Oxford: Pergamon Press.

Kumin, M. (1997). Woodchucks. In *Selected poems 1960–1990* (p. 80). New York: W. W. Norton & Company. (Original work published 1972)

Kureishi, H. (1997). My son the fanatic. In *Love in a blue time* (pp. 119–131). New York: Simon & Schuster.

Langer, J. A. (1994). A response-based approach to reading literature. *Language Arts, 71,* 203–211.

Lazar, G. (1993). *Literature and language teaching*. Cambridge: Cambridge University Press.

Lazar, G. (1995). Close analysis: An activity for using novels and film in the language classroom. *IATEFL Literature and Cultural Studies SIG Newsletter, 12,* 22–25.

Lazar, G. (1999). *A window on literature*. Cambridge: Cambridge University Press.

Lee, J. F. (2000). *Tasks and communicating in language classrooms*. Boston: McGraw-Hill.

Lemann, N. (1999). *The big test: The secret history of American meritocracy*. New York: Farrar, Straus and Giroux.

Lim, C. S. (2001). Grammar in the English language curriculum in Singapore. Paper presented at the 36th Regional Language Centre International Seminar 2001. In J. James (Ed.), *Grammar in the language classroom: Changing approaches and practices* (Anthology No. 43). Singapore: SEAMEO Regional Language Centre.

Lin, B. T. L. (2001). *Re-inventing the relevance of literature in secondary schools in Singapore: The appraisal of three poems using stylistic analysis*. Unpublished doctoral thesis, National University of Singapore.

Littlejohn, A., & Windeatt, S. (1989). Beyond language learning: Perspectives on materials design. In R. Johnson (Ed.), *The second language curriculum* (pp. 155–176). Cambridge: Cambridge University Press.

Lotman, J. (1972). *Analiz poeticheskogo texta* [Analysis of poetry discourse]. St. Petersburg, Russia: Prosveshenie.

Lyon, G. E. (1999). *Where I'm from: Where poems come from*. Spring, TX: Absey & Co.

Mackay, R. (1992). Lexicide and goblin-spotting in the language/literature classroom. *ELT Journal, 46*(2), 199–208.

Maley, A. (1989). A comeback for literature? *Practical English Teaching, 10*(1), 59.

Maley, A. (2001). Literature in the language classroom. In R. Carter & D. Nunan (Eds.), *The Cambridge guide to teaching English to speakers of other languages* (pp. 180–185). Cambridge: Cambridge University Press.

Maley, A., & Duff, A. (1989). *The inward ear: Poetry in the language classroom*. Cambridge: Cambridge University Press.

Mant, A. C. (1993). The little blue bag. In J. Mark (Ed.), *The Oxford book of children's stories* (pp. 23–41). Oxford: Oxford University Press. (Original work published 1825)

Many, J. E., & Cox, C. (1992). *Reader stance and literary understanding*. Norwood, NJ: Ablex.

Marshall, G. (Director). (1990). *Pretty woman* [Motion picture]. United States: Touchstone Pictures.

Maslow, A. (1987). *Motivation and personality*. New York: Harper & Row.

Massie, A. (1993). The caravan siege. In J. Mark (Ed.), *The Oxford book of children's stories* (pp. 297–303). Oxford: Oxford University Press. (Original work published 1926)

Mattix, M. (2002). The *pleasure* of poetry reading and second language learning: A response to David Hanauer. *Applied Linguistics, 23*(4), 515–518.

McCarthy, M. (1991). *Discourse analysis for language teachers*. Cambridge: Cambridge University Press.

McKay, S. L. (2001). Literature as content for ESL/EFL. In M. Celce-Murcia (Ed.), *Teaching English as a second or foreign language* (pp. 319–332). Boston: Heinle & Heinle.

McRae, J. (1991). *Literature with a small 'l'*. London: Prentice Hall.

Moll, L., & Gonzalez, N. (1994). Lessons from research with language-minority children. *Journal of Reading Behavior, 26*(4), 439–455.

Narayan, R. K. (1985). The mute companions. In *Under the banyan tree and other stories*. Harmondsworth, England: Penguin Books.

Neelands, J. (1999). *Structuring drama work*. Cambridge: Cambridge University Press.

Nunan, D. (1992). *Research methods in language learning*. Cambridge: Cambridge University Press.

Nünning, A. (1998). Von "teaching drama" zu "teaching plays" [From "teaching drama" to "teaching plays"]. *Der Fremdsprachliche Unterricht Englisch, 27*(1), 5–13.

Nuttall, C. (1996). *Teaching reading skills in a foreign language* (New ed.). Oxford: Heinemann.

Olson, D. R., Torrance, N., & Hildyards, A. (Eds.). 1985. *Literacy and language: The nature and consequence of reading and writing*. Cambridge: Cambridge University Press.

Palim, J., & Power, P. (1990). *Jamboree*. Walton-on-Thames, Surrey, England: Nelson.

Paran, A. (1999, September). *Towards an appropriate methodology for literature in ELT*. Plenary talk given at the GRETA conference, Granada, Spain.

Pastan, L. (1989). To a daughter leaving home. In *The imperfect paradise: Poems*. New York: W. W. Norton & Company.

Peracchio, A. (1990, September 16). A world apart: Segregation on Long Island. *Newsday*. Retrieved October 7, 2005, from http://www.newsday.com/

Peterson, R. (1992). *Life in a crowded place: Making a learning community*. Portsmouth, NH: Heinemann.

Pinter, H. (1979). *Betrayal*. New York: Grove Press.

Propp, V. (1981). *Morfología del cuento* [Morphology of the folktale]. Madrid, Spain: Editorial Fundamentos.

Protherough, R. (1983). *Developing response to fiction*. Milton Keynes, England: Open University Press.

Pulverness, A. (2000). Showing and telling: Joyce's *The Dead* and Huston's *The Dead*. *IATEFL Literature and Cultural Studies SIG Newsletter, 20*, 6–14.

Purves, A. C. (1979). *Evaluation of learning in literature*. Oxford: Pergamon Press.

Qiping, Y., & Shubo, C. (2002). Teaching English literature in China: Importance, problems and countermeasures. *World Englishes, 2*(2), 317–324.

Quirk, R., & Widdowson, H. (Eds.). (1985). *English in the world: Teaching and learning the language and literatures*. Cambridge: Cambridge University Press.

Richards, J., & Renandya, W. (2002). *Methodology in language teaching: An anthology of current practice*. Cambridge: Cambridge University Press.

Rifaat, A. (1987). An incident in the Ghobashi household. In *Distant view of a minaret and other stories* (pp. 23–27). Oxford: Heinemann.

Rinvolucri, M. (1984). *Grammar games*. Cambridge: Cambridge University Press.

Rodari, G. (1979). *Gramática de la fantasía* [The grammar of fantasy]. Barcelona, Spain: Reforma de la Escuela.

Rodriguez, R. (1983). *Hunger of memory: The education of Richard Rodriguez*. New York: Bantam.

Rönnquist, L., & Sell, R. D. (1994). Teenage books for teenagers: Reflections on literature in language education. *ELT Journal, 48*(2), 125–132.

Rosaldo, R. (1989). *Culture and truth*. Boston: Beacon Press.

Rosen, M. (1974). *Mind your own business*. London: André Deutsch.

Rosen, M. (1995). *Count to five and say I'm alive! The poetry video resource for primary schools key stages 2–3*. London: Team Video.

Rosenblatt, L. M. (1938). *Literature as exploration*. New York: Appleton-Century.

Rosenblatt, L. M. (1956). The acid tests for literature teaching. *English Journal, 45*(2), 66–74.

Rosenblatt, L. M. (1978). *The reader, the text, the poem*. Carbondale: Southern Illinois University Press.

Rosenblatt, L. M. (1991). Literature S.O.S.! *Language Arts, 68*, 444–448.

Rosenblatt, L. M. (1993). The transactional theory: Against dualism. *College English, 55*(4), 377–386.

Rosenkjar, P. (2002). Adjunct courses in the Great Books: The key that unlocked Locke for Japanese EFL undergraduates and opened the door to academia for EFL. In J. Crandall & D. Kaufman (Eds.), *Case studies in TESOL practice: Content-based instruction in higher education settings* (pp.13–27). Alexandria, VA: TESOL.

Ross, N. (1991). Literature and film. *ELT Journal, 45*(2), 147–155.

Roy, L. (1993). Carousel. In A. Barlow (Ed.), *The calling of the kindred: Poems from the English-speaking world* (pp. 52–53). Cambridge: Cambridge University Press.

Ruiz, R. (1988). Orientations in language planning: Language diversity—Problem or resource? In S. L. McKay & S. C. Wong (Eds.), *A social and educational perspective on language minorities in the United States* (pp. 3–25). Cambridge: Newbury House.

Rumelhart, D. E. (1980). Schemata: The building blocks of cognition. In R. J. Spiro, B. Bruce, & W. F. Brewer (Eds.), *Theoretical issues in reading comprehension* (pp. 33–58). Hillsdale, NJ: Erlbaum.

Rushdie, S. (1990). *Haroun and the sea of stories*. London: Granta/Pengu.

Schock für die Schule: Die PISA-Studie und ihre Folgen [Shock for schools: The PISA study and its consequences]. (2002). *Zeit 3* [Selection of articles from *Die Zeit*].

Segal, J. (1997). *The ECB anthology*. Ra'anana, Israel: Eric Cohen Books.

Shaffer-Koros, C. M., & Reppy, J. M. (1994/1998). *Explorations in world literature*. New York: Cambridge University Press.

Shakespeare, W. (1992). *Hamlet* (B. A. Mowat & P. Werstine, Eds.). Folger Shakespeare Library. New York: Washington Square Press. (Original work published 1603)

Shakespeare, W. (1993). *Romeo and Juliet* (A. Quiller-Couch & J. D. Wilson, Eds.). Cambridge: Cambridge University Press. (Original work published 1597)

Shaw, B. (1941). *Pygmalion*. Harmondsworth, England: Penguin Books.

Short, M. (1996). *Exploring the language of poems, plays and prose*. Harlow, England: Addison Wesley Longman.

Smith, A. (2001, December 6). On tape, admits beating laborer. *Newsday*, p. A34.

Soll, W. (1999). Integrierte Fremdsprachenarbeit an den Grundschulen in Rheinland-Pfalz [Integrated foreign language teaching in the primary schools in the Rhineland-Palatinate]. In G. Gundi et al. (Eds.), *Jahrbuch 1999, Kinder lernen europäische Sprachen* [Yearbook 1999: Children learning European languages]. Leipzig/Stuttgart, Germany: Ernst Klett Grundschulverlag.

Spiro, J. (1991). Assessing literature: Four papers. In C. Brumfit (Ed.), *Assessment in literature teaching: Review of English language teaching* (pp. 16–83). London: Macmillan Modern English Publications (in association with the British Council).

Spiro, J. (2004). *Creative poetry writing*. Oxford: Oxford University Press.

Stake, R. E. (1995). *The art of case study research.* Thousand Oaks, CA: Sage.

Stern, S. L. (1991). An integrated approach to literature in ESL/EFL. In M. Celce-Murcia (Ed.), *Teaching English as a second or foreign language* (2nd ed., pp. 328–346). Boston: Heinle & Heinle.

Stoppard, T. (1991). *Rosencrantz and Guildenstern are dead.* New York: Grove Weidenfeld Press. (Original work published 1967)

The Storyteller Group. (1994). *Open talk: Talking about love and sex.* Johannesburg, South Africa: The Storyteller Group.

Sutton, E., & Dodd, L. (1973). *My cat likes to hide in boxes.* London: Puffin Books.

Svobodová, R. (1998). Strukturované drama [Structured drama]. In S. Kotátková, M. Provazník, R. Svobodová, A. Tomková, & K. Blahová (Eds.), *Vybrané kapitoly z dramatické výchovy* (pp. 119–147). Praha, Czech Republic: Karolinum.

Sydney, P. (1973). *An apology for poetry* (G. Shepherd, Ed.). Manchester, England: Manchester University Press. (Original work published 1595)

Thrilling, I. (1997). Advice to a teenage daughter. In C. A. Duffy (Ed.), *I wouldn't thank you for a valentine* (p. 28). New York: Henry Holt. (Original work published 1985)

Thurber, J. (1993). The unicorn in the garden. In A. Lurie (Ed.), *The Oxford book of modern fairy tales* (pp. 300–301). Oxford: Oxford University Press. (Original work published 1940)

Tobin, K. (1990). Changing metaphors and beliefs: A master switch for teaching. *Theory Into Practice, 29*(2), 122–127.

Tomalin, B., & Stempleski, S. (1993). *Cultural awareness.* Oxford: Oxford University Press.

Tomlinson, B. (1998). And now for something not completely different: An approach to language through literature. *Reading in a Foreign Language, 11*(2), 177–189.

Towndrow, P. A., & Vallance, M. (2004). *Using IT in the language classroom: A guide for teachers and students in Asia* (3rd ed.). Singapore: Longman.

Tucker, C. M. (1993). The green velvet dress. In J. Mark (Ed.), *The Oxford book of children's stories* (pp. 93–101). Oxford: Oxford University Press. (Original work published 1858)

Tutaş, N. (1996). *A transactional approach to the teaching of literature in EFL situations: The effects of aesthetic and efferent teaching approaches on EFL undergraduates' responses to literature.* Unpublished doctoral thesis, University of Reading, England.

Ur, P. (1996). *A course in language teaching.* Cambridge: Cambridge University Press.

U.S. Census Bureau. (2000). *State and county quick facts* [Online]. Retrieved September 3, 2005, from http://quickfacts.census.gov/

Vale, D., & Feunteun, A. (1995). *Teaching children English.* Cambridge: Cambridge University Press.

Vale, D., Mullaney, S., & Murphy, P. (1993). *Storyworld* (Teacher's book). Oxford: Heinemann.

van Wyk, C. (1995). On learning Sotho. In R. Malan (Ed.), *Poetry works 1.* Cape Town, South Africa: David Philip.

Vethamani, M. E. (1996). Common ground: Incorporating new literatures in English in language and literature teaching. In R. Carter & J. McRae (Eds.), *Language, literature and the learner* (pp. 204–216). Harlow, England: Longman.

Voortgangsrapportage: Ict in het onderwijs maart 2003–april 2004 [Progress report: ICT in education March 2003–April 2004]. (2004). The Hague, The Netherlands: Ministry of Education, Culture, and Science.

Weston, A. (1996). Picking holes: Cloze procedures in prose. In R. Carter & J. McRae (Eds.), *Language, literature and the learner* (pp. 115–137). Harlow, England: Longman.

Wheately, N. (1993). The convict box. In J. Mark (Ed.), *The Oxford book of children's stories* (pp. 424–435). Oxford: Oxford University Press. (Original work published 1992)

Whiteson, V. (1996). *New ways of using drama and literature in language teaching.* Alexandria, VA: TESOL.

Whitney, N. (1990). Editorial. *English Language Teaching Journal, 44*(3), 171–173.

Widdowson, H. G. (1975). *Stylistics and the teaching of literature.* London: Longman.

Widdowson, H. G. (1985). The teaching, learning, and study of literature. In R. Quirk & H. Widdowson (Eds.), *English in the world: Teaching and learning the language and literatures* (pp. 180–194). Cambridge: Cambridge University Press.

Widdowson, H. G. (1992). *Practical stylistics.* Oxford: Oxford University Press.

Wilde, O. (2003). The happy prince. In *Collins complete works of Oscar Wilde* (5th ed., pp. 271–275). Glasgow, Scotland: HarperCollins. (Original work published 1888)

Williams, J. (1994). *The practical princess and other liberating fairy tales.* London: Scholastic Children's Books.

Williams, R. (2002, July 23). The loss of childhood. *The Times,* p. 2.

Wright, A. (1995). *Storytelling with children.* Oxford: Oxford University Press.

Yin, R. K. (1994). *Case study research: Design and methods* (2nd ed.). Thousand Oaks, CA: Sage.

Zarrillo, J. (1991). Theory becomes practice: Aesthetic teaching with literature. *The New Advocate, 4*(4), 221–235.

Zarrillo, J., & Cox, C. (1992). Efferent and aesthetic teaching. In J. Many & C. Cox (Eds.), *Reader stance and literary understanding* (pp. 224–249). Norwood, NJ: Ablex.

Zipes, J. (1995). *Creative storytelling building community, changing lives.* New York: Routledge.

Zughoul, M. R. (1987). Restructuring the English department in Third World universities: Alternative approaches for the teaching of English literature. *International Review of Applied Linguistics in Language Teaching, 25*(3), 221–237.

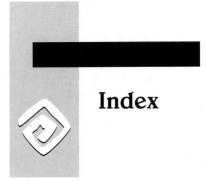

Index

Note: Information presented in tables and figures is denoted by *t* and *f*, respectively.